The Uncommon Touch

BOOKS BY TOM HARPUR

Harpur's Heaven and Hell (1983)
For Christ's Sake (1986; reissued 1993)
Always on Sunday (1988)
Life After Death (1991)
God Help Us (1992)
The Uncommon Touch (1994)

The Uncommon Touch

An Investigation
of Spiritual Healing

Tom
Harpur

M&S

Canadian Cataloguing in Publication Data
Harpur, Tom
The uncommon touch: an investigation of spiritual healing

Includes bibliographical references and index.
ISBN 0-7710-3944-1

1. Spiritual healing. I. Title.

BT732.5.H37 1994 615.8'52 C93-095210-3

The publishers acknowledge the support of the Canada Council, the Ontario Arts Council, and the Ontario Ministry of Culture, Tourism and Recreation for their publishing program.

Typesetting by M&S, Toronto.

Printed and bound in Canada.
The paper used in this book is acid-free.

McClelland & Stewart Inc.
The Canadian Publishers
481 University Avenue
Toronto, Ontario
M5G 2E9

1 2 3 4 5   98 97 96 95 94

To my brother, George David Harpur, M.D.

ὁ ἰατρὸς ὁ ἀγαπητὸς
(The beloved physician)
– Colossians 4:14

*"For with thee is the fountain of life:
in Thy light shall we see light."*

– Psalms 36:9

*"He gave them power . . . to heal all manner of
sickness and all manner of disease."*

– Matthew 10:1

*"The profoundest healing of all is
the healing of the human soul."*

– Anon

Contents

Preface

According to the January 28, 1993, issue of the prestigious *New England Journal of Medicine*, a surprising 34 per cent of Americans, or approximately 61 million people, used one or more unconventional therapies or forms of non-medical healing in 1990. The study, "Unconventional Medicine in the United States: Prevalence, Costs and Patterns of Use," included practices from acupuncture and chiropractic to homeopathy, massage, relaxation response, meditation, biofeedback, self-help groups, prayer, and the laying-on of hands. The researchers were astonished to find that the better-educated the people surveyed were, the more likely they were to have pursued such complementary or alternative therapies. Nine out of ten who saw a spiritual or other kind of healer did so without the recommendation of a medical doctor. Some seven out of ten did not tell their own physician about the unconventional therapy.

A similar study has not yet been done in Canada, but it is evident from a host of signs that the situation here, and indeed throughout the developed countries of the world, is no different. This demonstrates that there is huge dissatisfaction with Western medicine as it is currently practised, and also that bright, ordinary people find it almost impossible to discuss this discontent with their family doctors. As Canadian journalist Morris Wolfe pointed out in the March 16, 1993, issue of the *Globe and Mail*, one of the reasons for this lack of dialogue is that the medical establishment, at any rate in North America, takes a very dismissive or patronizing approach to anything other than allopathic (conventional) medicine. Wolfe notes that in the same issue of the *New England Journal of Medicine* as the report, a condescending editorial puts down these other therapies and states that "roughly a third of unconventional practices entail theories that are patently unscientific and in direct competition with conventional medicine." The editorial writer's list of "unscientific" therapies includes spiritual healing and acupuncture. But, as I have discovered in my research for this book, this commonly held view is simply no longer tenable. Certainly, there are a lot of fads and false "cures" out there, but there is hard, scientific evidence both for spiritual healing and for acupuncture, as well as for the ancient Chinese therapy known as Qigong. And this evidence has been written up in learned journals – for example, *Subtle Energies* – which, unlike most Western medical publications, do not depend on funding from advertising placed by the huge pharmaceutical companies. As Wolfe rightly noted in his article, given that the major source of their income is the drug companies, it's not surprising that major medical journals "rarely discuss non-pharmacological approaches to treatment." There is little or no money for research into unconventional therapies for the very same reason.

This book began as a quest for understanding but has ended as much more. It has become a three-fold challenge: to the medical profession, to all of the religious community (in particular the churches), and finally to each reader. What follows here challenges doctors and other health-care professionals to look beyond conventional approaches to a much wider paradigm or model of healing. It confronts the various faiths with their common traditions of healing and the present opportunities they afford both for growing closer to one another and also for becoming more relevant to modern men and women at the same time. Lastly, but most importantly, it summons every one of us to realize afresh the power of the "inner healer," to take responsibility for our own health, and in turn to become ourselves channels of healing.

A word of caution is needed about the term spiritual healing. Unfortunately, because of stereotypes and past associations, many people take the word spiritual to mean spiritualist or spiritualistic. It conjures up séances, table-rapping, and all the other oddities that characterize the religious movement known as Spiritualism. I make no judgements upon Spiritualism in this book, but want to make it perfectly clear that when the term spiritual healing appears in these pages it has nothing to do with that movement. (Nor has it anything to do with that vague, recent usage which puts everything strange or unusual, from fortune-telling with tarot cards to numerology, under the umbrella of the spiritual.) What I mean by the term is healing achieved not by physical intervention, as in the prescribing of medications, lab tests, surgery, or elaborate hi-tech treatments of various kinds, but by the laying-on of hands or other religious rites, by prayer, visualization, meditation, and the cultivation of the inner, spiritual qualities of hope, faith, love, forgiveness, courage, purpose, and meaning.

Throughout the course of my own journey and investigation, one guiding conviction and principle has become absolutely bedrock, and it may help the reader to have it laid out as briefly and simply as possible at the very outset.

All healing is ultimately self-healing. This principle remains true no matter how much either doctors or other kinds of healers may intervene in the treatment of the sick or injured. They and their expertise, medications, surgery, and technology on the one hand, or their ancient rites, sacraments, and prayers on the other, are simply instruments or channels. The human organism, like the earth itself, is self-renewing and self-healing. The body is constantly making new cells, repairing damaged tissues, fighting off diseases, repelling tumours, and working to keep everything in its proper balance. Our total organism wants and wills health. Thus, all healing finally flows from nature, if one is a non-believer. As Voltaire once put it wryly: "The art of medicine consists of amusing the patient while nature cures the disease." For the person with a religious commitment, ultimately healing comes from God. Theologically, healing is what God is all about. The Bible states it boldly this way: "I am the Lord who healeth thee."[1]

Acknowledgements

I wish to thank Al and Jenny Mowat for sending me their copy of *Forth in Thy Name*, the story of Godfrey Mowatt, to replace my long-lost edition, and also for providing me with further documentation on the life of this remarkable man. I owe thanks as well to Rev. Canon Robert Dann, Rector Emeritus of St. Paul's Anglican Church, Toronto, for so kindly making available his file of news clippings and other writings by or about Dr. Alfred Price, the former rector of St. Stephen's Episcopal Church in Philadelphia. The readers of my ethics column in the Sunday *Star* have once again assisted me in my research and encouraged me in the original undertaking of this project; my sincere gratitude to them all. Thanks are due also to Dr. Bernard Grad of Montreal and Dr. Frank Benor of London, England, for sharing both their time and their scientific papers with me. My brother, George, in spite of his own heavy schedule as a family doctor and coroner in a far-flung practice, graciously and thoroughly reviewed an early draft to spot any serious medical or technical errors, imprecisions, or mystifications. He also made a number of other valuable suggestions. Susan, my wife, was, as always, my unfailing encourager, perceptive critic, and wonderfully wise friend. To my editor at McClelland & Stewart, Dinah Forbes, whose patience, industry, and insight "pass all understanding," what more can I say than that the book would have been impossible without her. *Si monumentum eius requiris, circumspice!* If you want to see a tribute to her efforts, look for it in the book itself. The same can be said for her associate Alex Schultz, who did the painstaking task of copyediting the manuscript. In a stroke of genius, he also suggested the title *The Uncommon Touch*. My heartfelt thanks to both. The final responsibility for the views and theories expressed here, of course, is mine alone.

I

Roots of an Enquiry

"What the physician is doing today is attempting to duplicate what the healer did in times of antiquity. If the healer phenomenon is real, and I believe that it definitely is, then there is a mechanism inherent in the organism that permits things to occur that we cannot do with surgery or drugs. Availability of this information to medicine would markedly change the scope and efficiency of the medical care process."

– Dr. Robert O. Becker, Professor of Orthopedics, New York State University Hospital.[1]

"We have come to the conclusion that a vibration of a very high intensity and an extremely fine wave-length, with tremendous healing power, caused by spiritual forces operating through the mind of man, is the next thing science expects to discover."

– Agnes Sanford, healer, and author of The Healing Light.[2]

From the very earliest times, long before the first cities were built in Mesopotamia, in that part of the fertile crescent now known as Iraq, our ancestors recognized the presence in their midst of special individuals who possessed a gift of healing. The shaman phenomenon, still seen today wherever native cultures have preserved or revived their ancient lore, is as old as Homo sapiens himself. We see the evidence of this in cave drawings in Europe, dating from some fifteen thousand years ago. In caves in central and western France, the palaeolithic priest-healer artists have left a remarkable collection of paintings of hands.[3] The use of hands in healing is recorded in the earliest scriptures of all the major faiths, and, in India, Tibet, and China, the precise origins of healing practices involving variations of the laying-on of hands – still being passed down from teacher to student – are lost in time.

The major prophets of the Old Testament or Hebrew Bible were healers. So were some of the earliest advisers to the Pharaohs. For example, in the twenty-seventh century B.C., at Memphis in Egypt, a man called Imhotep is known to have served as sage, astrologer, healer, and chief minister to King Zoser (c.2686-2613 B.C.), the second king of Egypt's Third Dynasty. Imhotep, who must have been a physician of considerable skill, was described by Sir William Osler, M.D., as "the first figure of a physician to stand out clearly from the mists of antiquity."[4] Within a hundred years of his death, he was revered as a kind of medical demi-god, and by the time of the Persian conquest of Egypt in 525 B.C. he had been elevated to full deity, replacing Nefertum in the great triad of gods at Memphis. His cult reached its peak in Graeco-Roman times, when his temples at Memphis and on the island of Philae in the Nile were crowded with the sick. They prayed and slept there, believing their cures or remedies would be revealed in their dreams.

Some of the Roman emperors were reputed to have possessed healing powers, most notably Vespasian and Hadrian. In the Europe of the Middle Ages, kings were thought to have had the ability to exercise a "royal touch" that conferred healing. In China today, there are reported to be approximately sixty million adherents to the centuries-old Qigong movement (pronounced chee gong), whose practitioners claim to heal a vast range of illnesses by simply regulating with their hands the flow of Qi (also known as chi), the sacred life-force, through the bodies of healees. ("Healee," by the way, is a dreadful word, but it is widely used in the literature. I have searched in vain for a better term but, in the end, "healee" seems a necessary evil.) In England, in several former Iron Curtain countries, including Bulgaria and Poland, and in the United States, a startling coming-together of traditional healers and orthodox medical practitioners is quietly beginning to revolutionize the nature and scope of medical care.

Significantly, since the end of the Second World War, the mainline churches, particularly the Anglican and Roman Catholic churches, have witnessed a growing revival of ancient healing practices once abandoned because of fears of "witchcraft" or the rationalists' charge of superstition. In Britain today, the Churches' Council on Healing, an ecumenical body, is headed by none other than the Archbishop of Canterbury. On a recent visit to London my wife and I noticed a sign outside Westminster Abbey announcing a service of the laying-on of hands for healing every Wednesday in the historic cathedral. Similar services are now conducted without fanfare in Anglican (Episcopal) churches throughout the world, including a rapidly increasing number in Canada and the United States. The Pentecostal churches, which have been expanding worldwide since their beginnings in the early years of the twentieth century, have always emphasized the "gifts of the Holy Spirit," and hence the gift of healing. So, too, of course, has the Church of Christ Scientist.

But, as the reference to Qigong has already shown, healing of this kind is not limited to the Christian churches. In the course of my research, I met in England with members of the Jewish Association of Spiritual Healers (JASH), who hold regular healing sessions in synagogues in London, New York, and other major cities.[5] Indeed, JASH is a founder member of the British Alliance of Healing Organizations, which has about twelve thousand members. Many of them have some kind of religious commitment, but it's not a condition of joining. Keith Bailey, president of the 6,500-member National Federation of Spiritual Healers in the United Kingdom, told me that while he is a Christian his organization is open to healers of any faith or of none.[6]

At the same time as churches are reviving their practices of healing, an increasing number of scientists are now conducting research which appears to demonstrate that the old explanations of "placebo effect," or of superstitious people succumbing to the power of suggestion, are no longer an adequate response to account for the healing phenomenon. Something objective, something verifiable, seems to be going on. The question remains, however, is this really so? And, if it is, what exactly is it?

Before attempting any answers, I should sketch out the background to my investigations. This book is the result of an interest which, while it has greatly intensified over the past three years, really began many years ago. The first time I met with a publisher to discuss the writing of a book was in the early 1970s, when I raised the possibility of a book on spiritual healing with Jack McClelland, then the president and publisher of McClelland & Stewart. I told him what I had in mind, and he responded with typical enthusiasm. However, I had just recently left the halls of academe to become the religion editor of Canada's largest newspaper, the *Toronto Star*. Life there turned out to be much more exciting and demanding than I had ever anticipated, and so the writing of a book had to be put on hold.

But, during the twelve years (1971-83) I worked full-time at the *Star*, covering religion around the world, I had innumerable opportunities to observe and write features about non-medical healers of every description and faith. This included meeting with and covering the mass-healing crusades of such notable healers as the late Kathryn Kuhlman and Rev. Ernest Angley, to name only two. I went to a number of international conferences on non-medical healing, and visited several healing centres and shrines in Canada and abroad. One in particular stands out in my memory. It is called Burrswood, a Christian Centre for Medical and Spiritual Care. It's a stately, modern nursing home, with a full staff of nurses and a resident doctor, to which is attached a chapel where services of healing are held several times a week. Located in the depths of the English countryside, near Tunbridge Wells, Kent, Burrswood was built by Dorothy Kerin, a woman who, from 1907 to 1912, suffered from acute tuberculosis. In spite of the best medical attention of many doctors, she developed tuberculous peritonitis and meningitis, and lost consciousness for two weeks. One night, after being told in a vision to get up and walk, she was miraculously healed. Subsequent medical examinations, including x-rays, confirmed that her cure was complete. Shortly afterwards, Dorothy Kerin received what she believed was a commission from God "to heal the sick, comfort the sorrowing and bring faith to those without hope." Others caught her vision and together they eventually built Burrswood in 1948. Today, it is only one of many centres or retreat facilities in Britain that combine the best in modern medicine with prayer, the sacraments, and the laying-on of hands in care for the whole person.[7]

As a journalist, I have frequently met and interviewed people of all faiths (and occasionally of none) who have had seemingly miraculous recoveries from various intractable or "terminal" illnesses. In a few cases, the medical evidence, consisting of accurate diagnosis, prognosis, and final mysterious cure, was available and seemed convincing. When I say "convincing," of course, I mean it was clear something had happened. The explanations varied. The doctors, for their part, were non-committal. "Spontaneous remission" was their usual verdict. The intervention of prayer or other spiritual factors was, they said, probably just a coincidence. But, the number and nature of these coincidences eventually made me wonder.

Before becoming a journalist, I had spent seven years as a parish priest (Anglican) followed by seven as a seminary professor teaching New Testament and Greek. In the parish, as I tried to minister to a large and rapidly growing suburban congregation, it had quickly become apparent to me that there was a missing dimension in this pursuit. Faced constantly with the whole gamut of human needs that presented themselves in the weekly routine of home visiting, hospital visiting, personal counselling, instructing new-comers, officiating at baptisms, weddings, and funerals, and preaching, I soon came to appreciate more fully than before that what we all need most is the deepest possible assurance that we are loved and accepted – just as we are. At the verbal or intellectual level, this can sound obvious and trite. But, it remains bedrock all the same. Indeed, I faced what every minister faces: the problem that most of the institutional religion I was involved in was purely verbal and cerebral, instead of being experiential or practical as well.

In short, in spite of doing all the correct things and being judged as successful by my peers and superiors, I was acutely conscious of not filling the gap between the correct churchy rhetoric and the average member's often inarticulate longing for wholeness or heal-ing. This was particularly painful at times of crisis; with the sick, the heartbroken, the despairing, or the bereaved. Words, however glorious or potent, however comforting or hoary with age, were of limited help. I felt challenged by the fact that whereas Christ reportedly told his would-be followers to preach, teach, and heal, most of my efforts seemed to be concentrated on the first two (both verbal). My denomination was placing little or no emphasis on the command to offer healing of body and soul; that is, of the complete person. Certainly, my training at the seminary had given me no preparation whatever in this field. It had concentrated mainly on book-learning and on how to conduct church services. So I began to read as widely as I could about the subject, paying particular attention to the descriptions of early Christianity in the Book of Acts. The religious life described there seemed to have little in common with the rather dry and boring church experience of the modern age. Before long, I decided to introduce to my parishioners the ancient practice of the laying-on of hands for healing.

I did not feel or believe myself to be a healer. Nor had I any detailed, clearly thought-out rationale for what I had set out to do. Perhaps naively, I acted partly out of the awareness that something was missing in contemporary ministry and partly out of obedience to what the New Testament seemed to expect. Since, at its core,

being a Christian is supposed to be about attempting to be obedi-
ent to the will of God, it seemed to me to be incumbent on anyone
ordained to a position of leadership in the church to try to follow
the full commission to preach, teach, and heal.

I began holding a mid-week service of Holy Communion at
which those who wished could receive the laying-on of hands,
with prayer, either for themselves or on behalf of someone else.
There was no hoopla or fuss; those wishing the rite simply
remained kneeling at the altar rail after receiving the bread and
wine. Sometimes they would hand me or my assistant a slip of
paper with a specific problem or request on it. Sometimes they
would just whisper the nature of their illness or their desire for
wholeness so that only we could hear. Quite often there was no
direct communication at all. As we placed our hands gently on
their heads – or occasionally one hand on the head, the other on
one shoulder – we would pray either silently or just loud enough for
the person to hear. Similarly, in all hospital visiting of the seriously
ill, as well as in counselling sessions with the disturbed, the sad,
and the remorseful, I began to practise the laying-on of hands –
always, of course, prefacing this with an explanation of the rite and
asking for consent to proceed. It was never refused.

There were, at least to my knowledge, no startling cures,
no front-page-type "miracles," no dramatic throwing away of
crutches such as one hears of at certain shrines or sees on television
when the so-called faith-healers strut their stuff. That is not to say
that nothing happened. Right from the outset I had what can only
be called direct confirmation that those who had received the laying-on of hands were finding an energy, power, or "blessing" in it
that they had never found in their religion before. Time and again,
these ordinary, intelligent, not too-easily-carried-away folk testi-
fied that this rite had made all the difference in how they coped
with their daily lives. They found it made all the verbal assurances
that they were loved by God and in touch with a truly caring community suddenly come alive. The sick said it gave them fresh faith
and hope that they were on the road to fuller health; the dying
found it calmed their fears, brought peace and, not infrequently, a

sense of healing light at the end. There is and was no question in my mind that, whatever was going on, it made a tremendous difference to my own sense of the relevance of my work and to the congregants' sense of what their religion had to offer.

What confirmed the seriousness and importance of this approach for me was an event that occurred in May 1962, while I was still in parish work. An outstanding American preacher and healer, Rev. Dr. Alfred Price, the rector of St. Stephen's Episcopal Church in Philadelphia, was invited to hold an unprecedented series of healing services at Canada's largest and (at that time) most stuffily respectable Anglican church, St. Paul's, located on Bloor Street in Toronto. It was the church for the residents of nearby Rosedale, an enclave of the city's wealthiest and most prestigious élite. The church, originally built to compensate its first rector, Canon John Cody, for failing to be elected bishop in a squeaker of an election, holds roughly three thousand people. Today it is very rarely, if ever, filled to capacity.

As one of the clergy called upon to assist in the laying-on of hands during the service, I was sitting up at the front on the first night. I will never forget looking down and seeing that place crammed full. There was a hymn, a brief prayer, and then Dr. Price spoke for about twenty minutes about the relationship between inner, spiritual health, and bodily health. When he quietly and with great dignity invited anyone wishing the laying-on of hands to come forward, I wondered whether any in that vast throng of rather snooty-seeming Anglicans would allow himself to become involved in such an affair. But I wondered only for a moment, because there was a sudden, great surge as hundreds upon hundreds of people got out of their pews and came in a seemingly endless line up the chancel steps and into the sanctuary for the ancient rite. The same thing happened the next night, and the next.

On the third and final evening, after the last person had made her way back to her place in the nave, Price, a towering giant of a man, stood at the front and said, "Some of you have been here every night, others for one or two. In any case, and without making any pretence that this is in any way a scientific analysis of what has gone on here, let me ask you a question. How many of you – think carefully – have found that these services, and particularly the laying-on of hands, have been of some specific help to you in body, mind, or spirit?"

I looked on from the chancel, again fearing that nobody would move. But once more the effect was instantaneous and dramatic. Hands went up from every pew, hundreds of hands, a veritable forest of them. It was an extremely moving moment. There had been no attempt to stir emotions or to create the kind of hypnotic trance familiar to me from other healing crusades. Yet these people had found something that was deeply relevant to their hopes and fears. I wasn't quite sure what had really happened, but the experience rekindled my determination that if I ever got the chance I would one day take a much closer look at what the phenomenon of spiritual healing was all about.

One final point. Before leaving parish work in 1964 to teach at my old theological college at the University of Toronto, I returned to Oxford University, where I had done my undergraduate studies and had spent a year (1962-63) researching the Church of the first four centuries. Here, once more, I had an opportunity to deepen my understanding of the role of healing in religion in general and in Judaism and Christianity in particular. It struck me there as never before that healing, in the widest possible sense, is what religion and spirituality (a much wider concept than religion) are all about. *Religio*, the Latin word behind our English word *religion*, comes from roots which mean the binding together again or healing of the gap between the human and the divine ground of all being. The Latin word *salvatio*, from which the English word *salvation* is derived, signifies the state of having been made sound or whole. Holiness has at its root the concept of wholeness.

Even the most sceptical of modern scholars, in the fresh spate of books about Jesus now flooding the bookstores, agree that, whatever else Jesus was or was not, he was a healer. That is evident from the earliest accounts as preserved in Mark's Gospel. The reason all the Gospels stress the physical aspects of the healing ministry of Jesus is that, ultimately, true religion is not just about the spirit but about the entire psychosomatic organism, the total person, body and soul. The Holy Communion service in the Anglican Church includes, just at the moment of administering the Holy Communion, the words "The body of our Lord, Jesus Christ . . . *preserve thy body and soul* unto everlasting life." The same phrase is used at the giving of the cup of wine. The service for the sick, of course, is more specific still. The health of the total being is a primary religious concern.

Over the years, it has become increasingly evident to me that healing, both as a metaphor and as a reality, might well hold the key to the renewal of religion, and, more importantly, of spirituality, in the post-Christian world of the future. If there is anything to the non-medical healer, who has worked from antiquity both inside and outside of established religions, the way might lie open, not just for a fresh point of contact and communication between religious institutions and ordinary people, but also for a much-needed breakthrough for modern medicine. I found that I was far from alone in my thinking.

2

*Facing Some High
Hurdles*

Anyone interested in seriously examining the healing phenomenon today immediately comes upon some quite formidable barriers. The first of these is that the hierarchs and purveyors of our prevailing cultural and philosophical assumptions are for the most part strenuously opposed to any challenge or threat to present paradigms for healing. Western medicine has fought too long and at too great a cost down the centuries, with witchcraft, superstition, ignorance, and blundering stupidity, to look with kindness or approbation on any claim to heal that doesn't follow current scientific models and procedures. I have been fully aware of this scepticism throughout my research and during the writing of this book, and want to deal here with two of the most common reasons for dismissing the reality of spiritual healing. They are of crucial importance.

~ Frauds and Charlatans

Sometimes, when you are watching television very late at night or very early in the morning, your attention is caught by one of those extremely emotional people who claim to be God's special agents. Strutting up and down in front of the camera, usually with an enormous Bible in hand, they hold out the promise of miracles and healings. Some of them are so extreme that at times you find yourself wondering whether they're a genuine television evangelist or a comedian doing a satirical portrait. Rev. Ernest Angley, who appears regularly on dozens of stations in North America and elsewhere – in addition to his healing crusades in major cities – has become a kind of cult figure for thousands of young people who don't believe the message but enjoy what seems to them to be a campish send-up of an entire genre.

Certainly there are humorous moments in "Brother" Angley's performance. I remember once covering a crusade of his at the International Centre, near the Toronto airport, where a man who said he was deaf in one ear came forward for healing. Angley, who pronounces Jesus as Jeeeeezus and calls arthritis "arthuritis," had the man indicate which ear was the problem. Then, shouting "Jeeeeezus heal!" he clapped both his hands over the man's ears with considerable force. Though he only whispered it, the microphone picked up and amplified the man's voice as he blurted, "Oh my God, there goes my good ear!"

Having studied the operations of the major television preachers for many years now, I am well aware that many, if not most, of the self-proclaimed healers who leap out at us from the small screen are manipulative deceivers. I believe most of them start out with a sincere desire to serve and preach "the Word." They get seduced along the way by the same sins they originally denounced – greed, lust for fame and power, and, not infrequently, illicit sex. Nothing, however, has done more to deter intelligent people, including whole denominations of Christians, not to mention the vast majority of scientists and doctors, from taking the phenomenon of spiritual healing seriously than the antics of these Bible-thumping, money-grubbing hucksters. The extravagant lifestyles, the mass-mailed lies, and the scandalous tricks at crusades of these self-proclaimed wonder-worders are reprehensible – for example, getting people to sit in wheelchairs rented for the purpose, and then performing a "miracle" by telling them to stand up and run down the aisle. I wouldn't buy a used Bible from any one of them. Many of them, sadly, are an open disgrace to their religion and the God whom they profess to serve.

Oral Roberts, for example, has long been an embarrassment to many who call themselves Christians. They justifiably cringe at his crude attempts at fund-raising and at such notorious stunts as his ill-conceived, widely publicized "bargain" with God in which he asked Him to take his life if a huge sum of money he urgently needed didn't come in within a certain number of months. His letters soliciting funds are filled with claims of personal encounters and visions in which God or Jesus tells him to do seemingly preposterous things. He was seeking solace in the desert, he said, after the tragic death of his daughter in a plane crash, when God told him to build a medical centre called the City of Faith.

Roberts never consulted with anyone beyond those connected

with his ministry – let alone the authorities in Tulsa to see whether such a facility was needed – before at once proceeding with the project. The result, at a cost of more than $150 million, was a thirty-storey hospital, a twenty-storey research centre, and a sixty-storey medical school tower near Tulsa. The centre never attracted the enormous crowds Roberts had predicted and was forced to close in 1989, because of a severe financial crisis. About 40 per cent of the interior of the buildings was never completed. The director of commercial services at Prudential Properties of Oklahoma, who was hired in 1992 to try to sell the centre, was reported by the *Wall Street Journal* (in an item titled "News of the Weird") to have described the centre as a white elephant.

In a recent plea for cash for his television ministry, Oral Roberts actually told his followers to write the name of Jesus on the soles of their shoes. "As you put your foot down, know by your faith you're bruising the devil's head," said the dunning letter. "The devil should always see the sole of your shoe coming down on him." There was a blank space on the letter on which those being gulled were to draw the outline of their shoe. This is but one illustration of a kaleidoscope of gimmicks Roberts and his cohorts have come up with.[1]

The 1992 movie *Leap of Faith*, starring Steve Martin as Jonas Nightengale, an itinerant, Pentecostal-type healer, and co-starring Debra Winger in the role of his partner in deception, is an engrossing – the Gospel singing alone makes the film worth seeing – and fairly accurate depiction of the fraudulent antics of all too many tent and television evangelists. (Incidentally, the final episode where, to the fake evangelist's total consternation and surprise, a teenage lad is healed and recovers the power to walk normally has a profound insight at its heart.)

In his book *The Faith Healers*, James Randi, the ebullient former conjuror who is now best-known for his crusading efforts to debunk any and all exploiters of the paranormal, has set forth a classic exposé of the extraordinary range of chicanery practised by the television healers.[2] The most publicized fraud in Randi's long catalogue of deceit, however, is the one he uncovered and revealed live on "The Tonight Show" in February 1986. At the centre of this debacle was Peter Popoff, a well-known television healer.

Popoff, who operates his religious television empire across the United States and Canada from his base in Upland, California, has, over the years, sent out some of the most bizarre baubles – everything from holy ribbons and blessed shoe liners to sacred handkerchiefs soaked with his sweat – and some of the most extortive pleas for money I have ever seen.

Randi, who had been given some fairly convincing evidence that Popoff was faking miracles at his crusades and deliberately deceiving his audiences, decided to investigate. Along with two or three others, he posed as an ordinary member of the audience at a couple of Popoff crusades and made the following discovery. During the live services of healing, which were later aired on television, Popoff would run up and down the aisles calling out specific names, illnesses, and other data in what he let on was a demonstration of his having been given what the New Testament calls "the gift of knowledge." Sometimes he would correctly, and in great detail, identify as many as twenty individuals and their complaints before acting to heal them. Randi and his assistants, however, quickly spotted a tiny receiver in Popoff's left ear. With the help of an electronics expert and some behind-the-scenes sleuthing with a scanner, it soon became clear that there was a transmitter tuned to a set frequency being used by his wife, Elizabeth, behind the scenes to feed the healer all the relevant information.

Randi discovered that Elizabeth Popoff would go out to the foyer before the service and interview a number of ailing people as they came in. She made brief notes on these conversations, including descriptions of what the person in question was wearing, their name, approximate age, where they came from, and what healing they were hoping for. Randi and his team were able to record her reading this collected data to the evangelist as he, with seemingly supernatural insight, called out the names of these people and repeated the data for all to hear. According to Randi's sources, which included former Popoff employees, the evangelist's televised appeals for cash brought in an average of $1.25 million (U.S.) a month before the exposé on the Carson show. Income dropped off sharply following the revelation, but the healer has since bounced back and his programs can still be seen in most major North American cities. The Popoff scam, incidentally, is reproduced in the plot of *Leap of Faith* as Martin and Winger use similar electronic communication to con the crowds.

Randi's detailed exposure of what he calls "the faith-healing racket" holds no surprises for close observers of this particular aspect of religious or pseudo-religious practices. We know that many television healers prey upon the weak, the elderly, the lonely, and the despairing. We know they extort vast sums of money by exploiting people's need, guilt, and gullibility. However, those who are curious about the activities of such "biggies" as Oral Roberts, Pat Robertson, and their ilk will find Randi's book hard to put down. He makes his point, and he makes it convincingly. These charlatans are an outrage.

It is essential, however, to be careful here. It is too easy simply to write off healers and healing because of the gross conduct of certain so-called faith-healers. Randi's book, in spite of its thorough research and damning evidence, is decidedly not a piece of clear, logical thinking. Far from it. In fact, in his foreword to the work, Carl Sagan, himself no great friend of religion, dubs Randi's book a "tirade" and concedes that it is written in a style that is "rambling, anecdotal, crotchety, and ecumenically offensive." I would strongly warn the reader against Randi's conclusion that, because he has found many faith-healers to be imposters, there is therefore no rational argument for non-medical healing. This is a logical fallacy.

The misuse of something in no way establishes a case against its proper use. This truth becomes most evident when we apply the principle to modern medicine itself. The medical profession would be the last to deny the fact that abuses and mistakes abound in the practice of modern medicine. Like the clergy, a number of doctors in North America have recently been convicted of various forms of sexual abuse, and major tragedies, like those of the thalidomide victims of the 1950s and the women who have become ill as a result of silicone breast implants, are but a small part of a list of iatrogenic (doctor-caused) problems that have marred the medical escutcheon.

One of the most alarming stories of failures and scandals in the established medical system in recent times appeared in the April 1, 1992, issue of the *New York Times* under the headline "Hospital Errors; Tracking the Pattern." The article dealt with many instances of "well-publicized trouble" in New York City's hospitals. Some of the events recorded seem beyond belief. For example: a young Hasidic scholar died after emergency-room doctors failed to notice a stab wound in his back; a prominent Harlem lawyer, William Chance, died of a bleeding ulcer after waiting almost eleven hours in the emergency room and then being sent home; a psychiatric patient was found dead in an elevator shaft after wandering unnoticed from his room.

These incidents prompted the *New York Times* reporter Lisa Belkin to examine hundreds of records of unexpected deaths, injuries, and other problems in New York hospitals between 1986 and 1991. The resulting report, listing the events of a single month in 1990, reads like a Stephen King horror story. The list went on and on, and it got steadily worse. Some of the errors were caused by malfunctioning machinery, some by economic factors and the chaos resulting from being understaffed. Nearly all of them involved inattention by doctors or other attendants.

But nobody seriously suggests that the entire basis upon which modern medicine is built should be abandoned because of the possibilities for and past examples of abuse. It is an old adage that the more potential something has for good the more it hurts when it goes wrong.

There are a couple of other reasons why I have never allowed the activities of the bogus healers to settle the issue of spiritual healing for me. In the first place, the entire concept of "faith" healing – that is, healing that lays down as a precondition a certain measure of doctrinal orthodoxy or of self-generated confidence in the healer, God, Jesus, or some other divinity, teacher, or guru – does not seem to be what real healing and healers are about. Moreover, it can add enormously to the suffering of the sick to be told that if only they had enough faith they could be made well. (All too many of the popular self-help or "recovery" books flooding the bookstores at present fall into this same error.) What's more, this emphasis on faith gives the faith-healer a perfect out if and when nothing happens as a result of his or her intervention. From the scores of healers I have interviewed, it would appear that healing, if indeed it is genuine, requires no more than a kind of neutrality on the part of the sick. In other words, as long as there is no actual hostility to the concept of healing or to the healer, a positive result can be achieved. When Jesus spoke of people being saved by their faith, he was talking more about a sense of trust that wholeness is a possibility than about correct belief in his person and the claims to divinity ascribed to him by orthodox believers.

Secondly, and perhaps surprisingly in view of all that I have just said on the negative side about the television preacher-healers, as a journalist I long ago became aware that sometimes, in spite of all the froth and all the manipulation, there are people who are transformed inwardly and healed outwardly as a result of encountering one of these showmen. I hasten to add that I cannot prove this statement. But I have observed that the character or motives of the person up at the front at such crusades have not impeded certain individuals from finding physical or emotional release and well-being. Somehow, whether through the energy kindled by throngs of expectant people around them, or through a form of hypnotism and the strong power of the suggestion that healing might be possible – or both – long-standing physical and other maladies have, in my view, been cured. In some cases, these cures are temporary. In others, I am convinced both from observation and from my research, they are enduring.

∽ The Placebo Effect

When the phenomenon of non-medical or spiritual healing is discussed, frequently someone will argue that any apparent results obtained by this method are purely the consequence of the placebo effect. A placebo is any harmless substance or act which, while having no curative power in itself, nevertheless provokes a healing response in the recipient through the power of suggestion.

The Concise Oxford Dictionary defines it as "medicine given to humour rather than cure the patient." However, this completely misses the real point. Modern medical researchers have done innumerable experiments in which patients given placebos have experienced an extraordinary degree of pain relief, sound sleep, or general relaxation, depending on what they were told the medication was for. In his book *Quantum Healing*, Dr. Deepak Chopra notes that many heart bypass patients, even with still-clogged arteries, don't feel the return of their agonizing, frightening chest pain, because they are sure their surgery has cured them. He goes on to state that some surgeons have even experimented with placebo operations in which all they did was open the chest and close it again. A good percentage of patients so treated felt relief from their angina. It has been discovered that patients in pain can often be relieved by a sugar pill when they are assured it is a very powerful painkiller. "Not everyone will respond to this but generally between 30 and 60 per cent will report that their pain went away."[3]

In his attack on the faith-healers, James Randi describes the placebo effect thus: "A placebo effect takes place when a patient is exposed to a satisfactory 'bedside manner' and/or when medication, manipulation, or other means (any or all of which may be entirely ineffectual in themselves, but are seen by the recipient as unique, special or advanced) are applied to the problem." In his view, and in the view of the sceptics in general, this is the phenomenon at work in all forms of spiritual healing, particularly the laying-on of hands or prayer for the sick.[4]

It has to be admitted that at first sight this seems an entirely plausible explanation. And it applies to a lot of regular medicine as well. I have absolutely no doubt that what a patient is told to expect, together with the setting, the presence of an authority figure, and the proper "manner," can have an enormous influence in producing a greater sense of well-being and even observable physical improvements. The great physician Sir William Osler pointed out long ago that the doctor's bearing and approach to the sick has as much, or more, healing efficacy as anything carried in his little black bag. Both in medical and non-medical healing, the placebo effect plays a great part.

What will not do, however, is to argue or assume that, because something called the placebo effect can be discerned, the real mystery has then been fully explained. The "placebo effect" or the "power of suggestion" are umbrella words that hide the fact that science does not yet know fully what is going on. Now that we have learned that the human body is better able to produce a vast range of effective chemicals and drugs than any pharmaceutical company, including its own narcotics and cancer-killers, it appears that what is happening in the placebo effect is that the body is being stimulated to make its own medicines. Precisely how this works is still a matter of uncertainty. As the famous neurologist Sir John Eccles has asked, how does an insubstantial entity like a thought manage to move the various atoms of hydrogen, oxygen, carbon, and the other particles in the cells of the brain? Where is the link between non-matter (thought) and the "solid gray matter of the brain?"[5]

Even without the answers to these questions, it is still obvious that the cry of "placebo!" is not the valid objection to claims about spiritual healing it once appeared to be. If the non-medical healer, religious or secular, can manage to trigger the mechanisms of the healee's mind to produce (or strengthen the production of) whatever resources are available to the body to combat the illness or malady in question, is this any less welcome or marvellous than results produced by conventional medical interventions? The bottom line in both cases is the health and comfort of the patient.

But thinking through the precise implications of the placebo issue still leaves us with an unresolved question: is spiritual healing to be wholly explained in terms of the placebo effect? Two discoveries in my research have led me to say no. First, the subjects of some of the best research with healers I have encountered have been plants, enzymes, yeasts, and animals. The placebo effect is simply irrelevant there. Similarly, other top research done with sick babies in the United States has shown specific, positive results obtained by healers where the power of suggestion was never a factor. The infants were simply passive recipients of whatever was going on.[6]

Second, the latest evidence available, based upon careful research, shows beyond a shadow of doubt that some kind of subtle energy exchange is involved in genuine healing. Something physical does indeed happen in the laying-on of hands. The process itself defies exact measurement or description at this point. However, and this must be stressed, its results, as we shall see, can now be measured and verified by the latest scientific technology. Before turning to that, however, there is another aspect of my investigation I want to share.

First, though, one caution needs to be sounded. It affects all that I have already said about healing and all that is to come. Throughout my research I have been impressed by the insistence of those who take spiritual healing seriously, both researchers and practitioners, that it is emphatically not an alternative to conventional medical practice. Nobody I interviewed, read, or listened to is advocating the ignoring or abandonment of doctors and their growing arsenal of expertise and technology. They regard non-medical healing and healers as complementary forms of therapy and not as substitutes. As Dr. Bernard Grad, an eminent scientist who is fully persuaded from his own research that spiritual healing is a reality, told me, "If I were seriously ill, I'd want the best doctors available, but I'd send for a proven healer as well. I'd want to avail myself of whatever assistance and skill could help restore me to health and vigour again."[7] In other words, while it is convenient and important to have different names for different approaches to healing, human health is ultimately a seamless unity. Healing is healing, no matter where it comes from or who is used as its channel. Since, like drama and the theatre, the story of healing begins with religion, it was the obvious point of departure for my investigation. The following two chapters describe what I discovered.

3

The Religious Roots of Healing

T hroughout history, healing has held a primary place in religions around the world. Almost always, the key figure or founder of the religion is also the principal source of this healing. All the rest derives from him or her. For example, in the Pali Canon of Buddhism, the Sakyamuni Buddha is depicted as a great healer. His teaching, based upon the Buddhist belief that illnesses are rooted in psychic states that have gone wrong or that foster illusion, offers direct healing through fresh insights into the true nature of reality. Full awareness of this spiritual reality underlying the world of sensation and desire brings liberation from error and disease. Full realization or escape from illusion is the ultimate healing or salvation.

Zarathustra (Zoroaster) taught his followers in Persia, around 500 B.C., how to overcome illness through prayer and divine intervention. Indeed, it is Zoroastrianism – which so deeply influenced both Judaism and Christianity – that first developed the potent and eventually widespread religious idea that the whole process of the creation and the fall and redemption of humanity is tied in with the restoration and renewal of the cosmos. The word for this, *frashokerti*, signifies the healing and renewal of all things, a moment when humankind will experience the final abolition of death and of time itself. The cosmic consummation will be endless paradise. This concept is repeated by the Old Testament prophets, most notably Isaiah, and is taken to the limits by Paul in his Epistle to the Romans and elsewhere.

From its beginnings, Hebrew religion, with its profound understanding of the wholeness of the human person, laid great stress on health and on healing. This is best expressed in Exodus 15:26, when God tells Moses, "I am the Lord that healeth thee." It sounds again in the voice of the Psalmist when he exclaims, "Bless the Lord, O my soul. . . . Who forgiveth all thine iniquities; who healeth all thy diseases" (Psalm 103:3). The great prophets, Elijah and Elisha in particular, were acknowledged healers. In fact, as pointed out in my book *For Christ's Sake*, healing was expected of all true prophets. It was a kind of talisman or sign that their calling was genuinely from God.

Jesus inherited this Judaic background and gave it fresh dimensions. He was a healer, and the movement that sprang up in his wake was primarily a healing community for the first generation of Christians. The commission Christ gave to the Apostles, according to Luke (10:9), was to "heal the sick." Islam is also marked by a central concern for human wholeness and healing. Healing is a key part of the revelation given to Muhammad in the Qur'an. The book clearly refers to itself as a "cure" for the mind or heart of the believing reader: "It [the Qur'an] is a guidance and a healing for those who believe."[1] Although Muslims hold that Muhammad's greatest miracle was the receiving and transmission of the Qur'an, Islamic tradition specifically attributes several dramatic healings to him as well. From the tenth to the fourteen century of the Common Era, Islamic thinkers in both the Sunni and the Shi'a branches worked out fairly elaborate theologies of cure. Prayer played a pivotal place in these and still does today.

In a recent interview with the president and missionary-in-charge of the largest mosque in North America, Bait-Ul-Islam, which has just been built on the outskirts of Toronto, I asked him about the place of healing among Muslims today. Naseem Mahdi, who belongs to the Ahmadiyya sect of Islam, explained that in addition to the regular, formal prayers of the mosque there was a very strong emphasis on personal prayer in his community and that it, together with the best in modern medicine, was brought to bear whenever illness struck. He then told me of some quite striking instances of persons being healed as a direct result of his praying with them, combined with what can best be described as the laying-on of hands. He makes no claims to being a healer, and there was a frankness and a quiet sincerity about his description of the actual healings that convinced me something quite authentic had occurred. At this point, however, it's too early in our investigation to say anything further about such anecdotal evidence.

It is not only the major religions that exhibit this deep connection with the human need for healing. A broad survey of the relevant anthropological and medical literature quickly reveals that all peoples, tribes, and cultures in Africa, Asia, Oceania, and the

Americas have for untold centuries made the cure of the body and soul a fundamental, central expression of their religious beliefs and their attitudes towards the most profound powers in the universe. Their healers were and still are in touch with the hidden energies of God (or of the gods) and of the natural world. Whether one studies the ancient Egyptians or the modern inhabitants of the Kalahari Desert, one finds that healing and religion are inextricably bound together.

Sacred stories, myths, and rituals help the sufferer understand the origins and meaning of his or her illness in a wide context, and offer relief not just through this or that remedy but by enabling a fresh vision of connectedness to life itself. Of course, this is precisely what so often is lacking in conventional medicine today. It's enormously healing to see yourself as an integral part of the origin and purpose of the cosmos, to have the whole of your life and experience taken into account in therapy and not just your physical body, or worse, some particular part of it. Though some moderns may think of them as naive, the holistic approach of the traditional healers is the chief reason why many in our time are giving them a closer look.

~ Sacred Touch

From earliest times, the therapeutic power of touch has been recognized and has been raised to a sacramental significance in both the religious sphere and beyond it. Medicine men, shamans, healers from every culture and part of the globe have used – and continue to use – sacred touch as the medium of blessing, restoring health, and protecting against the ravages of evil. In the Hebrew Bible, or Old Testament, references to the power of touch to heal, to bind covenants, to transmit blessings and birthright, to set a seal on prophets, and to anoint kings abound. The widespread belief in the efficacy of the touch of the particularly holy is best seen in Mark's description of the mothers of Salem bringing their children to Jesus "that he might touch them" or in the story in Matthew of the woman who touched the hem of Jesus' garment. We are told that she had thought to herself, "If I may but touch his garment, I shall be whole."[2]

Touch in the form of the laying-on of hands was the normal method in the early church, not just of healing but also of imparting the power of the Holy Spirit to new converts and of ordaining deacons or elders for ministry. In a letter addressed to him, the young Timothy is told by the writer (traditionally believed to have been Paul) to "lay hands suddenly on no man." In other words, ordination conveys a certain power of the Holy Spirit and a privilege; the young man is to treat it cautiously. In the same letter, the author tells Timothy to "stir up the gift that is in thee by the laying on of my hands." The Apostolic Succession, a cardinal doctrine of the Roman Catholic, Orthodox, and Anglican churches, is based on the belief that there is an unbroken succession of priests and bishops, linked by the sacred touch of ordination, right back to Christ and the Apostles.

One of the most vivid and explicit forms of sacred touch in the Christian tradition is preserved in the Roman Catholic sacrament of Holy Unction or anointing with oil. For centuries it was called Extreme Unction and was reserved for those about to die. Since the Second Vatican Council, however, it has been restored to its proper place as a rite administered to any sick person who desires it. It's offered with a prayer, which says, significantly, that the rite is being done "for the health of body and soul." The priest dips his finger in consecrated olive oil, an ancient symbol of healing, and makes a small cross with it on the sick person's eyes, ears, nose, lips, hands, and feet.

As stated already, Muhammad is held to have had a healing touch, and Al Bakhari has recorded several healings of this type, including one where the prophet immediately restored the broken leg of a friend by touching it.[3] In Asia and in North America, most medicine men and shamans used sacred touch – often in the form of a kind of massage – as a part of their healing techniques. In Hinduism, the sheer physical presence of a guru or holy man imparts power. Often a disciple just sits nearby and meditates for hours in the orbit of this energy. Then, the guru may touch the disciple's forehead lightly or gaze intently into his eyes for a moment – and power is transmitted. At the investiture of a high-caste Hindu male there is sacred touching as a sign that the person, who is given a new name at the same time, is now a "twice-born."

The "royal touch" was part of what Shakespeare called "the divinity that doth hedge a king." From ancient times, for example, the kings of France had a specific healing rite in which they touched those of their subjects who suffered from scrofula, a serious, painful complaint, which the Concise Oxford Dictionary calls "a disease with glandular swellings. . . . Also called king's evil."[4] The custom of administering the royal touch for scrofula was introduced into England by the pious and saintly Edward the Confessor, in the late fifteenth century. Henry VII developed it further by instituting an official ceremonial approach, and it became a part of the Anglican Book of Common Prayer. The ritual, called simply "At the Healing," remained in the Prayer Book until a revision in 1719. It included not just the laying-on of hands on the assembled sick by the reigning monarch, but also the placing of a gold or silver token on a chain around the neck of each of the supplicants. As this was done, a court chaplain said the following prayer: "God give a blessing to this work, and grant that these sick persons on whom the King lays his hands may recover."

The whole process came to a peak under Charles II, who reigned from 1660 to 1685. He is reported to have touched nearly one hundred thousand people in this manner during these twenty-five years. According to the historian Lord Thomas Macaulay, at the royal ceremony of healing in 1684 there was such a crowd that six or seven of the sick were trampled to death in the crush. Boswell tells us in his biography of Samuel Johnson that the great lexicographer had been taken as a baby by his parents to the court of Queen Anne to seek the royal touch because of a disfigured face. Boswell himself called the custom "a superstitious notion," and he used to tease Johnson that it hadn't worked and that perhaps he should have been taken to the Pope in Rome instead.

When the French explorer Jacques Cartier first visited the site of the future City of Montreal, the Natives who belonged to the Iroquois Confederacy of Five Nations obviously thought he was gifted with special powers. Their chief, the *agouhanna*, who was completely crippled and lying on a deerskin, asked Cartier to touch his legs and arms, and then gave him the band of cloth studded with porcupine quills that served as his crown. "And at once many sick persons were brought to the captain [Cartier], some blind, others with but one eye, others lame or impotent." Moved to have such trust placed in him, Cartier, we are told, devoted "a pair of hours" to making the sign of the cross over the sick Natives and then reading the Passion of Jesus Christ in the Gospel.[5]

From something as near-universal as the simple act of shaking hands to the pat of encouragement or congratulation on the shoulder, from a sympathetic touch on the arm of someone just bereaved to the parent holding a child and rubbing or stroking "where it hurts" after a tumble, touch is obviously much more than a meaningless or impotent gesture. It is a means of communication, an expression of solidarity, a bonding of persons and communities, and a profound visual symbol of an unseen transmission of healing energy and power. It is sacramental in the deep sense expressed by the Anglican Prayer Book's definition of a sacrament as an outward and visible sign of an inward and invisible grace.

～ Healers and Shamans

Anthropological studies have made it abundantly clear that individuals charged with every aspect of the health of the whole clan, tribe, or nation appear universally wherever human beings have made their dwellings or hunted for food. Though often diminished in importance or all-but-forgotten through the spread and encroachment of modern technological civilization, these healers still practise their ancient art today. In the case, for example, of North American Indians, there is a growing revival of the ancient "medicine." These healers come in a wide variety. In some aboriginal cultures there is or was a high degree of specialization among bonesetters, herbalists, diviners, drummers, incanters, dancers, exorcists, and many others. In most cultures, however, a healer would use all of these skills, depending upon the nature and extent of the illness treated. Some priests were healers but not all healers were priests. Similarly, all shamans had healing at the centre of their role in their community – though it was not their only func-tion – while not all healers were shamans.

Before explaining what made a shaman different from the ordi-nary healer, it's important to say something about the way in which shamans and other healers were, and still are, "called" to this work. In this regard they have a great deal in common. There were a number of ways one could become a healer. It could be an inherited role, handed down carefully from parent to child through succeeding generations. Because it involved special knowledge and because knowledge always brings power, the heal-ing art was a source of enormous influence and prestige. It was jealously guarded in many communities, and making it the prerog-ative of a specific family or clan ensured proper transmission and authenticity.

In many places, however, even where inheritance was the nor-mal route, certain people felt a "call" from God or the gods to undertake the healing vocation. This inner compulsion, signifi-cantly, most often followed some outer sign, usually involving sur-viving some horrendous ordeal such as being struck by lightning, coming near death from a terrible illness, or recovering from an accident like falling over a cliff or from a high tree. The isolation, suffering, and deliriums, the visions such as those described in the modern near-death experience, and in particular, the sense of dying and rising again, all helped focus the future healer's psychic and spiritual energies. There was a sense of being special and of being "saved" for a purpose by the power or powers behind the universe. One could then aspire to bring others into touch with that same energy and so restore them to health.

This idea of initiation into healing through dramatic suffering or escape from calamity is by no means unique to aboriginal peoples. Over the years, one of the things that has struck me about recognized Christian or other religious healers I have met (not the television variety!) has been that most, if not all, of them have been people who have known the shadow of illness or accident. Indeed, if I think for a moment of the most striking of those I have encountered, including Dorothy Kerin and Godfrey Mowatt – Mary Baker Eddy, the founder of Christian Science, is another outstanding example – all of them faced some life-threatening or incurable disease and then went on to play an extraordinary part as a healer. From this comes the concept of "the wounded healer." The one who has been there, so to speak, knows the way out.

Significantly, among the !Kung people of the Kalahari Desert, all healers begin their vocation by an initiation known as "dying *kia.*" According to the *Encyclopedia of Religion*, this is an intense mystical state in which the healers-to-be come into full possession of a healing energy called *num*, which is believed to have originally been given to the !Kung by the gods. In a process that is both feared – it's quite painful – and yet also eagerly anticipated, they whip themselves up into a highly energetic dance in order to heat up or "boil" the *num*. It is already latent within them, residing in the pit of the stomach and at the base of the spine (note the similarity to the Hindu belief in *chakras* or centres of energy in the same places). As this *num* or life energy heats up, the initiates consciously direct it up the spine to the base of the skull, where it acts on the central nervous system to produce *kia*, a kind of ecstasy.[6]

Old Testament prophet-healers and Aztec healers alike found their cures through connecting with invisible, profound energies both outside and within the sick. North American Indians called it – and the objects used as points of contact for it – "medicine"; the Hebrew prophets such as Elijah and Elisha, as well as Jesus, called it the energy or power of the Spirit of God. The Melanesians called it *mana*, the Hindus used terms such as *maya* and *prana*. The names are without number; the reality is always the same.

In many cultures, the healer or shaman at times makes use of the whole community to facilitate healing. Through dances and other rituals performed by the entire assembly, a kind of group dynamic emerges in which the energy generated becomes much more than the sum of each person's. There is, of course, an enormous energy generated by any large gathering. What is important is how it is directed and to what end.

For tribes and peoples more closely in touch with their environment – not to mention their bodies and the energies of the cosmos itself – than those of us cocooned in the sanitized, techno-wonderworld can ever hope to be, certain geographical places were recognized as being more innately therapeutic than others. We speak in jest about good or bad "vibes," but for aboriginals many lakes, mountains, springs, or other places were thought to be particularly sacred because experience (sometimes accompanied by superstition) had taught them the sick found healing more readily there than elsewhere. This is still true among, for example, the Navajo today, but the same reality also lies behind some of the most famous spas or other putative healing sites of Christian Europe as well.

Finally, we come to the particular group of healers known as shamans. Since the study of shamanism and shamans has become extremely popular, even trendy, in the past decade, and since much serious scholarship has been published on the entire phenomenon, there is no need to give a detailed description of it here. But briefly, shamanism is a phenomenon originally occurring in Siberia and in what is referred to as Inner Asia. The word *saman*, from which the name derives, comes to us from the Russian, through the Tunguz people. There are also Siberian-type shamans to be found in North America, especially in the Arctic and in the Pacific Northwest, no doubt because of earlier migrations or contacts with those in Asia. However, if one realizes that the central aspect which marks the shaman is the emphasis upon trance states or ecstasy, in which the shaman's soul is believed to travel through the various levels and layers of the universe, making contact with the dead, with spirits, gods, and other cosmic forces, then the term shamanism can be more widely applied and covers a diverse range of spiritual leaders in most parts of the world.

The principal function of the shaman is healing, and their basic understanding of illness is expressed in terms of loss of soul. If the disease seems minor, the theory is that the soul of the patient has strayed but has not gone far. If there is serious illness, then the soul is thought to have departed or to have been seduced by spirits into altogether other dimensions. Hence the need for the shaman's ability to leave his own body and travel to the heights of heaven or the depths of the underworld in search of the missing soul.

But shamanistic healing is not restricted to physical or mental and spiritual afflictions. He, or she, in the case of some tribes in the American Southwest and elsewhere, is responsible for all factors that affect the well-being of the community, from the weather and the fertility of the crops or the success of the hunt to matters of warfare, defence against natural disasters, and protection from death itself. In short, the shaman stands as a kind of mediator between the worlds of light and of darkness. He removes the fear of death because, moving as he does between realms, he brings the dead and the living into communication with one another. In his essential role, he serves and defends the complete psychic integrity of his people. Their sense of meaning and of their place in the cosmos derives from his lore and his interventions.

The call and the initiation of the shaman resembles what happens to other healers, except that it is almost unbelievably extreme. "The shaman's vocation often implies a crisis so deep it borders on madness, and since a youth can't become a shaman until he has resolved this crisis it's clear it plays the role of a mystical initiation."[7] Candidates for shamanism often seem to be obsessed by what has been called the shaman's disease. The young person becomes increasingly aloof from his or her peers, disappearing for long periods of seclusion and carrying only a drum and a minimum of supplies. They often are marked by an unusual sensitivity and soon begin to hear voices, see visions, and experience altered states of consciousness.

Gradually, in the classic form, the inner turmoil builds to a shattering mystical episode in which the youth sees himself torn asunder by animals or spirits until only his skeleton remains. He then watches as his body is reconstituted and renewed, and he goes on to explore spiritual realms, where he acquires spirit helpers before he returns to his people. It is the kind of crisis for which the only resolution is to begin to shamanize. Once the initiate begins to practise this art – and only as long as it is continued – he finds health. Anthropologists report that shamans exhibit greater intelligence and overall physical energy than other members of their community or tribe.

The idea of being stripped to the bone and of contemplating one's own skeleton is totally foreign to most of us. Yet it is obviously a source of great strength and spiritual power. The Inuit, who believe that an animal, either a polar bear or a walrus, tears the shaman apart before the new flesh can grow on his bones, lay great emphasis upon this aspect of the ordeal. For example, the Iglulik Inuit are reportedly able to meditate for long periods on the image of their own skeletons. In truth, the idea of being dismembered, stripped clean, and then restored is a near-universal religious theme. Echoes of it can be heard in the Egyptian myths of Osiris, and even more clearly in the Passion and Resurrection of Jesus in the Gospels. The shamanistic initiation represents a passage from life to death to life again – a rising in newness, a dramatic second birth.

The wounded healer, the one who has plumbed the depths of pain and suffering and then has been "resurrected" by forces other than himself, is the one who knows the secret energies and the god or gods behind and through all things. He then becomes the person who can effectively bring others into contact or harmony with this energy. Because his consciousness has been stretched, allowing him to "see" new worlds, he has the wisdom others need for life and health.

From my own experience, as already hinted above, the healers I would judge most authentic have been nearly all wounded healers. They had all passed through some Calvary of illness, often recovering from a disease diagnosed as incurable by their physicians, or had been afflicted (like Paul) with a lifelong "thorn in the flesh," which kept them mindful of their dependence upon spiritual forces for their survival.[8]

The shamans may seem primitive to some. But shamanism embodies basic and profound spiritual truths. Above all, as we have seen, they bear eloquent witness to the deeply and widely held religious belief that there is some kind of energy or "power of being" in all things and that this power is concentrated in some objects, places, and people. This is a universal human way of experiencing the cosmos. Whatever one's doubts, one has to admit that shamans "are individuals with extraordinary access to spiritual powers."[9]

Just what the nature of these powers might be we will address shortly. First, however, we will turn to the origins of Judeo-Christian healing.

4

The Origins of Judeo-Christian Healing

"I have heard thy prayer, I have seen thy tears: behold, I will heal thee."
  – 2 Kings 20:5

"And at evening, when the sun was set, they brought all who were sick to him . . . and he healed many."
  – Mark 1:32

∼ The Judaic Tradition

The Hebrew Bible, the Old Testament, is the matrix out of which Christianity was born. There is nothing in the healing ministry of either Jesus or the Apostles that was not already anticipated in its pages, and one of the greatest strides forward of New Testament studies in our time has been the rediscovery of the profoundly Jewish roots of Christian thought. The Jewishness of Jesus and of Paul was neglected or minimized for many decades – even centuries – longer than New Testament scholars now like to admit.

What has struck me quite powerfully in my research is the prominence of the theme of healing in the Hebrew Bible. I'm not just referring to the obvious health concerns of the various food laws and other rites – from the prohibition against eating pork to the requirement of circumcision – but to the larger concepts of sin, salvation, and ultimate human destiny. What is at issue is the problem of human brokenness and how we can be restored to health. The dilemma caused by Adam's and Eve's disobedience in the great myth of the Fall, in Genesis, is that of a broken relationship with God, with one's inner self, with one's neighbours and, ultimately, with nature and the universe. What the myth really says is that humanity is in need of renewed wholeness. Thus, when the major Old Testament prophets looked ahead to a "Day of the Lord" when God's salvation or "making-wholeness" comes, they pictured a renewed cosmic harmony. Sickness and disease, war and famine, injustice and grief will be no more – and the lion will lie down with the lamb. In Ezekiel's great vision of the River of Life (echoed in the New Testament Book of Revelation), he speaks of the healing both of the earth and of all its creatures. Scholars in the past have not, it seems to me, paid sufficient attention to this emphasis on healing in trying to communicate to modern men and women what the Hebrew Bible is about. Words like redemption and salvation have little appeal or clout in today's world. But, as we all know, everyone has an interest and a personal stake in health, wholeness, and healing.

There are innumerable books about what are called the "Suffering Servant" passages in Isaiah because, for Christians, these are taken as prophetic of the coming of Jesus Christ and his eventual crucifixion "to save us from our sins." But, few, if any, have paid sufficient attention to the issue we are focussing upon here. In Isaiah (53:4-5), we read: "Surely he hath borne our griefs, and carried our sorrows; yet we did esteem him stricken, smitten of God, and afflicted. But he was wounded for our transgressions, he was bruised for our iniquities: the chastisement of our peace was upon him; *and with his stripes we are healed.*" Somehow, in the mind of the prophet, the vicarious suffering of the Servant (whomever he understood the Servant to be – according to some scholars he collectively stands for the Jewish people as a whole) is intended to bring healing to both Jew and non-Jew alike.

The overall thrust or preoccupation with the theme of healing in the theology of the Old Testament becomes intensely personal in the Book of Psalms, which is a collection of prayers and hymns flowing from the heart of Jewish spiritual life. It is far from accidental that these Psalms played so rich a part, not just in the devotional experience of the Jews in the centuries before the Christian era, but also in the life of Jesus himself (he quoted from them several times) and that of the early Christians. Through the ages since, the Psalms have been integral to Jewish and Christian worship alike.

The Psalms are a window through which we can view the inner wrestling of the human soul. All the emotions, conflicts, hopes, doubts, fears, and longings of our common humanity are laid bare in the presence of God or of what some theologians call the Ground of all Being, or the Depth Within. Pervading and overarching everything else is the yearning for wholeness and the healing of every aspect of the individual's life, body, mind, and spirit. There is a deep, explicit conviction in the Psalmist's outpourings that the natural will and bent of the ultimate cosmic energy is towards self-healing – both of the planet itself and of humankind (see Appendix III).

Finally, there are a number of instances of direct, physical

healings carried out by a variety of charismatic or prophetic individuals in the Old Testament narratives. In fact, one of the reasons
Jesus was given the title of prophet by his contemporaries – including some of the authors of the New Testament – was because working such miracles was a well-known mark of the classical prophets
of old. They were held to possess an extra measure of the Spirit of
God, and the inevitable outflowing of this energy manifested itself
in the restoration of others to full health. Moses, for example, had
been an instrument of healing, holding up a serpent of brass when
the Israelites were perishing of bites from a plague of "fiery ser-
pents" in the wilderness. Both Elijah and Elisha were involved in
remarkable events. There was not just the freeing of Naaman, the
Syrian army captain, from his leprosy, but two children, on sepa-
rate occasions, were raised from the point of death. Interestingly,
both prophets are described as carrying out something very close to
modern cardio-pulmonary resuscitation or CPR. In the case of the
Shunammite woman's son, it says, "And when Elisha was come
into the house, behold the child was dead, and laid upon his bed.
He went in therefore, and shut the door upon them twain, and
prayed unto the Lord. And he went up, and lay upon the child, and
put his mouth upon his mouth, and his eyes upon his eyes, and his
hands upon his hands: and he stretched himself upon the child; . . .
and the child sneezed seven times, and the child opened his eyes."
Elisha then called the mother in and said, "Take up thy son."[1]

⌒ Jesus as Healer

Mark's is the earliest of the four Gospels, written roughly about
65 A.D. It is simpler, more primitive than either of the other two
Synoptic Gospels or John. The frequent use of the word "immediately" to make connections between the various incidents lends
vigour and speed to the narrative, amounting at times to a kind of
breathlessness. This is supremely a Gospel of action. For Mark,
Jesus' communication of the "good news" of the Kingdom was

mainly non-verbal. Thus, while Mark frequently tells us that Jesus "taught them many things," scholars long ago noted the actual paucity of specific teachings. There are few parables, and Matthew's Sermon on the Mount, paralleled in Luke by the Sermon on the Plain, is not to be found.

All of this tends to throw the healings, exorcisms, and other signs or miracles that Mark describes – at times in great detail – into high relief. If a modern reader takes the time to read this Gospel through at a single sitting, the picture he or she will get is primarily one of Jesus as spiritual healer. Twelve healings are recorded in Mark (there are also more than a dozen references to the casting out of "demons" or unclean spirits), but the evangelist makes it clear by such statements as "and he healed many, all those who had a scourge of sickness" that the specific cases described are to be understood as typical of Jesus' whole ministry.

Jesus' first public act described in Mark (1:21), following the calling of the fishermen Peter, Andrew, James, and John, is the healing of a man possessed by an unclean spirit. The healing takes place right in the middle of a synagogue service at Capernaum.[2] In the so-called longer ending of the Gospel (16:9ff), which was included in the King James Version but is either omitted or marked as having been a later addition in the best modern translations, the Markan account concludes with the promise that all those who trust in the good news will cast out demons and lay hands upon the sick to heal them. Certainly, although this conclusion did not originate with the first author of Mark, it is in keeping with his overall view. It is clear throughout Mark's narrative that Jesus intended his disciples and all those who accepted his message that "the Kingdom is at hand" to carry out a ministry of healing.

A careful study of the individual healings in Mark shows a remarkable range of variables. There is no hard and fast modus operandi, no precise set of conditions to be met. True, the atmosphere in which every healing takes place is one of faith in the sense of trust, confidence, or expectancy. But it would be wrong to suppose that it is always the invalid who must have this faith.

There are several healings here – for example, in the case of the paralytic whose four friends lower him down through the roof of a house to get to Jesus – where the trust is supplied by someone else.

In the manner of secular healers of that day, Jesus sometimes, but not always, asks the sick person or, in the case of children, a parent about the duration of the disease. Sometimes he does a formal laying-on of hands, on other occasions he specifically touches the afflicted area; for example, the eyes of a blind man or the ears and tongue of a deaf-mute. But there are a number of healings described where he does not touch the person at all, and at least one (the woman with the "issue of blood" who had been ill for twelve years and had not only spent all her money on doctors but "was not helped but rather grew worse") where the recipient of the healing touched him.

That case, described within the story of the raising of Jairus' young daughter, has a number of fascinating features that add greatly to its feel of authenticity. The woman, who had had a gynecological problem of some sort, was convinced that if she could so much as touch Jesus' clothes from behind as he passed by she would become healthy or be "made whole." When she managed to do so, she suddenly "knew" within herself that the bleeding had dried up and that she was healed of her affliction. But Jesus, too, was aware of something having happened. The Greek text says that, having realized within himself that energy or power had flowed out of him, Jesus turned around and asked those immediately following, "Who touched me?" The disciples, often portrayed by Mark as none too bright, chided him sarcastically for such a question when he was being thronged by so many: "You can see the crowd mobbing you and you ask, who touched me!" Just then, the woman, timid and trembling, came forward and, falling at his feet, told her story. Jesus said to her, "Daughter, your faith has made you whole. Go into peace and be whole from your plague."

Occasionally, Jesus makes use of spittle – regarded as having healing, sacred power not just by healers of that time but by many aboriginal peoples today – and on one occasion mixes it with dirt to form a poultice. Since, presumably, he did not actually need such props, it seems likeliest that they were used for the sake of the patient. Able to read the mind of the person concerned, he seems to have had no compunction about using whatever means he judged effective in stimulating or increasing the patient's will and expectancy to be made whole. In the case of the blind man at Bethsaida, the original text says he "spit into his eyes" (so that the man would have no doubt that it was spittle and not just water being used) and laid hands on him.

This case is interesting because it is the only instance Mark records where the healing was incremental rather than instantaneous. Upon administering the spittle and the laying-on of hands, Jesus asked the blind man if he could see anything yet. He replied, "I can see people that look like walking trees." At that point, it says, Jesus put his hands on the man's eyes a second time and then had him look up. This time his sight was restored, and he could see everything "quite clearly."[3]

Nothing makes the case better for Jesus' flexible approach to healing than comparing this story of the blind man with the final healing in this Gospel, that of blind Bartimaeus. As Jesus and the disciples were leaving the ancient city of Jericho one day, a blind beggar, sitting by the roadside, began to cry out for Jesus to have mercy upon him. Instead of going to him, as in other cases, Jesus halted and told the others to call Bartimaeus to come to him. They went and delivered the message "Take courage, get up, he calls you." Bartimaeus jumped up, throwing off his outer cloak, and came to "the master." Then a curious thing happened. Jesus asked, "What do you want me to do for you?" In other words, he made him articulate what specifically he wanted. Did he want a hand-out, some sort of momentary comfort, or did he really want to get rid of the blindness that had become a way of life and a source of income? Bartimaeus immediately asked for restoration of his sight. Jesus replied, "'Go on your way; your faith has made you whole.' And immediately he saw, and he followed Jesus along the road." In this instance, Jesus used none of the techniques of the earlier healings.

He didn't even feel the need to use the laying-on of hands. Bartimaeus was ready and the healing took place.

The question here, of course, is the one that goes beyond Jesus' technique alone and asks what was the secret of his healing power. Before answering this, however, there is a prior question. Did he really heal at all, or are the stories of the miracles simply the later invention of credulous followers anxious to hype the reputation of their leader? Since many of them can be shown to have had a symbolic meaning – for example, people have their "ears" opened by the Gospel or their "blindness" gives way to spiritual sight – are we really dealing not with events but with theological insights put forward as narratives for greater dramatic effect?

This is a much more complex and tricky question than it appears at first sight. However, since there are plenty of scholarly works you can consult on the matter, here I will lay out as directly and as simply as I can what makes the best sense to me. I am totally convinced that in the presence of Jesus, often at his touch or command, sick people became well. Even the California-based Jesus Seminar, in its ongoing radical and controversial attempt to sift and test the Gospels in order to discern Jesus' precise words, has stated its conviction that he was a healer. In other words, even the most determined bid to get behind the New Testament tradition to the historic reality comes up against the fact that in the ministry of Jesus the lame walked, the deaf had their hearing restored, and the blind were made to see. Whatever else he was, whatever else he claimed to be, Jesus possessed an ability to free people from certain bodily and mental or emotional ills. Incidentally, given the conviction of the authors of the Gospels that Jesus could and did heal people, the restraint they show in narrating these stories is quite remarkable. To see this, one has only to read other, apocryphal gospels and writings from the first and second centuries that were eventually rejected by the Church. In them, Jesus is a wonderworker like Mandrake the Magician. For example, in one of them the child Jesus shapes doves out of clay. Then he claps his hands and they fly away!

This is not to say that all the healings recorded in the New Testament are necessarily historical. In my book *For Christ's Sake*, where I argue that working healings is by no means the same thing as "proof" of divinity, as some very conservative believers blithely suppose, I suggest that some of the miracles probably were included for theological rather than historical reasons; for example, the story of the raising of Lazarus told in John's Gospel. John tells us that for him the miracles are "signs" and that their true purpose is to bring people to belief in Jesus as the Son of God. Accordingly, he says that he deliberately chose the ones he did – out of a vast abundance – because of their suitability for promoting such conversions.[4]

Nevertheless, the truth remains that if the core testimony to Jesus' ability to heal is untrustworthy then the entire credibility of the Gospel record is undermined. Furthermore, as I have again pointed out elsewhere, the whole phenomenon of Jesus' effect on his contemporaries and the vigour of the movement which sprang from it become utterly inexplicable. Behind such a momentous effect there has to lie an extraordinary cause. One can only dismiss the healings if one has already decided that such things do not and cannot happen. There have always been, and still are, plenty of people, including biblical scholars, who take this tack.

But surely this assumption is a fallacy. If one already lays it down as a basic law (on faith alone) that there can be no such thing as spiritual or non-medical healing, one will never admit to having found any in the Gospels, or anywhere else for that matter. But the basis of this kind of thinking is a dogmatism of the most inflexible, inexorable kind. It has a façade of logic about it, but on closer inspection it is a materialistic assumption lacking solid proof of any type. What's more, it fails, among other reasons, because it simply does not account for all the data to be explained.

How, then, did Jesus heal? Mark's view is set out very early in his Gospel: "The scribes which came down from Jerusalem were saying that he [Jesus] was possessed by Beelzebub [a Philistine title for Satan] and that he was casting out demons through the power of the prince of devils. Summoning them to him, he said to them in parables: 'How can Satan cast out Satan? Surely if a kingdom is divided against itself it can not stand. And if a house is divided against itself it can not stand. Thus, if Satan rises against himself and is divided, he is finished. But nobody can go into the house of a strong man and plunder his goods unless he first binds the strong man. Then he will be able to rob his house. Truly I tell you, everything will be forgiven the sons of men, even whatever blasphemies they utter. But whoever blasphemes against the Holy Spirit has no forgiveness unto the age to come but is guilty of an ultimate sin.' He said this because they kept saying: 'He has an unclean spirit.'"[5]

Several points emerge from this passage. The representatives from the temple do not quarrel with the fact that Jesus was healing people of their bodily and mental or emotional diseases. They find the evidence itself too firm and obvious to be contested, and so their tactic is not to discredit the healings but the source of the energy or power at work in Jesus' ministry. Accordingly, they accuse him of being possessed himself and of working miracles through satanic means. In a shrewd piece of analysis, Jesus exposes the logical fallacies involved in their attack and then goes on to speak of the Unpardonable Sin. Tragically, down the ages, misunderstanding of this particular saying has caused more unnecessary heartache and despair than almost any other verse in the Bible. Overly sensitive and misguided folk have frequently and recklessly rushed to assume that they have committed the ultimate sin. I know from my own experience as a priest that for the most part these transgressions often turn out to have been sexual in nature and, in any case, truly minor in the scale of moral errors.

The truth is that anyone who is deeply worried he has committed the Unpardonable Sin most definitely hasn't. What Jesus is saying here is that the ultimate spiritual lapse is to mistakenly call good *evil*, to be unable to distinguish the Spirit of God from the spirit of that which contradicts and works against God. His claim in healing the sick is to be an agent or channel for the Divine Energy flowing from the heart of the universe, the very breath or presence of the dynamic Spirit of God. When Luke treats this same incident, he reports Jesus' saying: "If I by the finger of God cast out demons, the Kingdom of God has come upon you."[6]

Luke's Gospel takes this seminal concept of Mark – that Jesus acts and heals in and through the energy and power of the Holy Spirit of God – and develops it as the key to the entire secret of who Jesus was and what he came to do. He understands the phenomenon of Jesus' person and ministry totally in terms of his being filled and directed by God's Spirit.

Luke alone tells us that after the temptation in the wilderness, at the outset of his ministry, Jesus returned in the power of the Holy Spirit. In other words, he had opened himself in a unique way to the source of cosmic energy, wisdom, and healing. Almost immediately, Luke gives us the incident of Jesus' visit to his hometown of Nazareth and his attendance at the local synagogue. As was the custom, since he was recognized as a rabbi or teacher, he was invited to read from scripture and make comments upon the passage. In a description unique to Luke, we are told Jesus read from the Book of Isaiah in the place where it is written, "The Spirit of the Lord is upon me, for He has anointed me to make known good news to the poor, He has sent me to heal the brokenhearted." Then, putting down the scroll, he proclaimed to the stunned congregation, "Today this scripture has been fulfilled for you all to hear." Luke not only lays out here the program for the ministry described in the rest of his Gospel, he makes it absolutely clear that Jesus himself saw his gifts of healing and preaching as the direct result of an outpouring or "anointing" of divine power.[7] Many modern healers see their gifts in the same way. The difference is a matter of degree rather than of kind.

∼ Healing in the Gospel Tradition

A careful study of the Gospels reveals that their entire message is ultimately about healing; the healing of the individual, of the community, of the whole of humanity. Physical, emotional, and mental wholeness are all part of what it means to find salvation. They are both the signs and the results of the good news that, no matter what the "world" believes, the divine intelligence that created and sustains the cosmos is in ultimate control. They are the proofs and inevitable concomitants of the coming of what Jesus called the Kingdom of God. Healing in the fullest sense, spiritually and bodily, is what it means to be saved. The Greek verb *sozein*, to save, and its derivative *soteria*, or salvation, both come from a root meaning alive and well, sound in every aspect of one's being. It has been a tragedy that the Christian Church, and not just its more evangelical wing, has so often missed this truth and has interpreted being "saved" or "born again" in a narrow way that deals with the soul or spirit of the individual and neglects the psychosomatic dimension almost entirely.

In a manner that is totally in keeping with his Judaic background, Jesus' concern was with the entire person. For him it was actually a matter of indifference whether one spoke of someone's sins being forgiven or of their being restored to total physical health. He saw the two as different facets of the same reality. Hence his question to the critics after he told the man let down on a pallet through the roof of a house where he was healing the sick: "Son, thy sins are forgiven you; rise, take up your bed and walk." When the scribes complained that it was blasphemy to start announcing forgiveness of sins in this manner, Jesus replied, "Which is the easier, to say to the paralytic, 'Your sins are forgiven,' or simply, 'Arise, take up your bed and begin walking?'"[8]

Many moderns are put off by the frequent references in the Gospels, particularly in Mark (never in John), to demon possession and to the role of Jesus as an exorcist. Many conservative Christians of various stripes, on the other hand, especially those with a Pentecostal or Charismatic affiliation, have often gone overboard in their tendency to ascribe any condition or personal problem they can't comprehend – from homosexuality to serious depression – to the presence and work of demons. A leading Toronto

Pentecostal preacher once told me there would be no more hijackings of airplanes around the world. He said, with a totally straight face, that he and a preacher friend had fasted and prayed and then had "bound" the demons responsible for these terrorist acts. He pointed out that since their solemn act of exorcism there hadn't been a single hijacking. When I suggested that increased airline security probably had a lot to do with that, he looked at me pityingly and said, "That's exactly the sort of thing a sceptic would say." There have, of course, been many more hijackings and bombings of airplanes since then.

I believe that both camps, those who are completely turned off by the references to demons and exorcisms, and the extremists who see demons everywhere, are guilty of the same error. They are reading the text as literalists, with no feel for the rich symbolism that pervades the Gospels. There is no doubt that in the first century A.D. there was a widespread belief in the existence of demons or evil spirits. Exorcists were common. Diseases of all kinds were poorly understood, and the simplest solution was to regard them as the work of devils or of Satan himself. If you saw someone healing people assumed by you to be sick as a result of demons, it was only natural to suppose that the healer had exorcised the demons.

Jesus undoubtedly believed in the reality and power of evil. But there is nothing to suggest that he believed in a "personal Devil" or in the existence of demonic entities, à la Stephen King, capable of possessing individuals. It may be that the evangelists used the word "demons" in describing Jesus' healing ministry because that was the common language and symbolism of the day, especially where mental illness was concerned. It may be that Jesus used this symbolic language deliberately as a therapeutic technique. If a person sincerely believes his condition is due to demonic possession, it would be counterproductive not to convince him that the "demon" has been effectively dealt with! The story is told of one occasion when Dr. Norman Bethune was doing hospital rounds with some of his students. They came to a man who was absolutely convinced that his acute constipation was due to the fact that he had accidently swallowed a live frog. Bethune proceeded to give the poor man an enema. Then, when the desired effect had been achieved, he surreptitiously produced a frog from his pocket and slipped it into the bedpan. He told the students afterwards that the enema was for the patient's physical problem; "the frog was for his mind."

A final word about faith in its relation to healing in the Gospels. As I have said in *For Christ's Sake*, my study of the New Testament convinces me that Jesus saw fear as the chief enemy of human health and wholeness. His most characteristic sayings are exhortations to his disciples and others to have courage, to "be of good cheer," to let go of worry and anxiety and have radical trust in the "heavenly Father." He urges his followers to practise forgiveness and to lead their lives, one day at a time, based upon proper love of God, self, and others. But above all he stresses the therapeutic power of faith. This faith or trust has nothing whatever to do with belonging to any religious organization. It is not a faith in this or that set of creeds. It is a basic trust in the universe or in the life-force itself. It is a kind of expectant confidence that is quite aware of the injustices and perils all around and yet believes that God's Will will be done. It is not childishness but has the unqualified wholeheartedness that marks the trust of a child. Which, of course, is why Jesus once set a child in the midst of his disciples and told them that unless they became as little children they could not enter the Kingdom of Heaven. It is certainly much harder for a seriously ill person to get well unless someone, not necessarily the patient, believes and trusts that healing both can take place and is taking place.

Finally, it must be said that Jesus in no way thought of his healings as proof of his having a unique claim to divinity. Nor were they taken as constituting such proof by the religious leaders of his time. The temple authorities, fully aware of the number of sick being healed, nevertheless persisted in asking Jesus for more persuasive evidence. After all, they knew of lots of other healers, past and present. However, their repeated request for some irresistible, overwhelming "sign" from Jesus as evidence of his Messiahship was quite flatly rejected by him.

∼ The Acts of the Apostles

Jesus clearly believed that in the presence of the agents of the Kingdom of God, diseases of all kinds had to retreat and yield their debilitating hold on humankind. This reality was something all were meant to share in. Naturally, then, he insisted that the ministry of healing belonged to the whole community. It is quite evident from the Gospel tradition that he expected his disciples to go out and be instruments of healing. And this is precisely what we find the earliest Christians doing, not as an esoteric ritual rarely practised, but as a regular, natural, and expected part of their mission.

The only history of the early Christian Church is in the Book of Acts, one of the most dramatic and adventure-filled pieces of literature to have come out of the ancient world. For believer and non-believer alike it is an extraordinary read. I am reminded of the story told about Oscar Wilde as a student at Oxford. His classics tutor, worried that the young man was wasting his time and talent in carousing and skipping lectures, decided to humble him and bring him to heel. Without warning one day at the weekly tutorial, he gave Wilde a copy of the Greek New Testament and told him to begin translating aloud. It had been opened at the Book of Acts, which is filled with difficult Greek words, particularly in the story of the shipwreck of Paul. To the tutor's deep chagrin, his student was able to translate the text without difficulty. Foiled, and assuming that somehow Wilde had managed to read Acts in the original some time previously, he impatiently told him to stop translating. At which point Wilde exclaimed, "I can't stop now, sir. I want to find out whatever happened to St. Paul!"

Acts was written in all probability sometime between 70 and 80 A.D. The author was undoubtedly also responsible for Luke's Gospel, and there is no reason to reject the traditional view that this was the same "Luke the beloved physician" to whom Paul refers in his letters. Another title for this work could well be "The Acts of the Holy Spirit," because, while the Apostles are the central characters, the text makes it clear on every page that the same Spirit who empowered the ministry of Jesus was acting and working through the ministry of Peter, Stephen, Paul, and the entire Christian community. What Jesus was able to do in healing the sick and spiritually afflicted, Acts says, the Apostles were also able to do. In both cases, the source of the healing energy is declared to be God. Jesus was God's Spirit-filled agent; now the early Christians were his agents, healing in his name, having been anointed, blessed, or filled with the very same Spirit. In Acts, the Church is, internally, a self-healing community. Externally, as it reaches out into a predominantly pagan world, its power to heal, sometimes spectacularly, is its principal and most effective method of outreach. Those who had no previous idea of the strange message being proclaimed by the earliest Christians were attracted initially by either hearing of or seeking a "miracle" of healing.

Anyone who reads the Book of Acts quickly realizes that the vibrant, energy-filled Church of apostolic times is a far cry from the mainstream churches of today. In Acts, healing is not some peripheral activity for fanatics, sectarians, or mystics. It lies at the heart of what the Christian community is all about. There are almost as many notable healings recorded (eight) as in Mark's Gospel. In addition, just as in that Gospel, there are frequent statements to the effect that "signs and wonders" were a routine part of the apostolic ministry. There is no rigid schema according to which healing takes place. Sometimes, as in the case of the man "lame from birth" in Chapter 3, there is no mention whatever of the invalid having faith. It is the faith of the apostles James and John that releases the healing energy. When, however, Paul encounters a man similarly afflicted from birth at Lystra, the text says that Paul, *seeing the man had faith to be healed,* said to him in a loud voice, "'Stand up erect on your feet.' And he leapt and walked about."[9] Just as Jesus did, at times the Apostles healed through prayer and the laying-on of hands. So, in the case of the father of Publius, on the Island of Malta, where the man was suffering from high fever and severe dysentery, Paul prayed, then placed his hands upon him and healed him.[10] At other times, no touching is involved.

In one odd narrative, handkerchiefs and bits of clothing belonging to Paul are said to have been carried to the sick, with healing efficacy. (I must confess that until recently I had regarded this as superstition. As we shall see later, however, there is evidence today that some natural materials, most notably absorbent cotton, can retain a bioenergy field once it has been induced by a healer and have accordingly been used to facilitate healing.) In another passage in Acts, we are told how, as stories of the healings became known, people brought their sick folk out into the streets on beds and mattresses in the hope that the shadow of Peter might fall upon them as he passed by. This reveals the faith of the crowd, but it seems to the modern mind to border once again on rank superstition. Here again, though, I have found that research into what is going on in the world of non-medical healing today may throw an entirely new light on this story as well.[11] Incidentally, the author of Acts doesn't give us either the reaction of Peter or the results (if any) of Peter's shadow falling on the sick.

～ The Earliest Evidence of All

It may seem odd to leave this final, brief discussion to the end of this examination when, chronologically it belongs earlier. Because of the order in which the New Testament books are set out in the Bible, it appears that the Gospels and Acts were written before the letters of Paul and the others. The truth, however, is that all of Paul's letters were written before the earliest of the four Gospels. I have chosen to save them until now because the Christ Event described in the Gospels obviously preceded them even though the Gospels took their final shape later. The point is that

Paul was less than twenty years from the Passion and Resurrection of Jesus when he wrote the following passage:

"I don't want you, brethren, to be ignorant about spiritual gifts. . . . There are different gifts, but the same Spirit. And there are various ministries, but the same Lord. There are different kinds of operations, but it is the same God at work in all of them. To each is given the manifestation of the Spirit as is most expedient [for them]. For, to one is given by the Spirit a word of wisdom, to another the word of knowledge by the same Spirit. To another is given the gift of faith by the same Spirit, and to yet another *the gifts of healings* by the one Spirit. . . . All of these gifts are the work of that one, identical Spirit Who divides them out to each person individually as He wills."[12]

The early witness of Paul, then, is that God, described as an active or energizing Spirit, the same Spirit by whom Jesus healed the sick during his ministry, endowed various members of the fledgling churches with healing powers. Or rather, that God chose certain individuals through whom to channel or focus a ministry of healing. Paul writes here not only as one who is convinced of the reality of the phenomenon he is describing but also as a man who fears no rebuttal. He knows that the recipients of his letter at Corinth are fully aware that some of their number are being used to heal other people. The healings are not in any way at issue. They are a commonly accepted fact. Paul is not writing to convince anybody of their reality. His focus is on giving these new Christians a sense of perspective and balance on the matter of spiritual gifts in general. His emphasis on the one Spirit in and behind the "gifts," *charismata*, as he calls them in Greek, is intended to end squabbles over which spiritual gift is greater. Hence his great metaphor of the body, in which he shows how even the parts of our physical body that seem least important have an integral function and role to play. He asks, "If the whole body were an eye, where would the hearing be? If the whole were hearing, where would the smelling be?"[13]

When, in verses twenty-nine and thirty, Paul asks, "Are all apostles? are all prophets? are all teachers? are all workers of miracles? have all the gifts of healing?" the only possible answer is "no." He is acknowledging what modern studies confirm, that the capacity for psychic or spiritual healing is more fully possessed by some people than by others. One can develop or "stir up" an innate gift, but it cannot be attained through personal effort. Nor is it a cause for pride or self-congratulation. It comes as a charisma, a sheer gift of grace – to be used for others.

Significantly, there is nothing in the letters of Paul, or indeed in any other part of the New or Old Testaments, that would set up a dichotomy between medical science and other, non-medical forms of healing. There is nothing, for example, to suggest that Luke the physician felt any tension between his healing skills and the techniques of prayer or the laying-on of hands by the Apostles and others. Paul, the best-educated and most intelligent of all the early Christians, was the last man to be seduced by quackery or anti-intellectual fanaticism. Neither does he assume that since there is such a thing as a charisma of healing nobody should ever get sick, or that everybody who does will be instantly healed if they believe enough, pray enough, and meet the right healer. There are several instances of Paul's associates suffering illnesses of various kinds. He, or the unknown author of 1 Timothy (depending on which scholarly view you accept), straightforwardly advised the young man Timothy to stop drinking the local water on his travels and instead "drink a little wine for your stomach's sake and your frequent indispositions."[14]

Paul tells us that because of the richness and depth of his own mystical experiences – including visions and clairvoyance – there was a real risk of his becoming unduly "puffed up" or arrogant. As a result, he says, God sent him a "thorn in the flesh" to keep him humble. There has been endless speculation by scholars – some of it rather bizarre – as to the nature of this "thorn." The Episcopal Bishop of Newark, New Jersey, Rt. Rev. John Spong, has specu-lated that Paul's problem was latent homosexuality.[15] A more likely explanation is that it was some form of ophthalmic difficulty, perhaps going back to his temporary blindness at the moment of his dramatic conversion on the road to Damascus. For our purposes, however, the exact nature of this physical affliction matters little. The point is that Paul tells us he prayed many times for this problem to be removed or healed. The answer he got was that he had to learn to live with it. He reports that God said to him, "My grace is all you need. For my strength is being made perfect in your weakness." In other words, while one has a right and even a duty to seek for complete healing, there is no magic here, no instant solution to the things that may cause us pain. Yet, God is in and through it all.

∾ The Epistle of James

Martin Luther didn't care much for the Epistle of James, because it lays so much emphasis upon good works and says nothing about his favourite doctrine of justification by faith. In fact, he called it "a right strawy epistle." Nevertheless, some scholars date it very early, and it is important here because it has another, often-quoted reference to the reality of the healing ministry in the early church of the first century. In the fifth chapter, the author says, "Is any among you ill? Let him call for the church elders and let them pray over him, anointing him with oil in the name of the Lord. And the prayer of faith will save the sick and the Lord will raise him up. And, if he has committed sins, they will be forgiven him. Admit your faults to one another and pray for each other that you may be healed. The active prayer of a just person has an enormous effect."

In addition to underlining the fact that healing, through prayer and anointing with oil, was considered normal in the primitive Christian Church, this passage gives further witness to the near-universal religious conviction that there can be times when an illness may be the result or the symptom of unresolved sins or faults. An obvious example would be problems created by deliberate abuse of one's body through neglect, excess of any kind, or a bad diet. But James is not implying that sickness and disease are always somehow a sign of wrong-doing or wrong thinking. Overall, the Bible expressly denies such a view. What James is stressing is that confession of known sins – a frank facing up to the specific times and places when one has fallen short of what one knows one should have done or been – and the assurance of forgiveness remove the spiritual blockages that prevent healing energy from flowing in.

⌒ Summary

The New Testament ends with a remarkable vision of a renewed and healed cosmic order in which the past with its suffering has faded away and all things are made new. The King James Version puts it eloquently: "And God shall wipe away all tears from their eyes; and there shall be no more death, neither sorrow, nor crying, neither shall there be any more pain: for the former things are passed away."[16] The pinnacle of the vision is reached when the seer describes the pure river of the "water of life, clear as crystal," which proceeds out of the throne of God. In it and on either side of it grows up the "tree of life" whose leaves are for the healing of all the nations of the world. This is a fitting conclusion to a religious or spiritual saga which began with the myth in Genesis of the brokenness of humanity caused by Adam and Eve eating the fruit of the "tree of life" and their consequent banishment from the Garden of Eden. What is being said through all of this sublime symbolism is that, in spite of all the agony and tears of all the ages, the ultimate destiny both of the earth and of humankind is healing and wholeness in the presence of God.

The message of the Bible is that the energizing, creative intelligence "in whom we live and move and have our being" is constantly seeking us out to make us whole. Even though we "flee him down the labyrinthine ways" of our own minds, God moves towards us constantly in forgiveness and love. As the Divine Lover, he will not let us go.

Christians talk a great deal about "the Gospel" or "the Good News," but often without any clear understanding of what it really means or of how it can be shown to be good news to modern men and women. To me, the entire Judeo-Christian heritage constitutes good news precisely because it is about the healing of the individual, the community, the nation, and ultimately the world. The greatest single source of health and healing in the life of any person flows from knowing oneself to be accepted and loved by the very Ground of All Being. To feel at home in the universe, to experience forgiveness, to love and be loved, to have a sense of meaning and destiny for one's life – these all bring and foster wholeness of mind, body, and spirit. And these are the very things the Bible is about when you look to the core.

When the greatest preacher of the early centuries, John Chrysostom (literally, "golden-mouth"), reflected on the story of the Church of Acts and compared it with the Church of his own day (the late fourth and early fifth centuries A.D.), he lamented, "Our Church is like a very expensive, ornate jewel box. But the jewels are all gone!" Chrysostom was deeply aware that in the days following the decision of the Emperor Constantine to make Christianity the official state religion of the Roman Empire, shortly after 312 A.D., the vitality of the earliest Christians greatly diminished. The age of the Holy Spirit largely gave way to the age of conformity and of political compromise. Yet, down through the centuries, the Book of Acts has stood as a witness and a challenge to all Christians. Something transforming and new happened to human consciousness with the birth of Christianity. The "myth" of that is most powerfully described in the story of the first Pentecost, with which the Book of Acts begins. The meaning of the myth is that in the death and Resurrection of Jesus Christ, with its consequent lifting of consciousness, a vast pulse of energy was released. This outpouring or upsurge of the Divine Spirit – symbolized in the description of the Day of Pentecost as coming with a sound like a "mighty, rushing wind" and with tongues "like as of fire" – expressed itself in many ways and not least in the physical and emotional healing of those who opened themselves to or placed themselves in the path of its power.

Some, being sceptics, will accept none of this. That is their privilege. Amongst Christians, the majority believe – or act as though they do – that the Acts of the Holy Spirit may well have happened more or less as described but that they belong to a special time of dispensation. They're not for today. My own feeling is that this approach has been a cop-out for far too long. If there is to be a Christian Church at all as we close upon the new millennium, it will undoubtedly have to be one that has begun to take its own birthright seriously at last.

5

The Blind Healer

"The whole world is crying out for something better, something above materialism, something that can save them from war, cruelty and depravity, something that will heal men's minds and enable them to lead healthy and happy lives, not lives crippled by fear and dread."
    – Godfrey Mowatt[1]

I t is one thing to read about shamans and healers or to be aware of the biblical origins of certain types of non-medical healing. It is another to come face-to-face with an actual healer. That's what this chapter is about. The story you are about to read has impressed me very much. It is one surprisingly few people outside Britain know anything about.

During the early 1960s, I became friends with Herbert Mowat, an Anglican layman who was the executive director of the Canada-Israel Committee. Mowat, who died in 1975 at the age of eighty-two, was a tireless champion of the United Nations, of the cause of a homeland for the Jewish people, both before and after the founding of the State of Israel, and of world peace. His passion, energy, and his skill as an orator – he spoke in great cathedrals and in tiny churches, legion halls, anywhere he could get a podium, from Whitehorse to outports in Newfoundland – amazed everyone who met him. I mention Herbert Mowat here because it was he who first told me about one of the most remarkable figures in the modern recovery of a healing ministry by the traditional churches, Godfrey Mowatt.

Godfrey Mowatt (1874-1958) was the son of Sir Francis Mowatt, a civil servant of the British government who eventually rose to the post of Permanent Secretary to the Treasury. Since Sir Francis had attended Winchester and Oxford and had both a country mansion and a London home, complete with servants, carriages, and all the other marks of a highly successful man, it was assumed that Godfrey would follow in his father's footsteps – a privileged childhood, a top-notch education, followed by a brilliant political career. However, a terrible accident intervened and changed everything.

In her book *Forth in Thy Name: The Life and Work of Godfrey Mowatt*[2] (now out of print), Kathleen Lonsdale, who knew and worked with Mowatt for many years and who was appointed as the first secretary of the Churches' Council of Healing by the late Archbishop of Canterbury, William Temple, describes him as a child as "blue-eyed, with red-gold curls." She goes on to say he was unusually alert and intelligent. He grew up "sturdy, strong and good-looking" in the spacious estate of Withdeane Hall, his parents' country home.[3] His main passion as a youngster was his pony, Penelope, and his trips on her into the wilder areas beyond the estate. One afternoon, in his seventh summer, while his parents were away on a holiday in Germany, Mowatt broke a garter and tied a bit of string around his leg in its place. When he was getting ready for bed that night, he tried to undo the string. When this proved impossible, he took his penknife to it. The string was severed suddenly and the knife flashed up into his left eye, "doing irreparable damage." The child gave a cry because, although there was no pain initially, his eye was flooded with blood and he couldn't see out of it. A maid called the governess, and a doctor was hurriedly summoned. There was little he could do, according to Lonsdale's account, except to give Godfrey some whisky "to bring the blood to the surface and so clear the eyes for him to see." This caused excruciating pain and the child writhed about in agony for hours until he finally fell asleep, exhausted.

By the following day, both eyes were horribly swollen, and the boy was kept in his bed with the room darkened to keep out any light. The doctor gave him sedatives to help him sleep, but not much else could be done, given the state of medicine at the time. Unfortunately, the sympathetic nerve of his other eye was soon affected, and he lost all sight in it, "leaving only a glimmering of sight in the eye he had stabbed."[4] By the time his anguished parents had rushed back to be with him, Mowatt was already beginning to realize that the darkness wasn't going to pass. It was a permanent "horror" that would deprive him of light and freedom of movement and action. His mother and father were devastated. Their fond hopes for him were shattered, and they (somewhat selfishly) at first feared that instead of adding glory to the family name he was destined to be a burdensome responsibility.

Nevertheless, they did their best. Godfrey shared a governess with his older brother and a younger sister. He was taught to read by feeling words made of big letters cut out of cardboard. After two years of this, he shared a tutor with his brother, Frank, until he was twelve. Mowatt was then sent to Worcester College for "Blind

Sons of Gentlemen," run by an Anglican cleric, Rev. Strong Foster. In spite of the snobbish name, the college took blind boys from diverse backgrounds. Being "somewhat spoiled" and over-protected, the young lad found the school a great shock, and he became bitterly unhappy. Their suffering seemed to have hardened some of the other students and he found them rough and abusive. He did, however, learn something about independence and that he was not alone in his condition. Although his own home had not been particularly religious, Mowatt became preoccupied with confused thoughts about God, religion, and the meaning of his own life. Lonsdale reports: "He wandered in an uninhabited wilderness, seeking to recapture something, Someone he had once known, and finding in the life of the college little or nothing to point the way out of his spiritual desert."

By age sixteen, Mowatt's right eye had become such a disfigurement that his parents agreed with the doctor it should be removed. A new technique was tried in which the muscle of the eye was left to give movement to an artificial eye. The procedure failed, and a long illness followed during which his studies lapsed. He was withdrawn from Worcester College and returned home to be tutored by a succession of top university students.

One of them, J. Kindersley, was an oarsman who, in addition to history, taught Mowatt the art of rowing. He seemed to have a natural aptitude for it, and it remained a source of exercise and great pleasure for most of the rest of his life. (Anyone familiar with this sport knows that part of the training involves rowing "blind" with your eyes closed in order to develop timing, poise, and balance. It gives one a quite extraordinary sense of weightlessness – like flying). Kindersley also introduced Mowatt to the joys of a tandem bike, and the pair regularly went for long rides through the English countryside. At the same time, one of Withdeane's stablemen, a man called Henry, undertook to be his companion during the local fox hunt. Henry would alert Mowatt when fences were coming, watch as he took them, and come to his aid whenever there was a spill. All in all, his late teens proved a rich time. Looking back on this period, Mowatt said he was always grateful to his mentors.

They brought a sense of proportion back to his life, humour to his mind, light to his soul, and the means of keeping his body active and fit.

Just before his twentieth birthday, Mowatt decided it was time he did something for others. He joined a small committee which had just been founded and had begun to manage the Barclay School for Blind Girls in Brighton, Sussex. From this small beginning there gradually developed a far-reaching work for the blind, which he carried on for the rest of his life. At the same time, he continued to ride regularly with the Southdown Foxhounds. On his twenty-first birthday, his father gave him a big mare, a trained hunter called Speckles, who became a devoted companion and guide. She often brought him safely home from distant villages without guidance – at times her trail taking her across the neighbours' lawns and flowerbeds.

What is important for our enquiry, however, is the way compensations for his blindness were rapidly developing. He soon came to have a keen sense of direction, acute hearing, and an unusual sensitivity of touch. Above all, he was beginning to acquire a remarkable, intuitive ability to understand the people he met. It seemed that, with none of the distractions of people's appearance and manner, he could discern what they were really like and what was going on in their inner lives. He began to move about with more confidence at home and to take a normal part in the social gatherings both there and at the homes of his parents' friends.

Then, some unusual spiritual or psychic events began to occur. He wrote this description of his first direct experience of "divine guidance": "I woke in the night and heard a voice telling me that I must warn a young friend of the family who was our house guest at the time that she should go home. I must admit I was too scared of being laughed at to say anything to her at first. But the next night I heard the same thing again and this time I was more frightened of not telling her than of being ridiculed. Strangely enough, as soon as I told her, she went home. She found her brother lying across the dining table – he had shot himself. Had I warned the girl that first night, she might have had time to save his life. I made a vow that in future I would disregard all doubt."[5] Mowatt was to have this kind of telepathic insight or "guidance" again and again.

Much later in life he had a strong premonition startlingly similar to his first. He became aware of a sudden, inexplicable urge one day to see a certain friend. He felt the man was in some terrible danger. When he went to his friend's house, the butler insisted that his master was not at home. Mowatt, however, sensing something, felt certain that he was in the house and refused to be put off. They went through the large house together and found his friend sitting in his study with a loaded pistol lying in front of him on the desk. He was preparing to take his own life, and would certainly have done so if it hadn't been for Mowatt's timely intervention.

Yet, in spite of his growing capacity to accept his disability and the fact that certain spiritual gifts were now appearing as a kind of compensation, it would be wrong to suppose the young man was free from periods of depression, frustration, and loneliness. In the circles in which his family moved, all the young people were freely pursuing careers, courting, getting married, and establishing their own homes. Godfrey Mowatt spent many hours and days filled with mental anguish and even despair. He had already faced up to the question of marriage and decided that it would be unfair to ask anyone to accept his limitation as a life partner.

But eventually he did meet a young woman (by a strange coincidence her name was Constance Frend), for whom he felt an overwhelming attraction and, with the prompting and encouragement of his friends, he finally asked her to marry him. To his amazement – since he held the firm conviction it would be an "insult" and an "effrontery" for him to propose – she accepted him gladly. They were married in April 1898, and moved into their own house (a gift from his parents). They lived there happily for the sixty years of their married life.

Then a quite extraordinary accident happened, as a result of which he regained partial sight for just over a year. One day Mowatt was playfully flicking a whip, and the tip of the lash "caught his eye and performed an operation of the greatest delicacy in lifting a film from it." He saw his wife for the first time. He was able to go bicycling and riding by himself and to enjoy a freedom not known since he was seven. Although he and his wife were able to joke about it later and say that it was the sight of her that made him go blind again, after a year his sight began to fail. He was soon totally blind once more. Fortunately, before this happened in 1903, their only child, Mary Elizabeth, "Molly," was born.

His next few years were very full; he was now running his own business, a small transport firm in Wimbledon, and leading a public life that ranged from helping to train the world's first blind rowing eight at his old school to being made president-for-life of the local football club and, in 1914, becoming one of the youngest magistrates ever appointed in England to that time. On the outbreak of the First World War, he became a recruiting officer for the Special Reserve and chairman of various committees aimed at the war effort. Later, as war-blinded soldiers began to return from France he taught many to read Braille and was able to minister to their general well-being by sharing his own experience of coping without sight. He also talked with them about the strength he found in his own deepening faith.

That faith was soon to be tested. In 1917, as he was walking to meet his sister Maggie, a stray pellet from an airgun came over the hedge and struck the glass eye he was now wearing, fracturing it and driving tiny splinters deep into the socket. The glass fragments could only be taken out as they came to the surface, and so it took the surgeons almost three years of intermittent, extremely painful operations to remove them all. Mowatt went through a veritable hell of suffering. His heart was affected by the strain, as well as his nerves, and the doctors told him to give up all vigorous exercise, including climbing stairs. In 1918, his father died, and this, added to all the rest, precipitated an episode of deep depression. He had been able to cope with being blind, but being blind and a chronic invalid as well now seemed too much.

A prayer circle was formed by his wife and a few friends to support him. Feeling miserable, but prompted and encouraged by those around him, Mowatt gradually began to call on friends and others who were sick. To his surprise, he found that as he did so his own physical strength seemed to increase. He widened his visits to include nearby villages, and soon there were reports that people were finding themselves not only greatly cheered up by his presence but strikingly improved in bodily health as well. Many claimed their ailments had left them completely. What's more, in a short time Mowatt's doctors declared his heart to be perfectly normal once more, and he was able to take up sculling again. He won two events at the Worcester College Regatta (for the blind) that same year. The entire episode, from the moment of the shooting, was pivotal in the making of the healer Godfrey Mowatt was now becoming.

On March 19, 1919, just after recovering from his depressed state, Godfrey Mowatt had a vision. He found it very difficult to put into words but, as he later told his wife and friends, he had heard a command to "Go forth and serve your fellow men." The revelation was given to him that his own experience of suffering had equipped him to bring help to others in pain, illness, and grief. The entire mystical experience had been shot through and surrounded by a kind of "dazzling light." It seemed to him as though Christ had come and filled him with a new sense of an "indwelling love" and with the conviction that he was now to be a channel of the love of God to those in need of spiritual and physical healing.

Mowatt had been busy before, but the number of political, social, and educational enterprises he now became involved in is truly staggering. He was made chairman of the local chamber of commerce, president of the regional Liberal Council, and chairman of the Standing Committee of the National Institute for the Blind. When the British government set up a special advisory committee on the welfare of the blind he was appointed to this, and later he became a member of the Royal Commission on the Causes and Prevention of Blindness. He was then made a governor of the Royal Normal College for the Blind, chairman of London's Metropolitan Society for the Blind, and was given a host of other responsibilities at numerous colleges and institutes for blind youth and adults. In 1929, Mowatt represented England at a European conference, held in Vienna, for improving the lot of the blind.

Dismayed at the conditions delegates reported as "normal" in Europe at the time – little or no welfare work was being done, and blind children were used by beggars to solicit money on the streets – Mowatt attracted wide attention with his progressive ideas. Consequently, he was sent to New York for the 1931 World's Conference on the Blind, and was soon invited to act as chairman for the International Committee. In May 1935, his heroic efforts on behalf of blind people everywhere were recognized by the King and Queen. Mowatt was awarded a Silver Jubilee Medal at Buckingham Palace.

It may seem that this account of Mowatt's life and work is tangential to the central concern of this book. However, I have laid it out in detail because it is vital you see the kind of man he was. If you were to read only about the healing ministry that was at the same time evolving in and through him – and which we are now going to look at more fully – you could mistakenly think of Mowatt as some kind of one-dimensional religious or psychic phenomenon. The truth is, there has seldom been a more balanced, socially aware, and attractive person than he. His caring for others was so real, practical, and this-worldly that he impressed everyone who met him or saw him in action, whether they were Christians or atheists. I have never come across anyone associated with non-medical healing who has so convinced me of his personal wholeness and integrity as Godfrey Mowatt.

Mention has already been made of what at first report had seemed like mere coincidences. When Mowatt visited the sick – initially as a means of alleviating his own anguish – many began to recover. Lonsdale writes, "Friends . . . made remarkable recoveries, and soon it became obvious that it was more than mere coincidence. Local doctors also noticed the connection between his visits and a patient's return to health, perhaps unexpectedly rapid, perhaps not expected at all, and they began to send their patients to him when they made no progress."[6]

Mowatt, realizing that he had been given the power of healing, decided around 1936 to dedicate the rest of his life to using this charisma or "gift of grace" in the service of God and humanity. He made contact with the Guild of Health, a society that had been in existence in England for some time to promote an understanding of what it called Divine Healing. Here he was introduced to a man named Rev. David Workman, the guild's vice-president. As they met and shook hands, each greeted the other at the same moment with the words "We have a lot of work to do together." This proved to be prophetic. Much later, Workman commented, as he recalled that first encounter, that he was convinced the coincidence of their words of greeting was in fact a sign of the Spirit's presence making clear to them "His Will and Purpose."[7] In any case, he quickly realized that Mowatt was the leader for whom he and his associates had long been praying.

It was not long before Mowatt became Organising Secretary of the Guild of Health, and he began to take part in healing services held regularly in St. Martin-in-the-Fields, on Trafalgar Square in central London. With him were Workman and another Anglican cleric, Rev. Pat McCormick. The notable thing about these services – and all the healing work Mowatt was soon to do all over England and beyond – was their simplicity, dignity, and quiet reverence. There were no sensational claims, no promises of miracles, no blowing of trumpets or any of the hoopla associated with the television healers in North America today.

Godfrey Mowatt never solicited or took fees for any of this work. Wherever he went, Mowatt, guided by another man, usually the vicar of the parish, would give a brief sermon in which he outlined some aspect of the Church's ministry of healing – for instance, the importance of forgiveness of others or oneself for physical and mental health – and then he would invite all who wished to do so to come up and kneel at the altar rail. With the vicar guiding his hands, he would place them lightly on the head of each person as he passed along the line. He always said the following prayer: "May the mercy of God, which is present here with us now, enter into your soul, your mind, your body, and heal you from all that harms you." When all had been prayed for in this way, there would be a final period of quiet prayer, the recital of the Lord's Prayer, an act of thanksgiving, and a blessing. There was no emotional appeal, no badgering or exploitation – and people were remarkably helped. They were often healed physically, as the flood of letters Mowatt constantly received attests. But, more important to him, they were healed inwardly as they caught through this blind healer a fresh vision of the Light.

Mowatt once wrote: "It means more to me when people write to say they have found new peace and happiness, such as they have never known before, through the Light penetrating their darkness, than when they write that they have received some wonderful healing." Having witnessed the horrors of two world wars, Mowatt knew that physical health in and of itself is not everything. As he once said, "We may have strong, healthy nations and yet plan to use our youth in defensive or offensive wars." He knew, he said, from his own experience, that it was only the presence of God's love or "the Living Christ within" that brings healing to the minds of people and drives out "the terrible thoughts and fears that possess them. It is in this Divine Healing that the world can be saved." Basic to his whole approach was his insistence that the power of God is always "with us and around us" – the fundamental teaching of Jesus regarding what he called the presence of the Kingdom of God in our midst. To understand truly the reality of this divine, cosmic light or energy surrounding one, Mowatt said, is to know that help is available to free us from fear and dread and to assist the mind to free the body from physical suffering.[8]

Before documenting the experiences of some of the many thousands of people Godfrey Mowatt reached in his ceaseless ministry, which he undertook in his early sixties and continued almost to the day he died in 1958 at the age of eighty-four, it is crucial to report an event that ensured he was no lone ranger of healing but strongly tied to the mainstream life of the major churches. In 1942, Archbishop William Temple – who was Archbishop of Canterbury for little more than two years (1942-44) and yet has already been recognized as one of the greatest scholars and most loved men ever to hold that office – approached Mowatt with a remarkable proposal. He had heard of the blind layman's healing gifts and, after making exhaustive enquiries of his own, invited him to come to his residence, Lambeth Palace. The archbishop asked Mowatt whether he would be prepared to take on a much wider work, travelling to churches throughout the country as his official healer.

Mowatt, who was now sixty-eight, accepted the challenge, and on March 26, 1943, a most unusual service took place in the archbishop's newly refurbished chapel at Lambeth. In this small, private sanctuary, a group of clergy and friends were witnesses as the head of the Church of England commissioned Mowatt for the unusual task. It was moments before noon. There was a brief time of silence, then Big Ben boomed out the hour from directly across the river. They said the Lord's Prayer, recited a couple of other prayers, read a short passage from John's Gospel, ending with the words: "Without Me, you can do nothing," and then Temple laid his hands on Mowatt's head saying, "Go forth, and in the power of God bring healing to the minds and bodies and to the souls of men."

Temple's endorsement of the ministry of spiritual healing, and his strong desire to see it restored to a position it once had held in the Church of earlier times, is of vital significance. Because of his intellectual stature as a theologian and the enormous respect he gained with the entire nation during the war years, first as Archbishop of York and then as Archbishop of Canterbury, Temple could never be dismissed as a mere pietist or religious enthusiast. He made it very clear that this was no odd-ball or extremist concern at the first meeting of a committee he and Mowatt formed to co-ordinate and promote the Church's work of healing. Temple said that his primary concern was to use this new and practical approach to people's needs as a means whereby the Church could truly meet their spiritual hunger.

Temple was particularly careful to stress that the Church was in no way trying to usurp or belittle the work of the medical profession. There was, he said, no question of one mode being superior to the other. He noted, however, that it was doctors attesting to the cures wrought through Mowatt that had first attracted his attention. Also, it was doctors attending the wounded troops who had pressed the archbishop for action because, as they said, medicine and surgery had no remedies for the mental and spiritual scars left by the horrors of war. They pointed out that patients' response to physical treatment was often slowed or blocked where there was anguish of the soul. Temple's aim was always full co-operation between doctors and spiritual healers, because of his conviction that treating one part of the human reality apart from the other would eventually prove disastrous. By insisting on a holistic approach, he was in this as in so many other things a man ahead of his time. Some six months after Temple's death, officials of the major Protestant churches in England joined with the Anglicans, under Mowatt's guidance, to form the Churches' Council of Healing. The new Archbishop of Canterbury, Dr. Geoffrey Fisher, became its first president.[9]

The council thrashed out a policy statement on healing, which included the following three cardinal points:

(1) "All healing proceeds from the activity of the Eternal creative Power of God ever seeking to restore harmony to His world. God's will for man is perfect health, but sickness and disease are facts which must be faced. . . ."

(2) "God's infinite power can work . . . to remake the whole human personality. Divine Healing means essentially the healing of the whole person by the power of God, through a clearer understanding of His love and purpose and in obedience to His laws."

(3) "Doctors, clergy and ministers are instruments of God's healing power in the faithful exercise of their skill and patience; and all members of the churches can be used by God for healing, through their ministries of prayer . . . meditation and direction; and through the sacraments and other means of grace."

Mowatt, as an increasingly devout Christian, naturally expressed his philosophy of healing in specifically Christian terms. His answer to the question, "What has Christianity to offer me?" was direct and firm: "Come and be healed. Surrender yourself to receive of God's mercy in faith and trust – for which of us has not need of healing? . . . It is my experience that everything in the Christian's life turns upon healing. . . . It is healing of outlook we need; healing of our attitude towards life; healing of our conception of things. That is the vital truth, and we Christians have to go forward and testify to this truth, and prove to the world that the power of God and his love in Christ is a living force to help and heal the spirit, mind and body."[10]

Behind these words is a universal language with which those of nearly any creed, or indeed of none, can identify. He believed in a Divine Ground of Love permeating the universe, a Power in and around every living creature, available to all. It was as real as the power of gravity or unseen electrical waves. "Whether we are conscious of it or not, the Power of God is as inevitably with us as the power of gravitation," he said. "It has been proved to me over and over again that in prayer we are in tune with the greatest force in the world, a force which can alter our thoughts, our material worries, and our distress in spirit, mind and body."

He was frequently asked by anxious, ordinary people, "Why can't I realize this unseen power? Why can't I tune in to Divine Love? How can I escape from a materialistic outlook and from fear?" His reply was, "By prayer; not praying into space, but tuning in to Divine love – *the life within us, which is of God* [my emphasis] – to the life all around us, which is the existing God, and so to take in the Life as all nature takes in life. As we begin to realize these great truths we are opening up to receive more and more inspiration and help."

That people were healed in body and soul by and through the work of Godfrey Mowatt is in my view beyond question. There is a wealth of credible and compelling testimony from the thousands of people who wrote to him expressing their thanks and deep appreciation. I have interviewed people who attended Mowatt's healing services and are convinced they found healing. My conclusion is that he obviously had a natural gift of healing. It was greatly enhanced, however, by the extraordinary, intuitive insight he had into the hearts and minds of the people who came to him, as a result of his own experience of blindness. This knowledge helped him to deal with the sources of their problems in a profoundly individual manner. What resulted was a genuinely holistic healing rather than a superficial attempt at physical healing alone.

This phenomenon itself may explain the one question that naturally comes to mind (and no doubt has occurred to the reader long before this): How is it that if God or the Life Force healed people through the channel of this man he himself was never healed of his blindness? Wouldn't such a miracle have been the very thing needed to convince sceptics of the truths about spiritual healing? Those who knew him most intimately and who worked with him at various healing missions say that Mowatt was convinced his blindness was a great asset in his ministry to others. Watching him in action in 1948, during healing services in Denmark, the Lutheran Dean of Maribo noted, "It really seemed to me as if his blindness made it easier for him to concentrate upon the need of the patient." He went on to say he was amazed at Mowatt's sure instinct for finding each person's real trouble during his interviews.[11]

Once, a group of Mowatt's closest friends suggested to him they should organize themselves into a group of intercessors who would, with prayer, fasting, and self-denial, seek for the restoration of his eyesight. He would not allow them. He had even refused at one point to pursue the possibility that the thin film on his remaining eye, once removed by the accidental whip lash, might be remedied by further surgery. He had already suffered too much.

Certainly, however, he was no masochist and, at times, ardently longed for sightedness. But on one of the rare occasions when he spoke about his physical challenge, he said, "I, myself, maintain I have been healed, though my blindness has not been taken away. I have been lifted above it, and it has become no handicap to me. I am healed." Whatever else was true, his blindness kept the focus where he wanted it to be, not on himself but on the source of all life and healing, the Power of God. Mowatt for the same reason refused to call himself a healer. He was simply an "instrument" in the hands of the universal Divine Physician.

∽ Some Specific Cases

From the letters and records preserved by Kathleen Lonsdale I have taken the following accounts of Mowatt's ability to heal:

• A woman who had suffered from rheumatoid arthritis for thirteen years, but had been able to keep it under control through constant medical treatment, suddenly had a flare-up that turned her into a complete cripple. She wrote, "Every part of me was affected, even my hands, and so for three and a half years I have been a semi-invalid – although I have always tried to do things for myself. I had always said that if a chance ever came to go to a Healing Service I would go. Then you [Mowatt] came to our parish church. To me it was a most impressive service and I felt, although you were blind, that you could see right through me, and I felt great power and peace in your hands. Towards the end of the service, I felt quite different in myself. The pain in my back had disappeared and in my knees. My balance had been restored and I walked out through the churchyard without my stick – and I haven't used it since! I am still a little stiff but so much better that my family are astonished. The healing is still going on." The woman, in her fifties, said she "now feels a new woman," and not just physically but spiritually as well. "I came away with a wonderful sense of peace."[12]

• A naval officer wrote to Mowatt: "Thank you for your unselfish action in helping me on Monday. . . . The neck and back are better as I knew they would be, and the mind is no longer part of a seemingly dual personality."

• During a break for tea after one healing service in a parish church, several people came up to greet Mowatt personally. When introduced to one woman, he shook hands with her, whereupon she broke into tears. She had just realized that she had used her paralysed arm for the first time in many years.

On another occasion, at the back of a church after such a service, an invalid told Mowatt he could scarcely believe the gradual improvement which had started after a private meeting he had had with the healer a few weeks before. He then turned and, though very carefully and with obvious apprehension, he made his way downstairs to the church basement. It was only when he got to the bottom that he realized fully that by walking down stairs he had just done something doctors had said he would never do again.

• One of Mowatt's cardinal teachings was that anyone truly searching for total healing should begin to give to others as they receive themselves. He stressed that healing most often is gradual, with inner healing preceding the physical recovery. The following example illustrates this principle at work. Mowatt met one day with a woman who had twice tried to commit suicide. She had palsy so badly that she couldn't even feed herself, and her life had become a kind of hell. He helped her to believe that there is a divine energy or power in and around us; she came to a new understanding of the love of God and, at the same time, to be aware of the great number of sick people who were suffering just as much as she was.

Mowatt asked her to pray for a few people whose names he gave her, and later she asked if she could write to them occasionally through a friend. From her own experience of despair and isolation, she had an ability to empathize with and encourage others. She lost her former absorption in self-pity and, as she saw a new meaning for her life, began to know happiness. Mowatt lent her friend a typewriter for the letters, but before long the woman herself was able to type. The healing to her body seemed to be coming in direct proportion to the amount of loving interest and energy she expended on other people. Her strength improved and there is a letter from her to Mowatt one summer, saying, "I am digging in the garden and singing along with the birds – the happiest woman in the world."

• Another case, submitted, along with many others involving Mowatt, to a special commission of the Archbishop of Canterbury on the Church of England's Ministry of Healing, went like this:

"I had disseminated sclerosis from January 1937 to April 1949. It was diagnosed, queried, re-diagnosed, and finally confirmed by an eminent neuro-surgeon after three weeks of exhaustive tests. In April 1949, I asked the rector of our local church if he could hold a service of healing some time. . . . Eventually I was put in touch with Churches' Council on Healing and I asked for the help of Mr. Godfrey Mowatt. On April 13, 1949, Mr. Mowatt came out to where I was staying, in Essex, and took a service of the laying-on of hands. I could not walk, my legs were thin and wasted, I was nearly blind and extremely ill. During the service it seemed that Godfrey Mowatt and all earthly things disappeared. I was conscious only of the presence of the Lord, forgetful even of my needs, whether spiritual or physical. I do not know how long this lasted, nor do I remember literally thinking I was healed. But, when Mr. Mowatt rose to his feet after prayers, so did I, greatly blessed and quite whole. Every symptom had disappeared, I could walk and see. That night I slept soundly as I had not done in years. Moreover, when I noticed my legs the next day there was no sign of the wasting. They were quite normal. My doctor, cautious because D.S. is a disease that has remissions, said he would not confirm the 'miracle' for 12 months. But, five months later, seeing me running, he agreed to the fact of the cure. That was five years ago and I am now 42, whole and strong and well."

There are plenty of other cases recorded which are equally remarkable or in some instances even more remarkable than these. However, since these are all in the past and, essentially, come to us secondhand, I want to conclude my account of the blind healer with the direct testimony of two people whom I have known for many years and in whose ability to make an objective assessment I have the greatest confidence. Both of these men had an encounter with Mowatt. Each was tremendously impressed – and influenced – by the experience.

∼ Harrison

During my years of teaching at Wycliffe College, University of Toronto, my Old Testament colleague was Dr. Roland K. Harrison. Until his death in 1993, he was editor-in-chief of the *New International Commentary on the Old Testament*, which is being published by Eerdman's in thirty volumes. I vividly remember talking with Harrison in his study one day at the college. We discussed a couple of routine college matters, and then I happened to mention I had just been reading about Godfrey Mowatt. Harrison, whose scholarly demeanour contrasted sharply with the lively passion and infectious humour with which he attacked most subjects, burst out, "Godfrey Mowatt! I met him once and I've never forgotten the experience. It was quite remarkable." He went on to describe his encounter in some detail. Some time before his death, Harrison related the story to me again. What follows is his unedited account:

"In the spring of 1943, a few weeks before graduating from the University of London with my Bachelor of Divinity degree, I heard of a healing service to be held at St. Helen's Church, Warrington, a small town just outside of Manchester. [Harrison was ordained later that year for the ministry of the Church of England. He had been in a group interested in "divine healing" for some time, most probably associated with the Guild of Health.] I was twenty-two years old at the time, and I recall going to Warrington by train. The dignified, low-key service began, and almost immediately outside the air-raid sirens sounded, followed shortly afterwards by a German bomber attack. They dropped a lot of bombs, some of them quite close to the church, and kept it up for nearly an hour.

"Godfrey Mowatt, guided by another man, came to the chancel steps, said a few words about spiritual healing, and then people were invited to come up and kneel at the communion rail as they would when receiving the sacrament. Mowatt went from left to right, and, as the man guided him, put his hands on the head of each and prayed briefly. I watched as two or three full rails went up.

I thought to myself, 'I'm in good health, but since I'm about to be ordained, and on the principle that I need all the blessing I can get, I'm going to go up as well.' I went to the front of the church, knelt down, and waited. The moment I felt Mowatt's hands there was a sensation like a weak electrical current flowing down my neck and spine. It went down my arms to my fingertips and down my legs to my toes. It remained like that for a few seconds until he lifted his hands from my head. It was really a terrific experience of a kind I had never had before nor have had since. The surge of 'current' felt slightly warm and left me with a sort of inner glow for a long time afterwards. Of course, when I told others about this they were highly sceptical. They said, 'Why doesn't he heal himself, then?' But, on deep reflection, I think that that might have marred his extraordinary, unique ministry."

～ Crabb

By one of those strange coincidences of life – the kind Jung called synchronicities – just a few days after my original conversation with Dr. Harrison about Godfrey Mowatt, I was dining in the college refectory at Wycliffe. In addition to the usual students at the table, there was a guest, Rev. Dr. Fred Crabb, who was at that time the principal of Emmanuel College, an Anglican seminary in Saskatoon now called the College of Emmanuel and St. Chad. In the course of conversation, I said that one day I hoped to do some research into the whole subject of religion and healing, because I had been greatly intrigued as a result of reading a booklet on the work of a man called Godfrey Mowatt in England. To my complete surprise, Crabb immediately interrupted to say that if it hadn't been for Godfrey Mowatt "I probably wouldn't be here today." I was truly startled. There was a moment of silence, and then I asked him to tell us about it. He held the attention of the whole table as he recounted a quite remarkable healing in his own life that coincided with attending a service presided over by Mowatt in 1952. Not long ago I wrote to Crabb, who had recently retired as the

Metropolitan Archbishop of Rupert's Land in western Canada, asking whether he would consent to telling the story himself for my readers. What follows is his full account:

"I had just returned to England after nearly ten years as a missionary in the southern Sudan. I was in very poor health, a victim of tropical diseases. Dr. Donald Coggan, later to become Archbishop of Canterbury, had recently taken over as the principal of my old seminary, London College of Divinity. Since he was about to lose his vice-principal, Ralph Dean, to Emmanuel College, Saskatoon, Saskatchewan, he invited me to take the post, and though I was anything but well, I accepted. However, the medical officer of the Church Missionary Society, under which I had served my time in Africa, then gave me the official report on my condition. It seemed to change the future for me radically. Years of dysentery and malaria, I was told, had taken a very serious toll. The prognosis was that I had perhaps six months to live. As gently as it could be said, I was told to go home and put my house in order as soon as possible. My 'house' was a wife and three small children.

"When I conveyed this news and my decision not to become vice-principal of London College of Divinity to Dr. Coggan, he replied in a few terse sentences. 'Are you going to waste the next six months? I shall expect to see you on September 8th at the college to begin the term.' That was in the fall of 1951. So, I took up my appointment at the college as arranged. But it quickly became apparent that the doctors were right. I struggled through that first term and found myself in St. Luke's Hospital in London at the end of it.

"It was early in the second term, early 1952, that a new colleague of mine at the college, Douglas Webster, who later became Canon and Chancellor of St. Paul's Cathedral in London [and a distinguished Anglican theologian], suggested that I attend a service of healing at a parish church in North London where, once a month, in the context of a regular, weekly communion service, a layman named Godfrey Mowatt laid hands on those seeking the blessing of healing. Mr. Mowatt, it turned out, was not only a layman, but he was old (in his seventies then, I guess) and completely blind, the result of an accident when he was a boy. But he was ordained, not to so-called Holy Orders but to the ministry of healing, by no less a person than Dr. William Temple, the former Archbishop of Canterbury.

"Very reluctantly, with little faith and no expectations, but under pressure from Douglas Webster, Donald Coggan, and my wife, Margery, I accompanied Douglas and Margery one cold and discouraging Thursday to St. Luke's Church, North London. The service of Holy Communion, taken by the vicar, was reverent and traditional. But – why, I still don't know – my whole soul cried out in total protest when the elderly, whitehaired old gentleman moved along the row of kneeling communicants, laying his hands, as they were guided by the vicar, on the head of each worshipper, including mine. A brief, quietly spoken prayer, and he passed on to the next. I felt no exultation, no impact of virtue or spiritual power, no difference – nothing! Just as I expected, I thought to myself. I clearly recall a sense of self-justification. We returned to Lingfield in Surrey where the college was then functioning in a rented manor house, the original buildings in London having been destroyed in the Blitz, and I resumed the pattern of the past days. Except that . . . I was doing better!

"There was no particular turning point. Never did I experience anything like the experience recorded in the New Testament of a blind man suddenly recovering sight, or a cripple throwing away his crutches. Certainly, nothing like Lazarus coming out of the grave. And indeed it was a long time before I admitted even to myself that, in spite of my lack of faith, God's healing grace had been at work in me because of the ministry of this very ordinary and yet singularly extraordinary old blind man, Godfrey Mowatt. I knew at the time that my wife had faith that God could use this man to heal me. So did Douglas Webster. It was some time later that I learned that as soon as we left for London that winter Thursday morning in early 1952, Dr. Coggan had cancelled all classes at the college and called the entire faculty and student body to pray for me. This they did throughout that entire day.

"Godfrey Mowatt came every summer whilst I was at the college to lecture for a week on healing to the graduating students. I was by now convinced of my own healing and that, in some way I have never been able to understand, this man had been God's instrument in my healing as in many others. We became friends. But I never asked him the question that bothered me from the start. How come an elderly blind man, who apparently was unable to heal himself, could be so used to minister healing to others? And the healing was not just of physical ills. As I got to know him, and to observe his simple, transparent faith, his love for his God and for all people, it became apparent that his ministry was to the whole person – body, mind, and spirit. He knew his Lord as a friend knows a friend; and his chief object in ministry was to bring others to his own experience of his Saviour. Whether or not they received healing of their physical ills – he never claimed this to be inevitable – he gave them all an introduction to the One who heals all things. For he ministered to body and soul alike."

Archbishop Crabb appended this "epilogue" to his account: "All this took place in 1951-52. It is now late 1991. In between, I have been given several responsible jobs. Enough of my physical weaknesses have remained to keep me humble and remembering from whom my resources have come. But not enough to prevent me having a full life and giving a reasonably good account to those to whom I have been accountable. I have known for a long time that Godfrey Mowatt was the instrument in the hands of a healing God who admitted me back to health. I do thank God for him. But, as that humblest and gentlest of men would expect me to add, 'To God be the glory.'"

6

The First Scientific Evidence

"In healing we are dealing with an energy that knows what it wants to do."
  – Bernard Grad, Ph.D.

G odfrey Mowatt has been dead for a number of years. The stories of Harrison and Crabb, however interesting or even remarkable, are nevertheless anecdotal and so constitute "soft" rather than "hard" evidence. Much of the material one sees on healing is of this nature, and it is time now to move onto more solid ground, that of science and scientific research. Contrary to what the critics of non-medical healing suggest, there are indeed leading scientists who have investigated complementary therapies, including such techniques as the laying-on of hands. They have conducted most-rigorous experiments under laboratory conditions and have accumulated an impressive array of hard data.

One of the top figures in this field in the English-speaking world, the man whose name keeps popping up in all the literature, is a Canadian biologist, Professor Bernard Grad, who worked for thirty-six years at McGill University, in experimental morphology in the gerontology unit of the Allan Memorial Institute of Psychiatry. Until he retired in 1991, Grad was also associate scientist at the Royal Victoria Hospital, Montreal, and an associate professor at the University of Quebec. During this time, he published ninety-two learned papers on cancer and on the aging process. In the past three decades, he has also published thirty-five papers on healing. Grad, who describes himself as a "ferocious experimentalist," and who has two sons who are doctors, has little patience with those who attempt to mysticize non-medical healing. His attitude is summed up in his recent remark to me: "I don't deny the spiritual side of healing, but I want objective verification. Ironically, I have found over the years that scientists who belittle such phenomena as healing aren't willing to do the necessary experiments. I'm the one who finds himself saying let's do the experiments, while the critics steadfastly refuse!"

I first became aware of Dr. Grad's work some time ago, when my predecessor as religion editor of the *Toronto Star*, Allen Spraggett, did a feature on his double-blind experiments involving a renowned healer named Oskar Estebany. Spraggett later described some of this work in a book called *The Unexplained*.[1] During the mid-1970s, I went to Montreal and interviewed both Grad and

Estebany for the religion page in the *Star*. I met with Grad at his laboratory at McGill and was impressed by his commitment to the scientific method and by his enormous curiosity about the unseen bioenergy or force he had been able to demonstrate was at work whenever Estebany's powers were tested objectively.

Recently, I determined to track him down once more and discover whether the intervening years of study and experimentation had confirmed his original findings and what he thought today about healing. When contacted, he graciously agreed to an interview at his home in Montreal.

Though he has recently retired from his post at McGill, Grad finds himself busier today than at any other time in his life, he says. Between travelling to speak at the increasing number of international conferences being held today on non-medical healing and related topics, he is working hard to publish the results of years of work that have hitherto remained in the bulging files in his office. From his manner and bearing, I would say he is thriving on it. At seventy-two, he gives the impression of great vigour and a deep, compassionate humanity. He has an ongoing passion to play an effective part in relieving human disease and suffering.

Before looking at Grad's work itself, it's helpful to know how and why a biologist, trained like all the other scientists of his day to think in purely mechanistic terms, came to be interested in researching a religious practice such as the laying-on of hands. What made a man, whose professional life largely comprised studies on aging and cancer, spend so much time and effort researching the claims of healers? In our interview, he began by saying that he certainly "had no intention of going where I did" when setting out on his scientific career. Yet, on looking back, he marvels at the "skill" of the process or plan that eventually led him into it.

As a young child, he had an unusual awareness of being surrounded by a "power or energy in nature." At times, he remembers, he felt he could actually see this force pulsing in the air around him. In a paper presented at the second annual conference of the International Society for the Study of Subtle Energies and Energy Medicine, in Boulder, Colorado, in June 1992, Grad told the assembly he could still remember vividly at the age of four sitting on the grass in a city park and feeling energy flowing into him from the ground beneath. "At still other times, I could sense this energy by touching a wet pavement stone, or perceive its pulsing sound – like when a seashell is placed next to the ear, except I heard this sound without the shell." He told me a quick and unexpected "rush of energy" up his back was also a fairly common experience during his youth.(Some of these energy sensations remain with him to the present.)

He never mentioned these experiences to his peers or his parents while growing up, but from as early an age as he can remember he had "the conviction of a strong power in and around us," a kind of bioenergy which was not God but which could be said to flow from or be caused by God. During the discipline and training of his public- and high-school years, however, Grad says he was gradually taught to repress this sense of being in contact with a sort of cosmic energy field. He had a brilliant academic career at university, winning many scholarships, but all the while he was adopting all the prejudices and distrust of anything that cannot be explained wholly in terms of mechanistic causality. He remembers that when a medical student told him about Dr. William Osler's deep conviction that a doctor's bedside manner could play a role in the healing of his patients, he found himself snapping back that this suggestion supported witchcraft. It was not for another three decades that his own experiments proved that emotional states can have profound effects, not only on people but also on materials.

Grad's undergraduate years as a science student were difficult. He was extremely poor, with the social isolation this entailed, and the picture of the universe he was learning from his professors was bleak, since everything was devoid of God or purpose and was destined, according to the second law of thermodynamics, to become a burnt-out cinder. And the world was on the verge of the Second World War. All of this finally got to him, and he succumbed to a serious attack of tuberculosis. Grad was bedridden for sixteen months in a sanitorium, and then stayed on a further sixteen months, recuperating and learning to become mobile once more.

To aid in fighting the disease and recovering his health, he began using his imagination to call up pictures of some of his heroes. A strange thing began to happen. It seemed that none of these persons – whether famous historical figures or outstanding contemporaries – was "up to the task," and they faded away as the disease raged on. But he noticed that "it seemed that with the dissolution of each 'hero' some layer in my personality was being stripped from me. Indeed, the process could be compared to the peeling of an onion, with the removal of one layer after another." Surprisingly, this process continued, until suddenly there arose in his mind the image of the four-year-old child he had been. This image, instead of fading like the others, grew stronger daily. He knew then that "if I was going to rebuild my life, I would have to do it on the basis of the child."

Grad began to conjure up the sense of being alive and of the pulsing universe he had experienced in his early youth. He started to read avidly all the books in the sanitorium library relating to disease in general and tuberculosis in particular. Most were academic and highly technical. One, however, struck him because its view of the world was so in tune with his childhood beliefs. Entitled *Doctors, Disease and Health*, it was written by the English pianist Cyril Scott. Among the many topics Scott treated were the possibility of life after death and alternative modes of healing.

Little by little, Grad's former sense of a bioenergetic connectedness between him and his surroundings returned. "While still confined to bed, I could begin to feel the ebb and flow of energy into and out of my body, with corresponding effects on my sense of wellbeing." He began to realize what many today would call a cosmic consciousness, an awareness of being at one with all things. Grad still doesn't think of himself as being religious, but he reveals a mysticism of the sort that marked Walt Whitman's poetry when he says how "on one summer's day, while I was still confined to bed, I heard a bird singing and, in a moment, its song and I seemed to unite with the pulsing of the Earth's atmospheric energy into one cosmic rhythm." His health returned, and he went back to complete his science degree. The following year, he graduated from the Bachelor of Science course with honours in biochemistry.

Grad then commenced work on his doctorate, but the need, in that pre-antibiotic era of tuberculosis, to safeguard his health constantly and avoid a relapse from insufficient rest became increasingly frustrating. One morning, however, during a break in his studies, he suddenly experienced a "bioenergetic event" of such power that it still remains vividly etched in his mind years later. Here it is in his own words: "Up to that time, I kept totally silent about my bioenergetic experiences, which I tended to take for granted. However, the event of that day became a pivotal factor in determining much of my behaviour in the years that followed. It happened about midday – I was lying quietly on the bed when, without warning, I felt a concentration of energy move from my heart down the left side of my body and down the left leg, cross over to the right leg as if there was no gap between the legs, travel up the right leg and right side of my body, and back to the heart. This circuit was made two or three times, and then stopped as abruptly as it began. I thought it meant I was going to die, especially as the energy was passing through my heart. The feeling might be compared to putting one's finger in a socket, but I had done nothing of the kind. I sought the advice of medical doctors about this matter but received no help. Incidentally, the date was one most people find easy to remember. It was August 6, 1945, the day the bomb was dropped on Hiroshima. If at any time since then I ever had any doubt about the existence of an energy in the body, I needed only to remind myself of this experience."

The "bioenergetic event," which nobody could explain to his satisfaction, left him with one question. Where could he find information about an energy that could surge and move in the body? At the same time, he knew that a lot of inner work had to be done to close the gap between the child he had just rediscovered and the young man he had become. He began a two-year process of self-analysis (without benefit of a therapist), and started reading

the works of Freud and articles in current journals of psychoanalysis. It was in the latter that he first came across the person and
thinking of Wilhelm Reich.

Reich (1897-1957) wrote many books himself, and a whole literature has sprung up about him. Unfortunately, his ideas, which
were in many respects brilliant and miles ahead of his time, and in
others so eccentric and controversial as to invite public anger and
persecution, would take much more space than we can afford here
even to give in outline. He was writing articles on the human
psyche even before he took his medical degree in Vienna in the
early 1920s. He became a student of Freud's while still in medical
school, and gained considerable fame soon after graduation as the
training analyst of a number of the first-generation American psy-
chiatrists who came to Freud's clinic to learn psychoanalysis. He
later became more independent of Freud and began developing
the concept for which he was to become best known, the orgone
theory.

Put briefly and at its very simplest, Reich postulated a mass-free
energy which is omnipresent in the atmosphere, is related to the
sun, fills the whole of space in varying concentrations, is drawn in
or used by all organisms, and accounts for the pulsing contraction
and expansion of all living things. In his 1989 book on Wilhelm
Reich, *Vital Energy and Health*, Professor W. Edward Mann, of York
University, Toronto, says of Reich's view of orgone energy: "It
flows through organisms, creates a field around them and can be
transmitted from organism to organism (among human beings, by
the laying-on of hands, for instance). It governs the total organism
and expresses itself in the emotions as well as in the purely biophysical movements."[2] Orgone is the medium for gravitational and
electromagnetic activity, according to Reich, and is the medium
in which light moves. Matter, he believed, is created from orgone
energy – a point at which he came very close to the more recent
definition of matter by some physicists as a dance of energy. Grad
was excited and intrigued by Reich's ideas, because here was a
powerful voice saying that contrary to the prevailing view of science at that time the universe was totally alive and throbbing with

a vital energy that lent meaning and unity to everything. The orgone theory or something very much like it seemed to explain his own bioenergetic experiences and their relationship to his recovery from tuberculosis. He studied all of Reich's work he could obtain, and then, on learning that Reich, who had come to the United States in 1938, had moved in 1945 from New York to a small town in Maine called Rangeley, where he had a small laboratory, Grad determined to meet the great man himself.

In September 1949, one week after receiving his Ph.D. at McGill, he drove to Rangeley and spent seven or eight days questioning Reich and repeating some of his basic experiments. These included viewing atmospheric orgone through a telescope or binoculars pointing out the window onto a field. Beyond the field was a dark, forested mountain which served as a backdrop against which the subtle energy could be seen. Grad recalls: "That first view on a beautiful summer's day of the powerful, pulsing atmosphere flowing past me, like a river, up to the height of the mountain was an unforgettable event. My childhood's intuition of an atmosphere that was alive was wonderfully confirmed."[3]

Grad returned to Montreal and to his new post as a biologist researching the process of aging for the Allan Memorial Institute of Psychiatry. As time allowed, he enthusiastically began his research on orgone energy as well. Just a few weeks before Reich died, in 1957, Grad happened to overhear a conversation in his Montreal laboratory in which one of the technicians, a Hungarian, was talking about a countryman of his, a cleaner in a nearby hospital, who did healing by the laying-on of hands. Up to that time, Grad had never met anyone who actually claimed to heal by that method. Excited by the prospect of persuading someone to co-operate in properly controlled experiments, he asked the technician to arrange for a meeting with the healer. That was how he first came to meet Oskar Estebany, a man who played a prominent part in his researches over the next decade and more. Grad was impressed by Estebany at that first meeting when he asked the healer how he believed his "gift" worked. The Hungarian told him he believed we are surrounded by a living energy, which humans and all other living organisms pick up. He said in his experience as a healer – he first discovered his gift when serving as a colonel in a cavalry regiment in his native Hungary – the laying-on of hands seemed to facilitate the transmission of that energy from the atmosphere to the person. "There is an energy all around us; I just draw on it," Estebany told him.

Grad still recalls his surprise that this relatively uneducated man, who had never even heard of Wilhelm Reich, was making similar statements about an atmospheric and organismic energy. Estebany believed that while this energy flows into everyone, some people, healers for example, either have a surplus of it or are more open to its transmission. I, too, was impressed by the matter-of-fact attitude Estebany had towards his ability to heal when I interviewed him in the early 1970s at his home in Montreal. I asked him whether he prayed either before or during the laying-on of hands. His answer was succinct. He said, "No, I don't." Then he explained, "It's not that I don't believe in prayer. I do. However, I've come to accept this gift as something that is there as a natural part of my being. People who know they have a skill or an ability to act in a certain way – for example, a violinist or a surgeon – don't pray before playing or operating. I mean they could, of course, but they don't need to. Either they can do something or they can't. That's precisely how I look at healing."

One thing that made Grad feel his meeting with Estebany was in a way predestined was the eager way in which the healer responded to the suggestion that his alleged powers be tested objectively. "Estebany was extremely curious about the mechanisms involved, and this naturally made him an ideal person to work with. What followed opened up a whole new world for me and, I believe, for the understanding of what is going on in such age-old rituals as the laying-on of hands." Not all healers will agree to being tested. Estebany, however, was not only willing to submit to examination of his technique by conventional experimental science, he had the enormous patience required for the extensive and demanding protocols devised by Grad for a long succession of rigorously controlled experiments.

Before giving a few examples of these experiments and their results, it should be pointed out that once some of Grad's work with Estebany began to be published, other researchers immediately sought Estebany out, most notably Professor Justa Smith, of Rosary Hill College, Buffalo, New York, who did some valuable work with him on enzymes. Later, Grad told me, Estebany also visited Dolores Krieger and Dora Kuntz, which began their development of the technique now known as Therapeutic Touch, an adaptation of the laying-on of hands that is now practised by more than thirty thousand nurses in the United States and by many elsewhere.[4]

Estebany, like many healers today, believed he could detect the presence of disease in the body, because of changes in the sensations in his hands when placed on or near the site of the disease. Grad reports, "Such reactions involved increases in the sensation of heat, sometimes even a sensation of burning (or, surprisingly, sometimes its opposite, that is, a feeling of cold), a prickling sensation in the fingers and/or palms of the hands, a sensation of moving down the arms to the hands, where it sometimes moves in vortices." Estebany felt the energy flow increase when he worked with a group of sick people. He would say it was as if "disease itself may be a cry for help." Its presence called forth the energy. Thus, he habitually kept those with the most difficult problems to the last, when his healing energy would be at its peak. Some day others will catalogue and describe in detail some of the healings claimed to have been done through Oskar Estebany. My primary interest here is with his experimental work in the laboratory. (Incidentally, Oskar Estebany lived until his early nineties and died in Montreal in 1990.)[5]

Grad deliberately chose to test Estebany – and over the course of years several other healers as well – not with human subjects but with animals, plants, water, and yeasts in order to avoid all possibility of hypnotism, suggestion, and other psychological factors. He doesn't deny that there may well be a part played by the power of suggestion in non-medical healing, just as the white coat and stethoscope of the doctor or the mere fact of being given a pre-scription play their part in medical therapy. But today, just as when he began, Grad's primary concern is to devise and conduct experi-ments aimed at discovering the extent to which it can be said something objective and scientifically verifiable happens when a healer goes to work.

Grad's initial experiments with Estebany, called simply Mr. E. in his first published accounts, were done to determine the effect of the laying-on of his hands on the rate of wound healing in mice and on the germination of barley seeds. There was nothing in sci-entific literature to guide Grad on some key questions. For example, in the case of the animal experiments, he had to calcu-late how long to expose them to the laying-on of hands, how often, and in what manner. It should be said that before meeting Grad, Estebany's healing had been mainly of large animals; horses and dogs, and of course people. However, Grad decided to use mice because of ease in housing and handling and because more of them could be used and so provide the kind of data where statistical dif-ferences could be significant.

After much study and trial and error, he decided to treat the mice in groups of eight while they were temporarily confined for the purpose in a galvanized sheet-iron cage divided into compart-ments each large enough for one animal. (The number of animals that could be treated at one time was determined by the size of Estebany's hand, which had to cover the mice during treatment.) A sliding lid of galvanized wire mesh kept the animals from escap-ing or from entering adjacent compartments. Estebany placed the treatment cage between his hands, the cage resting on his left palm while he held his right hand several centimetres above the wire mesh covering the mice. Subsequent observations showed that when the mice were treated in this way for fifteen minutes each time, twice daily at least five hours apart, five days a week and once on Saturdays, it was sufficient to reveal "observable and statisti-cally significant differences."[6]

Forty-eight female mice, all between two and two and a half

months old, and from the same genetic strain, were divided into three groups of sixteen. The first group, A, was treated by Estebany in the described manner. The second group, B, served as a control group. These animals were placed in transfer cages identical to those in which the A group were treated and placed on a table in the same room in which they were housed. However, they did not have the laying-on of hands from Estebany or anyone else. By transferring this control group the same number of times as the A group, Grad was trying to ensure the same amount of disturbance or stress for all the mice. The third group, C, got the same treatment as the B group, except that they were heated to the same degree and for the same amount of time as the A mice, the only difference being that the latter were warmed by Estebany's hands and the former were warmed by an electrothermal heating tape covering the transfer cage and attached to a variable transformer. The temperatures were kept exactly the same for the two groups. When not being treated, the mice were housed singly on the same cage-rack kept at the same temperature. All animals were fed the same food and water.

Following a training period to accustom the mice to their environment and to being moved about, they were deliberately wounded. "The animals were anesthetized with ether and an approximately one half by one and one half inch area of hair was removed from the back of each. The wound was made by cutting out with scissors an oval of full skin about half an inch in diameter along the spine and with its centre about one and a quarter inches from the base of the tail." The skin removed was weighed immediately and the wound measured by tracing its outline with a grease pencil on transparent plastic. The wound outline was then transferred to paper, which was cut out and weighed on an extremely sensitive balance (to .005mg). Measurements of the mice were regularly taken on the first, eleventh, and fourteenth days following the making of the wounds. All procedures were done in the room in which the mice were housed. In his very detailed report, Grad has a series of tables and graphics illustrating the results obtained.

There was no significant difference in the size of the wounds among the three groups on the day the wounds were made, or on the day after. Nor were there any significant differences in wound area between groups B and C eleven days or fourteen days after the wounds were made. "However, the wounds of the A group treated by Estebany were *very significantly smaller* . . . eleven days after wounding and fourteen days afterwards." (Italics mine.) This experiment was repeated with similar results. Following these experiments, a research project was mounted at the University of Manitoba by Drs. Remi J. Cadoret and G. I. Paul of the department of physiology. It involved Estebany acting upon mice wounded in the same way as in the original experiments but in strictly double-blind conditions. The results once again demonstrated that the healer's intervention had a profound effect on the rate of healing.[7]

I have related this preliminary aspect of Grad's research with Oskar Estebany at some length in order to provide to the reader a feel for the kind of thoroughness involved in his experiments. Some of his other experiments can be now be cited much more briefly. Following the experiments with mice, Grad tested Estebany with plants. He had two reasons. One was to see how widely this energy effect could be observed in nature – free from any possibility of auto-suggestion – and the other was to attempt to find a method of measuring the effect that was less time-consuming and complex than the wound-healing approach. Once again, since there were no clear precedents, he had to feel his way in designing proper experiments and there were several stages before he arrived at the final method. One result of these pilot studies was the demonstration early on that it wasn't necessary for Estebany to treat the plants directly to obtain significant results. It was enough simply for Grad and his assistants to moisten the seeds with water that the healer had previously held in a beaker between his hands for a specific amount of time.

Several double-blind experiments were carried out on barley seeds, some of them watered with a beaker of water treated by Estebany (he held one of two identical beakers between his hands for fifteen minutes, his left hand supporting it from below and his right hand three or four centimetres above the surface of the liquid), the rest with untreated water. Thereafter, the twenty-four pots of seeds were all watered with untreated tap water every second day until the end of the experiment on day fourteen. The seedlings were counted, measured, and photographed at several points in their growth. The experiment demonstrated conclusively that there were more plants, that they grew taller, and produced more plant material in the pots originally given the water treated by Estebany.[8] When this experiment was repeated exactly, except that none of the water was held by Estebany, there were no significant differences found among any of the seedlings. The remaining four experiments followed the main outline of the first, but with an enormous amount of fine-tuning for each. For example, instead of an open beaker for the water, it was placed in glass reagent bottles sealed with glass stoppers. Both the control bottles and the bottles to be treated were enclosed in sealed opaque paper bags. Estebany held the bottles he treated while they were still protected in this way from both air contact and from his view. Once again, the number, height, and yield of the plants given treated water were significantly better than the controls.[9]

In the discussion section of the published results of these animal and plant experiments, Grad stresses that what happened with the mice was not to be confused with normal gentling. There is no doubt that animals gentled – held loosely in the hand and stroked for about ten minutes a day for several weeks – do resist stress better than non-gentled controls. However, in the Estebany experiments, all the mice, both the controls and those held by Estebany, were gentled up to – but not after – the point of the wounding. In none of the experiments was any gentling done by the healer. In fact, Estebany's hands never touched the animals directly. There was a sheet-metal floor below and a screen above them. As in the case of the water sealed in the glass bottles, there was no chance of any chemical or other physical interaction between the healer and the mice or water. Grad points out that the most reasonable conclusion to be drawn is that the biological effects observed in these experiments were caused by a force or energy released or exercised by the laying-on of hands.

This corroboration of his earlier intuitions and of the general thrust, if not all the specifics, of Reich's orgone theory led Grad to further life-energy research in the decades that followed. His subsequent laboratory experiments with Estebany included the effects of the laying-on of hands in inhibiting goitres in mice, on the capacity of yeast to produce carbon monoxide, on the stimulation of growth in rats, and on the healing of mice and rats sick with intestinal infections. Assured that the energy itself was an objective reality, his goal became to determine what kind of energy this was and how it achieved its effects. It is this intriguing and elusive problem that drives him today.

Grad told me he is now more hopeful of arriving at a scientific explanation of how the energy works than at any stage in the past nearly forty years. He's encouraged that more scientists today are ready to shed their former reservations and fears of "getting into witchcraft or mumbo jumbo" when they look beyond the once-staid boundaries of conventional medicine. Grad says, "there is a process at work in non-medical healing – such ancient practices as the laying-on of hands – and some scientists are getting nearer to it today than ever before. I have just done some research and discovered that there have been over 190 articles on this kind of healing by nurses and doctors in regular medical journals since the mid-1950s."

He doesn't believe that the laying-on of hands and other non-medical techniques are any kind of panacea. They're one tool among many, he says. "But this kind of healing is real. I believe the energy involved exists in a variety of different modes or frequencies. Prayer may stimulate it or be a form of it. It can be transmitted over long distances. It doesn't depend upon the "faith" of the recipients. They need to do or believe nothing as long as they remain open or neutral. The fact is, we are being healed all the time by various energies in our bodies. Cells are being replaced constantly, cuts are being healed, tumours are being thrown out, and various bacteria resisted." In other words, our healing system is already in place. What happens in the laying-on of hands or other treatment by a genuine healer is that this system is stimulated. Just as a walk in the country or listening to a piece of music can give us a fresh surge of energy, so, too, can the energy flow provided by a healer, Grad believes. "This is an energy that knows what it wants to do," he says. "It has a wisdom of its own."[10]

7

A Psychiatrist's Case for Healing

"If spiritual healing were a drug, they'd have put it on the market long ago."
  – Daniel Benor, M.D.

I telephoned Dr. Bernard Grad in October 1991, on the eve of leaving for a hiking tour in the English Lake District with my wife, Susan. When I told him we would be in London for a few days in order to take a look at the remarkable Healing and Counselling Centre, officially opened by Prince Charles a few years ago, in the crypt of the Anglican Church of St. Marylebone, he said excitedly, "You must try to see Dr. Daniel Benor while you're there." I had never heard of Dr. Benor before and so I listened with great interest while Grad explained who he was and the kind of work he was doing. Instantly intrigued by this introduction to the man, I called Benor in London. He graciously agreed to a lengthy interview. Here, slightly condensed and edited, is the substance of our two-hour session. It throws light not just on the phenomenon of spiritual healing but on the extent to which Britain is far ahead of North America in adopting non-medical healing practices.

Benor, a man of slight build, medium height, with a beard and a quiet, laid-back manner, was born in New York City in 1941. He trained first as a physician and then studied psychiatry. Most of his work was focused on family and Gestalt therapy before a life-changing event happened to him in the summer of 1980. Benor had been curious for some time about parapsychology or the study of paranormal phenomena. So, when he and a doctor friend learned there would be a "psychic fair" called Life Spectrum at Elizabethtown, Pennsylvania, that year, they decided to go. A woman healer there, Ethel Lombardi, was demonstrating spiritual healing. They watched idly for a while as several people were "treated," but their interest suddenly perked when a young man of about twenty-two went forward and told the healer he had a painful lump or cyst on his chest. Benor and his friend saw it clearly when the youth opened his shirt. Since this was a case where medical observations could be made and results evaluated, the two of them identified themselves as doctors and asked to be allowed to examine the lump "before and after" any healing activity took place. The healer agreed, and so they went up, looked at the cyst, palpated it and measured it. It was situated just under the man's left nipple. Benor told me, "He felt some pain when we touched the cyst. To us, the lump felt a bit like an eraser; it was fixed or non-mobile. In size, it was approximately one centimetre by two centimetres."

The healer never touched the cyst at any time. Rather, keeping her hands a few inches from his body, she worked instead on what are called in yogic thought the body's *chakras* or energy centres. As she did so, she suddenly said to the young man, "I'm getting the sense that there is some unfinished business between you and your father." At this, the youth nodded a "yes" and began to sob. He did so for what seemed a long time. After thirty minutes of "treatment," the two doctors re-examined the cyst. "We were amazed to find that the lump was already less than half its original size," Benor said. "What's more, it was no longer tender or sore, and it was soft and completely non-fixed. I know that if I had not had another doctor there to verify my own examination I would have begun to think I must have made some error or miscalculated in some way. It was a very impressive change and improvement."

It was so impressive that Benor decided there was something to non-medical or spiritual healing that justified a closer look. He began eagerly reading anything of a scholarly nature that dealt with the topic. At the same time, he started to formulate a research project, using leading healers, to put the issue to some objective testing. He persuaded a hospital to sponsor the affair and received a grant of $66,000 to fund it. But then a new chief-of-staff was appointed who had some rigid traditional views on what he would tolerate in the research programs at his hospital and he issued a veto with no chance of appeal.

Disappointed but not discouraged, Benor began to experiment with non-medical healing in his own practice, through relaxation techniques, meditation, visualization, and the laying-on of hands. He took courses in Therapeutic Touch, LeShan, and Reiki healing methods.[1] He became keenly interested in spirituality and in a holistic approach to health. As time went on, he found himself increasingly in demand as a lecturer on spiritual healing. Benor eventually came across the hard evidence we have just looked at produced by Dr. Bernard Grad in his work with Oskar Estebany at

McGill University. Benor immediately began corresponding with him. As a result, he became more certain than ever that the objective nature of spiritual healing could be even more fully demonstrated scientifically if only the medical establishment could be persuaded that it was time to take this age-old phenomenon seriously. However, he was at the same time becoming increasingly frustrated by the unwillingness of the medical profession in North America to look at anything outside the rigid parameters of its own approach to healing.

In 1987, encouraged by what he had read and seen in Britain, where, he says, "the healers were much more professional than in the United States, where the doctors were more open, and where the government itself had given some measure of recognition to non-medical approaches," he decided to move there. Benor has been living and working in London ever since. Today, in addition to his private practice in which spiritual healing is an integral part of his psychotherapeutic technique, Benor lectures to British doctors, medical students, nurses, and other medical professionals on Therapeutic Touch and spiritual healing.[2] Significantly, this is often at the invitation of medical schools or associations. He showed me a poster advertising his next all-day seminar. Billed as a Workshop for Stress Reduction, Therapeutic Touch and Spiritual Healing, the seminar was to feature Benor and Paulina Baume, a healer who teaches at and is the chair of the Leamington-Warwick Healing Centre of the National Federation of Spiritual Healers. The whole event was approved for doctors (as health promotion) by the British Postgraduate Medical Federation.

In addition, Dr. Benor now co-ordinates a network of doctor-healer teams across England. There are five regional groups: London-Rustington-Sevenoaks; the Chilterns; Yorkshire; Exeter; and Bath-Bristol. As we will see later, these teams meet regularly to discuss patients – often those treated by doctor-healer pairs – as well as theoretical and personal questions and to see demonstrations of healing methods. As Benor noted, this provides a forum for information and progress in integrating spiritual healing and conventional medicine.

It will come as news to many in North America that there are now at least three general-practice surgeries in England with spiritual healers paid by the government under the National Health Plan. A growing number of British doctors now refer their patients to healers at the healers' treatment rooms. A dozen or so doctors to date have declared they are developing their own innate healing powers. Two hospital pain centres and two hospital cancer centres have healers on the staff of the health team.

Britain – for a variety of reasons, not the least of which was Godfrey Mowatt's life and ministry – has always been in the forefront of the modern movement to recover lost healing arts. Since the mid-1970s, according to Benor, some fifteen hundred healers have had access to British hospitals. There are sixteen different spiritual healing associations, which together form the Confederation of Healing Organizations. The largest of these, the National Federation of Spiritual Healers, has five thousand healers in its membership. The rest together have about three thousand.

Benor has just published Volume One of a major four-volume work on healing, the first of its kind and ten years in the making.[3] In it, in addition to developing his own views and theories, he brings together some fifteen hundred references to books and articles on healing, including detailed discussion of nearly 150 research projects that offer objective evidence of the efficacy of non-medical healing methods. His research and his personal experience in his practice have convinced Benor, "emotionally and intellectually," that spiritual healing works. He says, "If spiritual healing were a drug, they'd have put it out there on the market long ago. There's more evidence of its effectiveness than there is of all the other complementary therapies together – from chiropractic or shiatsu to aromatherapy – except perhaps for hypnosis."

The problem, according to Benor, is that vastly more research should and could be done, but there is, as we have already hinted, great reluctance in academia to allocate funds for something it considers beyond the pale. Benor says, "Basically, medical science has not caught up with what's really going on. It's out of sync with modern physics. Ever since Einstein, modern physics has admitted that matter and energy are interchangeable and that mind is an essential player in how we view the universe. The observer influences what he sees. Mind can work at a distance. It's ironic, I believe, that the science of biology today seems increasingly materialistic in its approach to mind just when physicists are understanding matter in a much more spiritual or mystical way."

At the same time, Benor doesn't begrudge doctors their scepticism about spiritual healing. "After all," he says, "they have invested an awful lot in the opposite view." It usually takes him "about half a day" of lectures and discussion to convince a roomful of doctors that there's more to this kind of healing than they previously thought. With nurses, it's a simpler task, because, according to Benor, they already know from their more intimate dealings with patients that such things as massage and an atmosphere of positive, loving care often have better results than do drugs. "It's easy for them to move from that to a more active, healing role through learning about Therapeutic Touch techniques," he says. "There are thousands of nurses now in the United States who are using the method described by Dolores Krieger in her book *Therapeutic Touch*."

Defining spiritual or psi healing as "capitalizing the improvement in body, emotions, mind or spirit of another living organism without intervention through physical means [that is, drugs, mechanical devices, or surgery]," Benor describes briefly how he combines orthodox psychotherapy with this approach in his own practice. (Psi, the twenty-third letter of the Greek alphabet, is the symbol generally used to refer to the whole field of the so-called paranormal.)[4] He begins in the normal way by getting a case history or outline of the problem from the patient – "a sort of thumbnail sketch" – and then, because he looks at people as "pieces of families," tries to get a feel for the larger setting. Often, he sees the whole family at one or more sessions. As the process unfolds, he teaches visualization techniques for self-healing, and offers his intervention as a spiritual healer. Sometimes he and the patient meditate together. Then he does the laying-on of hands and, if the patient belongs to a church or other religious group where healing is practised, Benor encourages him or her to participate in it. He also gives the patient a reading list that deals with spiritual healing, stress management, and related matters. Noting that when he practises the laying-on of hands he can actually feel heat in his hands (a phenomenon reported by most, but not all, spiritual healers), the doctor says, "Somehow this procedure helps the person in distress to focus their progress; they get to the roots of their problem more quickly; they can digest past hurt, release it, and then make changes faster."

～ Fears of Spiritual Healing

Before turning to the "hard" evidence Benor cites in his lectures, it's important to consider for a moment the kind of answers given by someone such as he to those who wonder why there is such resistance to the idea of spiritual healing, not just from doctors and nurses but from the public – even from many parapsychologists. Why, indeed, do we fear it while, perhaps, at the same time, feeling a fascination for it? Benor referred me to his article in the October 1990 issue of the *Journal of the Society for Psychical Research*.[5] I have summarized his arguments here as succinctly as I can, since I have yet to discover anyone who has given the matter more thought or who has tackled the problem more directly.

Benor cites first of all the general difficulty encountered by anyone who wants to evaluate the work done by healers. Healers are nearly always people with strong intuitive faculties who have little use or proclivity for linear thinking. They don't seem to care about keeping records or documenting medical histories. They confidently make "broad claims for their successes in treating any and all of the ills of man," while offering little or no proof that would withstand scientific scrutiny. Thus, they're a broad target for criticism and scepticism. Benor says he admits and indeed welcomes any fair criticism of healers' unsupported claims or sloppy research methodology, or of defects in various theories. At the same time, he contends – and I strongly agree – that those who simply dismiss spiritual healing out of hand stand in need of criticism themselves. It is both dishonest and unscientific for critics to "cloud the evidence with any excuses to support their disbelief rather than examine either the phenomena or their own discomfort with them."

The Specifics:
• Spiritual healing conflicts with the prevailing paradigms of medical science and so forces us to look afresh at our fundamental hypotheses about how matter, energy, and the mind interrelate. "Healing suggests we may have to postulate new scientific paradigms which include information transfer and action at a distance without physical intervention." (My own view, based not just on the research for this book but on that done for my book *Life After Death*, has persuaded me that Benor is right. The near-death experience is compelling a similar re-examination of our basic paradigms as well.)

• Our materialistic culture dislikes the thought of non-material interventions. Our medical establishment has been extremely wary of what are called Type I research errors, "fearing to accept as being valid any treatments which might possibly be mere placebos." Thus modern psychology, which also deals in non-material, interpersonal and intraphysical problems and relationships, has bad-mouthed parapsychology out of fear of finding it more difficult itself to be accepted by the medical establishment. For the same reason, parapsychology has been uneasy dealing with healing. Benor notes that as early as the seventeenth century, Francis Bacon warned us that the mind is not simply an impartial observer but projects its own constructions onto what is supposedly objective reality. Einstein, as Benor notes, later put this same truth more succinctly: "It is the theory which decides what we can observe." In other words, you see what you are prepared to see.

On this point, the doctor adds an important comment on the nature of the placebo: "A placebo . . . represents a combination of clinical suggestion *and of self-healing* [italics mine]. Viewed in this light, it is not to be avoided, but rather explored, refined and utilized to maximum benefit – especially as it has no known dangerous effects."

• The Western materialistic outlook excludes the possibility of spiritual healing. Our culture in general is biased against anything mystical or spiritual. It tolerates them but in a way that places them outside the realm of "really real" matter, which is what counts. "We see ourselves as existing only in the flesh and come to fear excursions outside of or potential intrusions into our bodies, be they through healing, bioenergy, out-of-body and near-death experiences or death." Because non-medical healing wakens us to the limited range of our materialistic explanations of our world, it causes fear, even panic. A culture steeped in a mechanical, linear view of cause and effect "may fear that if psi energy is accepted (not having examined the evidence and believing psi to be a magical belief) then a Pandora's box of magical explanations will be opened for all science to be attacked on irrational grounds."

• It's human nature to resist change of any kind. When we all agree on a certain way of looking at something, life seems safer, more secure. Consensual views of reality provide a "psychosocial constancy." This saves one the pain of frequent readjustments, but can become rigid "and bind one into beliefs and manners of relating to the world which are limited, thus distancing oneself from reality and eventually stultifying." The possibility of spiritual healing raises the general issue of spiritual reality, and many, perhaps even some in need of such healing, shy from it because it challenges their agnostic or religious assumptions. Benor adds, "It is always easier to reject 'paranormal' evidence than to question accepted beliefs."

• The doctor cites the fear caused by cognitive dissonance. Cognitive dissonance occurs when there is "perceived conflict between several perceptions and belief systems," which often causes unease in the person experiencing it. There is always an inner urge to resolve such tensions. The simplest way to do so is to deny or reject one of the conflicting beliefs, then reduce the tension further by denigrating the rejected belief. Inasmuch as spiritual healing conflicts with normal sensory reality, "any exposure of a person to such experience creates cognitive dissonance." Thus, there is a strong tendency to reject the evidence for any such healing. Benor aptly quotes parapsychology researcher Jule Eisenbud: "Let something appeal to us and we'll make sense out of it. Let something offend us, disturb us, threaten us and we'll see that it doesn't make sense."

• As children we work hard to differentiate between inner and outer realities and then to integrate them, as Freud showed. Benor writes, "In crossing these boundaries, healing revives early childhood anxieties and conflicts associated with such confusions about these boundaries." In other words, having firmly established oneself in sensory reality, there is commonly "a fear of getting lost in the cosmic 'All' of mystical experiences."

• Healing or psi phenomena occur without the conscious control of the individual. This can be frightening to many people since "our conscious minds do not trust our unconscious minds." We moderns love to control.

• We fear that others might not respect or might somehow violate our physical and psychological boundaries through misuse of healing powers. This is similar to the fear some people have of hypnosis. "Reassurances that competent, ethical healers only produce positive results may be of little avail against such fears, especially if they are unconscious." Benor notes that studies of ordinary interaction between people show that we react with anxiety and withdrawal when our personal space is invaded. "How much stronger must this anxiety be with potential healing invasions of inner space on various levels of reality?" he asks. It is easier to avoid the perceived risks altogether.

• Some of those who are aware of having a gift of healing or who would like to explore ways of developing their healing potential have, at the same time, a fear that they might misuse or abuse such a power. They are aware of the temptation of thoughts of omniscience and omnipotence. As the English author Susan Howatch shows in her novel *Glamorous Powers*, healers and psychics face a strong spiritual challenge.[6] They need great discernment and humility to avoid pride.

Benor notes also that there is a parallel fear of what others may think. Historically, those who practise and believe in healing have been regarded with mixed feelings. "In other times, fears of looking inward were projected outward and even led to torture and murder in witch hunts as ways of eliminating sources of discomfort over these matters." Today, of course, there is no risk to one's life. However, when it comes to one's professional rights or status, the risks can be very real. This is particularly true for doctors, other health care professionals, and scientists.

Sophisticated psychological defences may be activated to deny healing. According to Benor and other experienced scholars in this field, there is a marked tendency for researchers to distance themselves from the material being examined. Rather than allowing that the power or energy being researched may also be flowing through them and being affected by their own emotions, conflicts, and relationships, they often engage in a type of projection. If there is anything to the "uncanny power" being researched, it is "out there" in mediums, healers, woods, and caves, in God's grace – anywhere but in the lives of normal people like the researchers themselves.

The second defence mechanism, Benor argues, is that of ideal-ization. Because of their own discomfort with the possibility that spiritual healing might be real, some researchers respond by mak-ing unreasonably strict demands of their tests and experiments. Take, for example, the idealized criterion often insisted upon that the healing be instantaneous and permanent. Benor adds that "by insisting . . . that healers perform on demand, researchers have assured themselves that they will be unlikely to encounter an event which might upset them."

• Students of Jung are aware of his personality analysis in which he pointed out that each of us has a personality style that is domi-nant in one or two out of four parameters – intuition, sensation, thinking, and feeling – paired in polar opposites. Where thinking dominates, it is usually paired with sensation, hence the reliance on sensory perception as a major basis for thought. Similarly, intui-tion and feeling generally appear together. It is a fact that aca-demics and scientists usually excel in the realms of thinking and sensation and are uncomfortable when called on to exercise their weaker functions, intuition and feeling.

The relevance to spiritual healing is obvious. The thinking-sensation person often, even usually, distrusts that which has to do with non-material influences and has "even more difficulties with spirituality, ineffability or mysticism." If something can't be labo-ratory-tested and measured, and produce results that can be repro-duced exactly, its reality is questionable; its validity is doubted. For such people to involve themselves in research of (to them) nebu-lous phenomena would mean activating the aspects of themselves in which they have least confidence and experience. The discom-fort often simply proves too great to overcome.

Benor comments that in exploring healing we have to accept our human limitations and settle for approximate results, mea-sured in probabilities over large numbers of trials. "No apologies are needed. These are the limitations of healing." Expressing the hope that further research will establish at least some minimum laws of healing, Benor says he suspects that one of them will be that we cannot know all of them in a given instance. "This is the healing uncertainty principle," he says. (The reference here is to Werner Heisenberg's Uncertainty Principle in physics.)

• Left-brain dominance may prejudice us against spiritual healing. Brain activity has been more widely tested and studied than Jung's personality style hypothesis. It is now accepted that the right brain is specialized in intuitive activities and the left brain is specialized in linear-type thought. Broadly speaking, in our culture men are more dominated by left-brain thinking than are women. Benor notes that in over a decade of discussing healing he has found that women intuitively accept its reality while men have difficulty and always demand a "logical" explanation.

The psychiatrist then quotes a number of studies that strongly suggest that psi activities are a right-brain function. Even more fascinating are the studies cited by him that show that experienced healers, advanced meditators, and yogic adepts "have balanced right and left brainwave patterns." Thus, he concludes, healing may involve either the right brain alone or the right brain in balance with the left. "In either case, the predominantly left-brain, linearly-thinking person will be uncomfortable with healing."

• The difficulties of reproducing healing phenomena in experiments and their "irregular occurrence" in clinical settings have been used as grounds for questioning their existence. The basic assumption of the physical sciences and, to a lesser degree, of the social sciences is that an aspect of nature is understood only when it can be manipulated to produce the same results predictably and repeatedly. But "healers have not been able to produce results with reliable consistency." Results may be repeated in some healing treatments and not in others, and there is little apparent regularity in the patterns whenever healing does recur. Benor has himself observed that the same healer "might succeed a number of times and we have not isolated the critical variables which can explain – much less predict – when healing will occur or not. Thus, critics can readily claim that what is happening is due to chance variations in the disease, 'spontaneous remissions' or other factors rather than the effectiveness of a healer's intervention."

Healers sometimes reply with the charge that sceptical observers hinder the healing effect. The sceptics respond that the healers are trying to avoid scrutiny with such "excuses." Patterns have been found in laboratory tests of psi effects, but they don't occur predictably, Benor says. "It is not uncommon to find that the first few trials in a series produce positive results, while subsequent trials may produce chance results."

At the same time, it has to be recognized that "unusual patterns" have also been found in conventional science experiments. "New processes for crystallization, developed in a particular laboratory, may be impossible to replicate in other laboratories – until the originator of the process visits personally to demonstrate how to do it." Consequently, Benor concludes, "it may be that beliefs and/or disbeliefs of the experimenters facilitate or block the reactions." Quoting Dr. Bernie Siegel, Benor says, "All healing is scientific. The problem is science's inability to measure or document what occurs." He is convinced that shifting and immeasurable factors such as the boredom, beliefs, and needs of the participants shape the results "along with numerous external factors." I tend to agree. I am also persuaded that the new Chaos Theory in physics, which is currently setting traditional science on its ear, may have important ramifications for healing as well.

• It may well be that healing has laws which differ from those of other sciences. According to Benor, "Procrustean demands are made of researchers of healing. It is ludicrous that scientists from other fields should insist that their own rules for evidence should be applied in healing – just because in their own fields these are the rules that have helped organize data into comprehensible and predictable units." Of course, it would be neater if this were so. The fact that it is not, however, is not proof that healing doesn't exist. Benor describes how some researchers have insisted that there must be a "standard dose" of healing, in the sense that each treatment must occur for the same length of time. But healers proceed intuitively and make adjustments as they become aware of the needs and responses of the patient. So the length of time involved can vary widely from person to person or even with the same patient. (There are, as it happens, tests – like those by Dr. Bernard Grad – using uniform times which have produced positive results.)[7]

Benor points out that in nuclear physics experiments, the results are not absolutely precise and cover large numbers of molecules or particles. "If a nuclear physicist is asked about a single particle, he is often in the same position as a healing researcher and cannot predict with certainty whether that particular particle will or will not act in a particular way." In some ways, physics is in a more difficult position, because an electron can be defined either in terms of its momentum, but not its position, or in terms of its position, in which case its momentum becomes unknown. This is the basis for Heisenberg's Uncertainty Principle.

Consequently, Benor argues, the time has come to accept healing the way it is. It seems to be influenced by a wide range of factors – "so many . . . that it is virtually impossible to establish a repeatable experiment in which all would occur in the same combination more than once. As it is difficult to control any one of these, much less all of them in concert, it is little wonder that only approximately equivalent results have been obtained in experiments over numbers of trials."

• Healing has often been practised in religious settings which emphasize faith and appear contemptuous of healing outside their belief systems. Many have presumed, and still do, that healing only happens as a result of religious faith. But Western science has viewed itself as having escaped from the "murky, magical thinking" of mystical beliefs and religion. Scientists see themselves as dealing with facts not faith, and so reject spiritual healing. There is, however, more faith involved in science than scientists care to admit. There are untestable axioms in science that are as questionable as any other. Indeed, in modern physics there are many theorists whose outlook is closer to mysticism than anyone would have dreamed possible fifty years ago.

• We all tend to be self-satisfied in our ignorance. Because it is militarily and economically dominant, the West assumes it has the only valid grasp of reality. We easily dismiss other ways and other wisdoms. We forget, too, that "all information is subjective." Indeed, as W. C. Ellerbroek has pointed out, "the word 'fact' is merely another statement of an opinion as to the validity of an opinion." By refusing to open ourselves to new possibilities we become victims of "self-validating feedback loops." Our minds thus become closed systems.

• Career success and financial support are based upon acceptance of particular worldviews. As Benor himself discovered in the United States, "research grants, professorships and products (such as drugs) are built on conceptual models. If these are threatened by competing models, funding might become scarce." Thus, it has to be faced that economic motives and wider political concerns militate against investments in exploring all kinds of new territories, not just spiritual healing. It's an old principle: If you want to get ahead, don't rock the boat.

• Healing, both physical and spiritual, threatens to remove potentially useful symptoms. People may insist they want to be healthy, but counselling often reveals unconscious motives for becoming sick in the first place and for staying that way. In other words, there are secondary gains which may, in some instances, outweigh the drawbacks. Illness may bring otherwise unobtainable attention and concern and improve communication with loved ones. It can provide an acceptable excuse for not doing difficult things. Consequently, Benor notes, "healing may be rejected because people fear it will take away their secondary gains quickly and completely. They do not realize that instantaneous, total cures are very, very rare." In his view, spiritual healing usually boosts the body's defences and enhances recuperation "but generally can only reduce the recuperation time by a factor of a quarter or a half of the expected."

It must be emphasized that both in the conclusion to his article and in my interview with him, Benor stressed the need to examine and probe the evidence there is for spiritual healing. Nothing in the above seventeen points negates that. His sole concern is with those who reject out of hand all evidence. I share his concern. It is unscientific to refuse to consider a subject carefully simply because it contradicts one's own unexamined belief system.

~ Scientific Evidence for Healing

It is time now to look at some of the more recent evidence that has helped convince doctors such as Benor that this mode of healing is a reality. In an article first published in the September 1990 issue of *Complementary Medical Research*, Dr. Benor produced the results of his extensive survey of spiritual healing research.[8] Ranging over everything written in English on this subject (from doctoral theses to detailed reports in the parapsychology journals), he found that there was documentation for 131 controlled trials of spiritual healing. Of these, he discovered some 56 showing "statistically significant results" at a probability level of ^.01 or better, and another 26 at a probability level of ^.02–.05. The 131 studies surveyed include research into the results of spiritual healing effects on enzymes, cells, yeasts, bacteria, plants, and animals, as well as on human beings.

One study, culled from *Human Dimensions* magazine, deals with the effects of healing on enzymes.[9] Titled "Paranormal Effects on Enzyme Activity" and written by Dr. Justa Smith, it describes an experiment using the healer Oskar Estebany and four samples of a solution of the enzyme trypsin: (1) a control sample, left untreated; (2) a sample treated for seventy-five minutes by Estebany in the same way as when giving a laying-on-of-hands treatment; (3) a sample exposed to damaging ultraviolet light, which severely reduced its activity, and then treated by Estebany as in (2); and (4) a sample exposed to a strong magnetic field (3,000–13,000 gauss). Samples were taken from these four at intervals to determine the degree of activity of the enzyme. Samples (2), (3), and (4) showed a 10 per cent increase in activity compared to (1).

Several other studies cited by Benor also deal with enzymes. Glen Rein, a British researcher, working with a well-known healer, Matthew Manning, reports "significant results" in the case of near-the-body healing on the nervous-system enzymes of laboratory mice. The enzymes in question were dopamine and noradrenaline. He also did tests involving the enzyme monoamine oxidase in human blood cells. In tests with the dopamine, enzyme activity increased up to 130 per cent in five mice and decreased down to 25 per cent in five mice. In the case of noradrenaline, there was an increase of up to 130 per cent in five mice and no change in five. With monoamine oxidase, from human platelets, there was an increase in activity in nine trials, a decrease in seven others, and no change in two.

These are only two of ten studies on enzymes and, while the results are not spectacular, the overall evidence is that changes can be made by healers to what may be important links in the body's healing process. As Benor notes, more research is clearly needed, if funding can be found. "If healing can enhance activity of enzymes in vitro, it may similarly improve their action in vivo." Monoamine oxidase is involved in the function of the nervous system and may influence neuronally controlled processes in the body. It has also been found to have a correlation with depressed moods. Benor says, "A healer might thus improve a healee's mood, thereby producing the reports by healees that they feel better, though no objective improvements may have been noted by others."

Benor goes on to examine a series of experiments done with various healers who, under controlled conditions, attempted to effect changes in different cells, including red blood cells and cancer cells. Cancer cells stick to the surface of the container in which they are cultured. Changes in the metabolism of, or the injury or death of, such cells causes them "to slough off into the surrounding fluid medium." Microscopic counts are then done of the number of cells in this medium to get a measure of the "state of health" of the cultures. Healer Matthew Manning reportedly was able to bring about changes of 200 to 1,200 per cent in *in vitro* cervical cancer cells. The effects occurred both when Manning held his hands near the flask containing the cells and also when he was isolated in a distant, electrically shielded room. Benor believes the studies done on cells and healing – he cites eleven – "suggest another mechanism for healing." If, as some of these studies indicate, a healer can sometimes increase haemoglobin levels by protecting red blood cells from haemolysis, the enhanced oxygen-carrying capacity of the blood will improve the body's ability to cope with stress and illness. Similarly, if cancer cells can be killed *in vitro*, as the above study with Manning suggests, it may be possible that they can be selectively killed *in vivo*. Given the vast sums donated for cancer research, surely it should be possible to allocate some for a thorough follow-up on this line of research.

8

Therapeutic Touch

"We are into high-touch care for the elderly; we call it the four-hugs-a-day approach."
— Nora Boyd, R.N., infection control officer, Sarnia General Hospital, Ont.

During my inquiry into spiritual healing, several times I had the odd sensation that I was engaged in a kind of detective mystery in which clues were being thrown up and then repeated in a pattern. That was the case when I turned to investigate a remarkable recent development on the North American medical scene known as Therapeutic Touch (TT). There are now estimated to be approximately thirty thousand nurses in the United States and Canada using TT in hospitals and clinics. There are teams of doctors and nurses combining modern medical skills with TT's adaptation of the traditional laying-on of hands in most major cities in the United States. TT, sometimes written as the capital Greek letter pi (Π), is used to relax patients before they receive anaesthetic, on cardiac patients before the insertion of pacemakers, and on premature babies in an increasing number of hospital nurseries.

As I began to read about this phenomenon, I was surprised to re-encounter two people we have met already, Dr. Bernard Grad and Oskar Estebany. The founder and developer of TT is Dolores Krieger, a professor of nursing at New York University. Krieger's first contact with laying-on of hands in healing was through the research of an American woman named Dora Kuntz. Dora Kuntz has been described as having been gifted from birth – like Grad and others – with an ability to discern the subtle energies flowing around all living things. At a young age she decided to make a study of these energies in collaboration with the best scientific and medical minds available. In telling of her debt to Kuntz in her book *The Therapeutic Touch: How to Use Your Hands to Help or Heal*, Krieger says Kuntz studied the function and control of these subtle energies under "one of the great seers of the twentieth century," a man called Charles W. Leadbeater. When Krieger first met her, though, Kuntz was testing the claims of several healers, most notably Oskar Estebany. Kuntz (like Benor later) had learned of Estebany through some of Dr. Bernard Grad's published research and from a feature article in a 1974 issue of *Esquire*.[1]

Dora Kuntz contacted Estebany, and, together with a medical

doctor, Otelia Bengsten, decided to carry out a much larger study on a wide sample of medically referred patients. Since Krieger was a nurse and had just completed her doctoral degree, she was asked to join them. She reports that her duties were peripheral to the main study, and so she was able to watch Estebany closely. She spent a lot of time just talking to him and getting to know his background.

Estebany told Krieger that after he first discovered – while caring for horses in the Hungarian cavalry unit in which he was serving – that he could heal animals, it was a long time before he could be convinced to try his gift on humans. He was eventually persuaded when, one Sunday morning, a neighbour's child became very ill and no doctor was available. In desperation, the child's father brought the youngster to Estebany's house and asked him to heal him in the same way that he healed horses. Faced with the parents' insistence and the emergency situation, Estebany reluctantly treated the child. The child got well again, and Estebany said he decided then that his gift ought to be shared with people. By the time he left the army and emigrated to Canada, he had already established himself as a full healer in the traditional sense.

Instead of all the expected trappings – arm waving, incantations, a hypnotic glare in the eye – Krieger says she found to her relief that Estebany was a very normal, "well-built man with cheery blue eyes and a frequent smile." She was struck by the man's deep sense of commitment to his work; he often worked on the healees for sixteen hours a day and would be up again before sunrise ready to work. His healing sessions, which lasted about twenty to twenty-five minutes, were quiet, undemonstrative affairs. Estebany would sit on a small stool, either in front of or behind the healee, and place his hands over any area of the body that seemed to him in need of energy. If the condition warranted it, the process would be repeated the following day or as often as required.

When questioned by Krieger, the patients said they could feel "heat" flowing from Estebany's hands and a great sense of relaxation as he treated them. She noticed an "up-welling of vibrant energy that seemed to come from his person as the days went by; and, in addition, a felt energetic intensity built up in the rooms in which he did his healing, so that it was quite perceptible upon entering the house." Many patients reported later that they felt better, but there were no cures that could be labelled "instanta- neous" except one. A woman, who had sustained serious head injuries in a boating accident some years before, which damaged her inner ear and radically affected her sense of balance, had been examined and tested by various specialists without obtaining relief. Estebany met her for her first treatment late one afternoon at the retreat centre in the Berkshires where the study was being done. Afterwards, she sat out on the lawn chatting with other patients, then had dinner and went to bed early. When she came down the next morning she said she felt much better. The doctor examined her and could find no trace of her previous symptoms. She was cured and has remained so ever since, Krieger reports.

What most impressed Krieger, however, were the follow-up reports on the others treated by the healer. "I was to be astounded by the number of medical reports or first-person reports that told either of an amelioration of symptoms or of an actual disappear- ance of symptoms," she writes. "Part of my surprise was based on the complicated nature of the medical diagnoses of the healees in the sample." These included pancreatitis, brain tumour, emphysema, multiple endocrine disorders, rheumatoid arthritis, and congestive heart failure, among others. Krieger's comment is significant: "There was nothing in either my previous education or experience by which I could rationalize these results."

Krieger was so impressed by all of this that she spent several summers observing further experiments with Estebany. She also initiated a pilot study and later two large-scale studies of her own, using him as the healer. One of her earliest findings was that "when ill people are treated by the laying-on of hands, a significant change occurs in the haemoglobin component of their red blood cells."[2] This finding of increased haemoglobin levels was indeed groundbreaking. As she learned from each study, she tightened the controls and other aspects of the next, rendering it more reliable, more scientific. Krieger's appreciation for the efficacy of the traditional healing method grew, and she began to be interested in learning whether she, too, could become a healer.

Estebany spoke quite emphatically against this. Not because he jealously wanted to keep others from his "turf." Rather, it was his view that nobody can be taught to heal; either you are born with the ability or you are not. He consistently refused requests to teach his skill to others. Dora Kuntz, however, disagreed with his position, and began a series of workshops for any who wished to learn. Since the theory underlying her approach is simple and basic to our enquiry it's worthwhile summarizing it here.

Touch is essentially a therapeutic activity. We can see this in something as instinctive as putting our hand over a bruise or other injury, in a mother's caress of her troubled infant, or in the reassuring pat by the coach on the shoulder of a player who has just made a mistake. In our predominantly no-touch culture, touch can serve to soothe, re-energize, or encourage us. Supposing for a moment that what all pre-modern cultures and religions have held actually exists, that a special kind of energy can be imparted by touch – whether we call it *prana* as do the sages of India, spirit (*pneuma*) as do the biblical authors, orgone as does Wilhelm Reich, or bioenergy as do contemporary researchers into the field of subtle energies. Then it follows (and most of the experts I have read or interviewed believe this) that to some degree every one of us has the latent ability to heal. It's a little like playing the piano. Everyone can learn enough to play the piano after a fashion, but only those with talent and aptitude will ever become concert pianists.

What I am really saying is that you, the reader, could become a healer. Following Dora Kuntz's reasoning, you could discover, as Dolores Krieger did, that once you pay attention and learn some basic techniques, you have powers you never realized. We'll come back to that possibility later. For now, it's sufficient to say that the more Krieger experimented – the more she tried to be a channel for the life-force or healing energy she was coming to believe was both within her and all around – the more evident it became to her that something objective was happening. The response from the healees boosted her growing confidence.

Eventually, even when the patients in the experiments were blindfolded, they could recognize her as the healer (among several) because of the heat and energy flow they could feel from her hands – even when she passed them a couple of inches away from their bodies rather than actually touching them. She now defines TT as "the intelligent direction of significant life energies from the person playing the role of healer to the healee."

For a cross-reference to this aspect of TT, I recommend Agnes Sanford's book *The Healing Light*.[3] In it, Sanford, the wife of an Anglican rector, records phenomena in her own hands and arms that are very similar to what Krieger describes. Sanford's approach is, of course, wholly in terms of her own Christian faith. She points out, however, that yesterday's impossibilities and miracles are today's commonplaces. God only works according to laws, in her view. Each advance in our understanding of the laws of nature opens new vistas. She writes: "So it is with that power of God that works through the being of one person for the healing of another. It is not really 'unscientific' at all. It is only the channeling of a flow of energy from God's being through man's being. It is the entering of the Holy Spirit of God through the spirit of a man [or woman], via the conscious and subconscious mind of that man, via the nerves of his body, via the nerves of the patient's body into the patient's inner control centre and thence to his mind and his spirit. The nerves are the telegraph wires of the body. The one who prays connects the nerve terminals in his hands with the nerve terminals of the patient's body and through that simple and natural thought-track sends a message to the patient's subconscious mind."[4]

Sanford likes the electrical metaphor. She sees the healer as a receiving and "transmitting centre" for the power of God. She describes her healees as experiencing warmth or electric-like shocks from her hands, and describes her own sensations of a force like a current running down her arms and into her hands. Sanford warns, however, against getting too caught up in physical vibrations or other subjective feelings. God, she believes, is working in the healing whether the healer is directly aware of it or not.[5]

What I like most about Dolores Krieger – her approach and her work – is her determination to submit everything she does and believes in to the strictest kind of self-criticism and to the most stringent scientific testing possible. She continues to do extensive research into what is actually happening both to the healer and to the healee in the administering of TT. There is a reason her work has been so influential and why many nurses and hospitals now take it so seriously that they have incorporated the technique – it's based upon solid testing and proven results.

Krieger documents the results of experiments proving that during TT performed by herself and others (on out-patients at the pain-control clinic of a large American hospital) there were changes in the brainwaves both of the healer and the healee. The encephalographic readings show that the patients being treated went immediately into a low amplitude alpha state – a "state of calmness and well-being" – and stayed there throughout the treatment. The healer registered a high amplitude beta brainwave state "indicative of a state of deep concentration similar to those occurring in mature meditators." Krieger says even sceptics willing to be observers of these experiments were able to discern objective, outward signs of this "relaxation response": the voice of the healee went down several decibels; the healee's breathing slowed markedly and deepened; there was some audible sign of relaxation, such as a sigh, a very deep breath, or an exclamation like "I feel so relaxed!"; and there was an observable "peripheral flush," a pinking of the skin "apparently due to a dilation of the peripheral vascular system." This meant increased blood flow and hence more oxygen available to body tissues.

Krieger does not claim that this healing approach is any kind of panacea and is against any attempt to use it as a replacement for the best in conventional medicine. She believes that in the end "it is the patient who heals himself." The energy flow given in TT, in her view, "accelerates the healing process." She has seen it work repeatedly with fractious or ailing premature babies, with cases of asthma, and with pain of every kind, from toothache to the pain of terminal cancer.

While one can observe and tabulate the results of TT, however, *how* it works still eludes us. Krieger's theory is that illness is caused by a lack of or a congestion of subtle body energies, what Reich called "dead orgone." The function of the healer is to try to balance the patient's energy "field," infuse fresh energy, or free the energy that has become stuck. Many will find this satisfactory as an explanation; others will not. Before one is too critical of this explanation, one should remember that even the best of medical scientists are unable to give a full explanation of how the body's healing processes, or even drugs as commonplace as Aspirin, actually work.

Krieger's book gives lots of practical advice to the would-be healer. While the method requires some self-discipline and willingness to learn, it is not something that requires an enormous effort. In other words, it cannot be accomplished by trying to summon up one's own strength and then working hard to project it to another. There are four phases, according to the author:

(1) Becoming focused or centred by becoming relaxed and at the same time aware and alert – a meditative state easily arrived at.

(2) Using the natural sensitivity of one's hands to assess the energy field of the healee "for clues to differences in the quality of energy flow."

(3) Mobilizing areas in the healee's energy field that the healer may perceive as non-flowing; that is, sluggish, congested, or static. This is done by making specific sweeps or brushing motions with the hand over the affected area. Krieger calls it "unruffling the field."

(4) Deliberately and consciously directing one's excess body energies to assist the healee to repattern his or her own energies. No straining or gritting of the teeth is required, simply a calm, concentrated directing of one's will. As one researcher observed of Krieger's method, "It's really a healing meditation."

Throughout this discussion, I have deliberately focused on the work of Krieger because of her scientific approach to the healing power of touch. But she is far from alone in this. The world's first Touch Research Institute has just recently been founded at the University of Miami's medical school to explore and document the beneficial effects on health of massage therapy. "We are studying the positive effect of touch," says Professor Tiffany Fields, the director of the new centre. Fields, a psychologist and professor of pediatrics, told Reuters News Service that researchers at the institute have already had promising preliminary results from exploring the potential of touch therapy for promoting growth in premature babies, treating depression in teenage mothers, encouraging communication by autistic children, and boosting the immune system of people with AIDS.[6]

Fields is currently seeking corporate funding to research whether brief massages in the workplace could promote workers' alertness, safety, and efficiency. One study already done, working with hospital personnel, has found that people who got a twenty-minute massage during their lunch-break performed better on math tests than did their co-workers. Dr. Gail Ironson, a University of Miami professor affiliated with the institute, has been successful in her attempts to boost the body's immune responses in men carrying the AIDS virus. The institute is steering clear of the "leap of faith" approach of some television and other healers. Instead, it's concentrating on measurable, physiological responses to the massage form of laying-on of hands, looking for hard data to support "an ancient healing practice that is now enjoying a renaissance."

Fields' research grew out of her experience with her daughter, who is now a teenager but was born prematurely in 1976. In one recent project she initiated, premature infants in incubators in neonatal intensive care units were massaged for fifteen minutes a day for ten days. They gained 47 per cent more weight than the low birth-weight babies who were not massaged. They were also more responsive to social stimulation and showed better motor development – and were released from hospital an average six days earlier.

Similar studies have found TT to have beneficial effects on

babies born to cocaine-using mothers, on HIV-exposed infants, and on those whose mothers have post-partum depression. Babies with sleep disorders or colic have also responded extremely well to touch therapy. Cindy, a teenage mother who was severely depressed and who had great trouble coping after her baby, Albert, was born, is quoted in the Reuters report as having found that the massage therapy sessions at the centre transformed her situation. She had begun massaging the baby every night after his bath as she had been taught. Albert quickly stopped having his colic attacks and became a near-model infant. Cindy's depression soon gave way to a growing pride in becoming a better mother.

Fields admits many of her medical colleagues scorn what they view as a kooky therapy or cannot shake off their associations between massage and sleazy sex parlours. With the typical mind-set of those who claim to be scientific, yet can't keep an open mind, they refuse to look even at hard evidence when it's presented to them. But Fields also noted that doctors everywhere are becoming more receptive to touch therapy as part of the new emphasis on exercise, diet, and preventative medicine.

Professor Janet Quinn, a TT practitioner and clinical researcher at the University of Colorado Health Science Center, Denver, has done a series of controlled studies in which she has shown that the immune systems of both healer and healee are enhanced during the process of TT. Quinn, who has been using TT for about fifteen years, has also conducted a study of the effects of TT on the immune system of people in deep grief. It is a well-known fact that severe grief often depresses the immune system, leaving the sufferer open to a range of serious illnesses. This accounts, at least in part, for the way in which the death of one spouse in a close marriage is frequently followed shortly by the death of the other. Quinn employed the services of two established healers and worked with four patients who were in deep grief. The healers did forty-minute sessions of TT daily with each participant for seven days. Blood samples were taken from the four participants immediately before and after each session, and the blood was analysed in the hospital laboratory. What she discovered was that there was an overall, striking drop of 18 per cent in the population of suppressor T-cells in all four cases. (These retard antibody production and so hinder the body's ability to cope with disease.) The study showed conclusively that TT has a direct effect upon the immune system by altering the balance between the helper T-cells and the suppressors.[7]

9

The Spiritual Factor

"Since there are imponderables that elude scientific prediction, the patient is entitled to a full mobilization of resources, including his own. . . .

"Medical research is discovering that high determination and purpose can actually enhance the working of the immune system."
– Norman Cousins[1]

"Faith, hope and love are the things that really endure; and the greatest of these is love."
– St. Paul[2]

V irtually any general practitioner will tell you that the majority of illnesses and problems presented to him or her by
patients are actually the symptoms or the results of stress.[3] They
arise from mental, emotional, and spiritual problems, which seem
at first glance far removed from the arthritis, disk injury, or insomnia that are presented as the reasons for seeing a doctor. Indeed, as
much as 85 per cent of all illnesses cared for by doctors are believed
to be self-limiting (that is, originating from within the patient). I
have interviewed many physicians and have heard the frustration
expressed as they admit that, given the time they can spend with
any one patient – anywhere from seven to fifteen minutes on average in most medical clinics and offices in North America today –
there is simply little or no opportunity to do more than treat the
most obvious problem, the physical malfunction, or the mood dis-
order. Right now, about 75 per cent of all visits to a doctor in
Ontario end in the filling out of a prescription for some form of
medication. It's a simpler and quicker approach than thorough
patient consultation and long-term solutions. It can be argued
that since the fee schedule under the Ontario Health Insurance
Plan is the same for such cursory visits as it is for those where some
genuine exploration takes place, the consultation takes on the
form of piece work or assembly-line medicine.

Unless there is a referral to a psychiatrist or other counsellor, the
troubled relationships, inner turmoils, or other mental and spiritual conflicts underlying or accompanying the illness are simply
ignored. Any healing that takes place is thus too often partial and
temporary. The patient, of course, keeps coming back for more
drugs or other kinds of quick-fix solutions. The implications of this
for the quality, scope, and costs of medical care are truly staggering.

Gradually, however, the old mechanical and departmentalized
approach to medicine is being challenged and changed. Some of
the most exciting and important research of the past twenty years
is rendering it increasingly difficult for even the most sceptical of
doctors to ignore the part played by non-material or spiritual influences in preventing illness and in facilitating healing. It's no

longer a matter of blind faith or of some kind of pious, exhortative and forced optimism. The data are in, and the immediate linkage between the inner life of the mind and spirit and that of the body's healing energies is no longer a matter of conjecture but of fact.

This is a vast field, but we can attempt to simplify it somewhat by focusing briefly on the enormous contribution made to this area of knowledge by one man and those he has inspired, the late Norman Cousins, former editor of the *Saturday Review* (from 1940 to 1971). Through his now-famous book, *Anatomy of an Illness*, in which he described his recovery from a mysterious, "incurable" paralysing illness (ankylosing spondylitis) by taking responsibility for his own treatment and by doing everything in his power to develop his positive emotions, Cousins has become almost a household name.[4] Because part of his self-prescribed therapy was watching old Marx Brothers and other comic movies, Cousins, who has likened laughter to "inner jogging," was widely described in the popular media as "the man who laughed his way to health."

The medical establishment wasn't amused. Some doctors ridiculed the idea of laughter being a kind of medicine. But today the best laugh is at the expense of the critics. Cousins' theory no longer seems idiosyncratic or weird. On January 22, 1993, the *Toronto Star* carried a story about the cancer unit at Foothills Hospital, Calgary, Alberta, one of the leading hi-tech medical facilities in the country. The unit is adding laughter to its arsenal of weapons in the fight against cancer and other illnesses. Staff nurse Jo Fraser has brought in clowns and comics and has organized a humour room where patients can go when their prognosis or general situation is getting too hard to take. She told reporters, "It's a very comfortable space with funny books and with a VCR to watch comedy films." The cancer unit is the first in the hospital to have a "humour cart" that can be wheeled into any room. It carries comedy videos and books, games, and toys. The hospital is planning the first Canadian, hospital-wide laughter channel on its closed-circuit TV system. The idea is to make round-the-clock comedies and sitcoms available in every patient's room.

After reading this article, I did some further research and found that the idea of introducing humour as a therapy into the top hospitals and clinics in North America has caught on more widely than I had imagined. A story in the same newspaper on January 29, 1993, featured the best-known cancer hospital in Canada, the Princess Margaret in Toronto. Janet Manzo, co-ordinator of the hospital's new Humour Therapy program, was quoted saying that now that studies have shown that laughter does indeed have positive *physiological* effects, the medical staff "want patients to laugh, play games, and have fun." The program, based upon what is called the Humour Project in American hospitals, includes a "laugh wagon" and plenty of comic movies. Several patients, facing weeks and months of radiation or chemotherapy treatments, were interviewed about their reaction to the use of "merriment as a tonic." Their responses were overwhelmingly positive. One twenty-four-year-old man, who had just been told he needed several weeks of radical therapy and was feeling quite terrible when the program was launched on his floor, was able to smile and tell the journalist how much he appreciated it: "I could use a few laughs. It gets people more involved, lifts their spirits and gets them out of their rooms." It does even more. It makes a difference to their ability to fight the disease.

Less widely known is the extraordinary research project at UCLA's School of Medicine, which Cousins helped to create. The full story is told in his remarkable 1989 book, *Head First*.[5] Cousins was convinced, as a result of his own experience with a deadly disease, that our human brain and spirit can use positive emotions and thoughts to affect how the body deals with illness. But he had no proof. He knew that there was lots of research to show that the brain, under the influence of negative emotions such as hate, rage, fear, panic, hopelessness, frustration, grief, or depression could change the body's chemistry and set up mechanisms leading to serious sickness. "But, there was no comparable evidence to show that the positive emotions – purpose, love, hope, determination, faith, will to live, festivity – could also affect biological states." In other words, it was known we can make ourselves ill. What about trying to prove that we can also make ourselves well?

Cousins was aware his questions and concerns weren't original. After all, Hippocrates (c.460-c.400 B.C.), the father of medicine, had already noted the connection between thought and health. The Bible expressly teaches that "a merry heart doeth good like a medicine." But he knew, as well, that many if not most doctors trained in the conventional manner feel there is nothing more unscientific than suggesting that attitudes have something to do with conquering serious diseases. Nevertheless, his obsession gave him no rest. He continued to write articles not just for the *Saturday Review* but also such medical publications as the *New England Journal of Medicine*. He was invited to speak at various medical schools and, in 1978, made his first visit to the school at UCLA.

During this visit, Cousins so impressed the dean and several other key professors that he was shortly surprised by a unprecedented invitation to join the medical school as a member of the faculty of the Department of Psychiatry and Biobehavioral Sciences. The department was headed by Dr. L. Jolyon West, a former University of Oklahoma professor who had gathered together at UCLA a prestigious team of experts on mind-body research. Nearly thirty disciplines – from anthropology to zoology – were included in UCLA's Neuropsychiatric Institute, which he directed.

For a year, Cousins participated in a weekly think-tank, led by Dr. Milton Greenblatt, a leading authority in the area of psychosomatic medicine and former chief of psychiatry of the Massachusetts Department of Mental Health. The aim of the sessions, involving about ten other experts and occasional visiting specialists, depending on the subject under discussion, was to hammer out specific protocols or guidelines for the kind of research Cousins was most interested in. He was warned that, as the only layman on the faculty, there would be some faculty members waiting to cut him to pieces if his methodology didn't measure up to their standards of objectivity. He was cautioned, in particular, to avoid quoting his own almost miraculous case or other similar cases he knew about because this would be regarded as anecdotal not scientific evidence. As Cousins learned, the "quickest and surest way for a doctor to discredit or disparage an account of a single experience is to label it an anecdote." He needed to look instead for evidence based on the results of a substantial *series* of experiences.

In the early 1980s, at the University of Rochester, the term psychoneuroimmunology was coined by Dr. Robert Ader to describe the interactions between the brain, the endocrine system, and the immune system. Medical researchers around the world had been exploring this area for some years without the benefit of a name for their field of study. Cousins was introduced to the work of most of these during his first year at the university, and had the pleasure of meeting many of the key figures. He learned about the wonders and capabilities of the human immune system, with its "sentry" cells, which roam the body continuously to locate and identify intruders or abnormal conditions, and its cells which can poison or wipe out infecting cells or "arrest" viruses and call for additional back-up. He came to see that at least as much as 85 per cent of all human illnesses are within reach of the body's own marvellous healing system. What is needed is the knowledge of how all that potential can be best marshalled.

Over the next ten years – Cousins was sixty-three when he first became an adjunct professor at UCLA – the former editor and the team he worked with conducted or sponsored a range of scientific experiments on everything from the effects of laughter on the immune system to the effects on health of more patient control of their own treatment, a better relationship between patient and doctor, and better information to the patient about his or her condition and treatment. The project was called the Task Force on Psychoneuroimmunology. The results of this effort, described and documented in *Head First*, are solid. What's more, their significance for medicine and health is revolutionary.

Studies done both by others as a result of interest in *Anatomy of an Illness* and instigated by Cousins once he was at UCLA have continued to verify his belief that laughter would one day be scientifically proven to "do good like a medicine." One project, which he helped to fund out of research money made available to him at UCLA, was done at Loma Linda University Medical Center in California. Dr. Lee S. Berk was able to show that there were significant changes in "stress" hormones in ten healthy males after they were shown a sixty-minute comedy film. Berk went on to document increases in spontaneous blastogenesis – growth of immune cells – "accompanied by a marked decrease in cortisol, a hormone that has an immune-suppressing capability."[6] Other experiments at Harvard and at Western New England College have reinforced the view that a consistently cheerful approach to life significantly enhances the body's disease-resisting forces.

One of the most important studies dealt with a large group of cancer patients suffering from a particularly complex and deadly form of melanoma. The aim was to discover the influence of a strong will to live, hopefulness, and other factors – such as a sense of meaning and purpose for one's life – on the body's ability to fight this affliction. Proper protocols were set in place. The research, which lasted one year, involved taking blood samples from the patients at regular intervals and measuring the levels of various immune cells. The patients were simultaneously tested for levels of depression and anxiety according to a POMS (Profile of Mood States Scale) and on the PAIS (Psychosocial Adjustment to Illness Inventory).

The cancer patients involved in the experimental group called themselves the Society of Challengers and met regularly with Cousins and his assistants to share their life stories – in particular, their experiences, hopes, fears, and attitudes leading up to their awareness of their illness. Cousins shared his own experiences with combating sickness – he had a major heart attack at age sixty-five, two years after coming to UCLA, in addition to the earlier crisis described in *Anatomy of an Illness*. He told the stories of, and showed the group photographs of, patients he had known who had overcome the grim predictions of their doctors and had either beaten their illness or managed to prolong their lives far past the usual expectations for their particular malady. He stressed repeatedly his credo: "Don't deny the diagnosis just defy the verdict that goes with it!" He made abundant use of laughter and also of various biofeedback techniques to show the Challengers that mind can directly affect bodily functions.

Soon it became obvious. The more the patients helped one another, the more they realized they were not lacking in resources with which to do battle, the more they took responsibility for aiding the doctors in their fight against the illness, the more they gained confidence and strength. The blood tests showed marked improvement in the immune systems of the Challengers as their depression began to lift. Cousins writes, "The conclusion was inescapable: if you can reduce the depression that invariably affects cancer patients, you can increase the body's capacity for combating malignancies."[7] This finding is especially important, since the effects of chemotherapy, so often used in treating cancer, are generally harmful to the immune system. When, at the end of the year, the computer poured forth the final statistics, Cousins and his team were ecstatic. For example, whereas the patients in the control group (who received only the prescribed medical and surgical treatment) were, at 0.04, slightly below the baseline figure at the end of six months in regard to the number of natural, protective killer cells in their immune systems, the experimental group showed a marked increase of 2.09. The same trend continued in "many of the other cell categories."[8]

In all, the task force conceived and led by Cousins at UCLA undertook or directly sponsored more than two dozen studies on the effects of psychological and psychosocial factors on the immune system. The way in which the studies reinforce or replicate one another is little short of astounding. Cousins was aware that this research was only a beginning (though it tied in completely with studies done on the placebo effect which, as we have seen, have also shown that belief affects biology), but he was aware, too, that what had been shown was "that at last it was possible to talk scientifically about the importance of hope and the will to live as essential parts of a comprehensive strategy of medical care."[9] He wasn't claiming a cure for cancer, but he had demonstrated beyond all doubt that there was a whole arsenal of innate weapons available to those afflicted with cancer or any other disease.

∼ The Wider Significance

The kind of research conducted by Cousins and the UCLA task force demonstrates unequivocally the way in which influences, attitudes, and values – in themselves completely intangible and invisible – can directly affect that which is material and subject to scientific investigation. You can't measure or weigh love, purpose, courage, joy, faith, or hope, but their reality and power to change physical health is finally no longer a matter for conjecture or faith alone. Their results can be measured and assessed.

The significance of this for medicine, the need to work constantly to improve the doctor-patient relationship and to enhance the environment in clinics and hospitals is obvious and is expounded at length by Cousins in *Head First*. But churches, synagogues, temples, and all other institutions and groups concerned with spiritual truth have yet to appreciate fully what this means to them. If spiritual or non-material factors have this kind of effect on the body's power to heal itself, then the case for the closest possible co-operation between those entrusted with conventional medicine and those whose chief expertise lies in the spiritual realm has been convincingly made.

Since it is, and has been from time immemorial, the function of religion and its shamans, priests, ministers, or founders and leaders to provide the grounds for meaning, purpose, values, faith, hope, and love, by witnessing to an underlying energy or reality from which everything derives, it is clear that anyone claiming to be concerned with the healing of the sick has to regard the role of the religious or of spirituality in health with an entirely new respect. Historically, the function of religion has been to enable humans to make sense of life, to discover and maintain hope, to relate to one another with compassion, courage, and justice, and to face death fearlessly. These qualities have now been shown to be tremendously potent for our total well-being.

It's not just a matter of the kind of positive attitudes listed and so strongly stressed by Cousins. When I was a pastor engaged in counselling and visiting the troubled and the sick, I learned the power of the assurance of forgiveness – through the sacraments, private confession, or simply from "hearing the Word" – to release people from negative feelings, guilt, or depression, thus helping their immune systems to prevent or fight serious sickness. It would be extremely difficult to devise protocols by which the power of forgiveness to affect mental and physical healing could be measured or tested. But its reality is beyond doubt. What those people who keep returning to their physician or psychiatrist with the same symptoms need more than pills or other forms of therapy is to be helped to face the pain and cost of confronting whatever it is in their past or present that needs to be forgiven – and to be assured that such forgiveness is theirs for the taking. It is no accident that throughout the Old and New Testaments forgiveness and healing are viewed as complementary aspects of the same reality.

It would be quite wrong to argue that all or even most sicknesses are *directly related to* or *caused by* spiritual problems. To do so would not only be foolish but cruel as well. It's bad enough to be sick without someone suggesting it's one's own fault. (Although a lot of New Age-type books on healing do just that.) It's one thing to recognize, as I stated earlier, that there is often an inner "soul sickness" underlying or accompanying a physical complaint, it's another to begin to assess blame. Many physical complaints may actually be masking a depression, for example, but the depression itself may be a direct product of childhood trauma, loss of a loved one, or some other factor completely beyond one's control. Nevertheless, it's true that many patients would prefer a pill or other "magic bullet" rather than face the hard work of correcting a spiritual conflict that may be blocking the flow of life energy.

Dr. Alfred Price, whom we met earlier, once told me a story

which illustrates this point. A woman came to see him in his study one day. She said she had heard he believed in the laying-on of hands for healing and she "wanted to try it" because of a very painful arthritic condition for which conventional medicine had done very little. Price talked with her about her life, her hopes and fears, and the duration of her complaint. Everything was fine until the subject of her daughter-in-law came up. The woman's whole manner changed. With gritted teeth and considerable bitterness she described her sorry relationship with her son's wife and how she wished he had married someone else. After listening for some time, Price told her, "Look, I'm not saying all arthritis is caused by anger and frustration, but I don't think you'll ever get relief from yours until you go to your daughter-in-law and make up your quarrel." The woman looked at him with alarm, grabbed her purse and coat, and flounced from the room with these words trailing behind her: "The arthritis hurts, but it doesn't hurt enough for that!"

IO

Energy-Field Healing

"Bioenergy medicine is the transmission of human energy from one person to another to improve his or her health. It's a little like giving somebody with a weak car battery a boost."
— Mietek Wirkus, bioenergy healer[1]

"What we have seen and measured in our laboratory [as healers have been tested while healing] is not possible. But it happens anyway!"
— Elmer E. Green, Ph.D., Director Emeritus, Center for Applied Psychophysiology, Menninger Clinic[2]

The first time I covered a large healing service as a journalist, not long after becoming religion editor of the *Toronto Star* in 1971, the healer was the late Kathryn Kuhlman. (She died in 1976.) Kuhlman, one of the best-known of all the American television healers – she was seen weekly on more than fifty stations at the time – is dismissed by James Randi in about half a page of his book *The Faith Healers*. In an accusation, unsupported by any evidence, he credits her with inventing the "sit-'em-in-a-wheelchair" gimmick. I can only say I saw no evidence of that or any other kind of deception or fraud at her Toronto services.[3]

I would like to record here the impression she made upon me at that time. Here is the reason. The service was announced for a Sunday afternoon at the O'Keefe Centre, one of Toronto's largest auditoriums. Normally, it seats about a thousand people. However, that day it was crammed to the doors and there was still such a crowd outside it was decided to hold two services. As soon as the first ended, the hall emptied and then promptly filled to capacity again.

A frail-looking, almost ethereal figure, in her flowing gown with its long, filmy cape, Kuhlman nevertheless radiated enormous energy as she singlehandedly held her audiences spellbound for nearly four hours. It was a feat of endurance few actors or other performers could sustain in their prime. I was given permission to watch the proceedings from the wings, where I was out of sight yet only a few feet from her. I watched carefully as she spoke and as she laid her hands on those who wished to come up and receive her blessing or special healing. She never actually touched any of the many hundreds who came up row after row; she simply held her hands a few inches from their foreheads and asked God to heal them. As she did, many of them collapsed for a few moments as if poleaxed. This included some nuns in full, traditional habit, and a number of robust men.

Since the healees left the stage by stairs beside where I was standing, I was able to ask some of them why they had gone up and why they had suddenly fallen to the floor. Several of them said they had no idea. They were accompanying friends or had come out of curiosity. They had had no intention of going up to the front until the invitation was made. As far as the matter of being "slain in the Spirit" was concerned (this is the term given by Pentecostals and others to the phenomenon of slumping, apparently stunned, under the "touch of power"), they were totally mystified. When I asked one particularly burly man why he had lain down on stage for all to see, he looked embarrassed and said he didn't know. "I suddenly just felt my knees buckle, and when I came to I was on the floor."

Obviously, one could speculate endlessly about the likelihood of mass hypnotism, mass hysteria, or whatever being at work in all of it. It's not impossible; but I detected no evidence. Since that time I have attended or watched many healing crusades with a lot more emotion and evident manipulation than occurred there. Anyone, for example, who has seen the ubiquitous Florida-based television healer Benny Hinn in action knows what I mean. In any case, when the first session was over and the second had not yet begun, there was an interval during which Kuhlman remained on the stage. Quite suddenly she turned around and walked over to me. She had been told I would be there from the *Star* and had given her approval earlier by phone. As she came towards me, she spoke my name and, holding out her hands, took both of mine. As she smiled up at me, she said, "Welcome," and kept her grip while we exchanged a few words.

I will never forget the experience. The nearest I can come to describing it is to say that it was like holding onto the terminals of a strong battery or being plugged into some other source of electrical current. There was an unmistakable – and, for me, quite unexpected – surge of an electric-like current into my hands and up my arms. At six feet four inches in height, I towered over this elderly, petite woman. Yet she seemed at the centre of a force or energy field that was palpably alive and much stronger than I was. It's the particular task of a journalist to write about events as objectively as possible. Whatever the explanation, the facts of that encounter are exactly as I have just described.

Sceptics would likely say that this and all similar experiences at the hands of healers – for example, the sensations often experienced and attested to by those prayed over and touched by Godfrey Mowatt or Oskar Estebany – are self-generated because of certain expectations or because of the effects of hypnotism. I used to have considerable sympathy with that point of view myself, *until it happened to me*. But, in light of the published results of scientific experiments, the old arguments about such experiences being "purely subjective" have to be abandoned anyhow. We have already seen how the experiments of Dr. Bernard Grad, Dolores Krieger, and those following their lead have removed any doubt that there is a "healer effect" that can be scientifically demonstrated. We come now to a slightly different approach that validates the same point in a singularly convincing fashion. I'm referring to ten years of solid research with over a dozen well-known healers carried out at the Menninger Clinic's Center for Applied Psychophysiology by Drs. Elmer Green, Robert Becker, and Steven L. Fahrion.

I'm going to focus on one healer, a remarkable man by the name of Mietek Wirkus, because I have had the pleasure of meeting him and observing him at work over a period of several days during a conference in London, England. Mietek Wirkus is in his late forties, slim, of medium height, with dark hair and a quiet, unassuming manner. Although he was born and spent most of his life in Poland, where he eventually became licensed as a bioenergy therapist, working co-operatively with doctors at a medical clinic, he and his wife, Margaret, now teach and practise healing in Bethesda, Maryland. Their non-profit centre is called the Wirkus Bioenergy Foundation.[4] He has been and continues to be the subject of a number of scientific studies both by researchers at the Menninger Clinic and elsewhere in the United States.

Wirkus's natural talents as a healer became evident before he was five years old, he told a large gathering of doctors, clergy, researchers, and healers at the London conference. Wirkus's older sister had begun to suffer from severe asthma attacks, but whenever Mietek attempted to soothe her with his hands, she would quite suddenly recover. His parents told their doctor about this, who one day witnessed it himself. The physician at once took a great interest in the child and eventually asked him to come to his surgery and assist him with certain patients. Wirkus says that when he was young he often used to feel a patient's illness as a pain or illness in his own body. But, as he grew older, he learned how to protect himself and to feel the disease only in the energy field of the other person.

Later, he was instructed in breathing techniques and meditation by a monk steeped in the Tibetan tradition of healing. According to Mietek – and all those who share a bioenergy approach to healing – there is, surrounding the physical body, an etheric body which is a kind of double of the physical body. It is an energy field, silverish in colour, that flows all around the physical body and is about three or four inches in depth – at approximately the limit of where you can detect the body's warmth. There is, as well, a third energy field or "body," which is called the astral or magnetic body. It can best be described as an aura-like, egg-shaped cocoon around each of us. This is something anyone can train himself to see, he explained, and appears as shimmering flashes of colour, usually within the range of blue.[5] Those familiar with Kirlian photography, of course, and subsequent refinements of the art, know that researchers have long ago demonstrated the reality of the human aura and the way it can be seen to change as the individual's mood or energy shifts. (The concept of a human aura itself goes back to earliest times, and may well account not just for the halos painted by early Christians around the heads of saints and other holy persons but also for the strange emanations drawn or painted around the forms of god-like figures in many pre-literate cultures.)

The "Kirlian effect," the reality of flares of "pulsating, multicoloured lights" surrounding the human body and ebbing and flowing according to the health and vital energy of the individual, gets its name from a brilliant electronics expert from Krasnodar in the south of Russia. Semyon Kirlian and his journalist wife, Valentina, after more than twenty years of painstaking research and refinement, from 1939 onwards, succeeded in perfecting an entirely new method of photography – it involved fourteen fresh patents – which made it possible to "see" not just the human aura but the auras of other living things; for example, that of a leaf.

At first, the photography could only reveal static images of the various energy fields. But soon the Kirlians added a new optical device that enabled them to watch this amazing phenomenon in action. In their book *Psychic Discoveries behind the Iron Curtain*, Sheila Ostrander and Lynn Schroeder describe what the Kirlians saw: "The hand itself looked like the Milky Way in a starry sky. Against a background of blue and gold, something was taking place in the hand that looked like a fireworks display. Multicoloured flares lit up, then sparks, twinkles, flashes."[6]

By 1949, the Kirlians' work had attracted wide attention and a steady stream of scientists began to show up at their small one-storey house in Krasnodar. Ostrander and Schroeder write that over the next thirteen years hundreds of scholars came – "biophysicists, doctors, biochemists, electronics experts, criminology specialists" – together with hordes of the idly curious.

The Kirlians discovered, as their technique became more sophisticated, that the high-frequency photography was actually capable of showing up disease in plants, animals, and humans. There were discernible differences in the force or energy fields according to the organism's health. More recently, researchers at UCLA's Health Sciences Department, working with Kirlian photography techniques, have photographed healers before and after their healings. "These showed that the aura or electric corona around the healer shrank after a laying-on of hands, while that of the healee expanded."[7]

While I watched Mietek Wirkus engaged in healing, I was struck forcibly by several things:

• I could detect absolutely no sign of his breathing from his chest or of facial movements, yet there was an extraordinary sound as he did the very shallow, high-energy breathing he has been taught to use both to enable him to project his own bioenergy to the healee and to replenish it without fatigue (when he worked in the Polish clinic, he gave therapy to from eight to one hundred patients a day).

• He never actually touches the healee. Instead, he "reads" or follows the outline, first of the etheric body and then of the astral or magnetic body. Since the latter reflects the emotions, according to the theory, and extends much farther than the etheric body, especially at the widest part of its egg-shaped form, Wirkus feels or senses it with his hands at a distance of from two to four feet from the healee.

• Once he detects where the energy concerned is out of balance, congested, static, or weak, he concentrates on that general area, but again without direct contact.

I could at this point list a series of medically attested healings that demonstrate Mietek Wirkus's results. For example, I have seen the evidence and witnessed the corroborating testimony of the parents of three very young children – one with cataracts which threatened blindness, one with chronic cardiac problems (four open-chest operations in the year between the ages of two-and-a-half and three-and-a-half), and one with uncontrollable epileptic seizures (more than a hundred a day) – where the healer's intervention made a dramatic difference. But, rather than go into further details of that kind, I will turn to what interests me most for our purposes about Wirkus, which is not so much his own theories or even the results of his healing, but rather the scientific findings and the views of the researchers who have made him the subject of their hi-tech scrutiny.

This man has spent more hours rigged up by wires to state-of-the-art machines than any other healer I know. The results have been quite mind-boggling. Isolated from all extraneous electrical and other influences in a laboratory room with copper walls, Wirkus was meticulously monitored as he carried out his healing on a series of healees. In addition to the kind of changes in the brain waves of both healer and healee found in the experiments of

Dolores Krieger, Dr. Elmer Green and Professor Fahrion of the Menninger Clinic recorded sudden electrical surges in Wirkus that on a number of occasions registered eighty volts or more. These surges were synchronous with times when the healer (who was not at all surprised by the findings), in his own words, "was just conscious of creating a charge and sending it." As Green says, creating an electrical force of that magnitude "isn't really possible. But it happens!" Green notes that in China and Japan the traditional healing wisdom says the bioenergy of a healer comes forth from the abdomen, while in India and Tibet it's believed to come from the "third eye" or the part of the forehead just above the eyes and centred on the nose, and says that the next step in his research will be to try to pinpoint the source of the electrical flow from Wirkus. It may well be, he thinks, that the ancient yogic belief that there are energy-field centres at the "third eye," the throat, the heart, abdomen, and so on – the *chakras* – will shortly be proven scientifically.

Green says the fact that voltage surges occur in proven healers will one day not seem so surprising: "After all, we are electrical beings or entities. There's not a single atom, molecule, or cell where there isn't an electric charge. Indeed, if you want to think of it that way, we're really an electro-magnetic cloud. All of nature is electro-magnetic and electricity in motion." What particularly impresses Green about non-medical healing is that it works so well with babies and young children. "Doctors often see the results of healers and are impressed, but they go on to attribute them to the placebo effect. Well, if you can affect the body of a horse, a dog, or a baby and bring about physiological changes – as many of these healers can – that's certainly not just a placebo!"

Dr. Robert Becker, author of *The Body Electric* and professor of orthopedics at the State University of New York, has spent the last thirty years researching how the body heals itself. He believes that studying such healers as Mietek Wirkus can open a whole new path and paradigm for medicine. He's convinced that what the physician of today is trying to do with drugs and surgery is what the traditional shaman or healer has done without either throughout history. He says categorically that if the healer phenomenon is real, and his research has convinced him that it is, then there is a mechanism in the human organism that permits things to happen "that we cannot do with surgery or drugs." If this information can be made more widely available to medicine "it would markedly change the scope and efficiency of the medical care process." Not to mention the cost!

Becker says that because of the kind of experiments done at the Menninger Clinic and elsewhere, many scientists are now ready to concede that there are biological effects from electro-magnetic energies. They know something real happens in healing, because they have now seen not just the results but the electrical side-effects. But how it works is as yet unclear. Becker, Green, and those who share their views believe that the search for the mechanism behind this, if successful, will revolutionize medical understanding and practice. According to Becker, "Later in history, this will be judged to have been the primary discovery of the twentieth century, I believe; that is, that the human organism is sensitive to electro-magnetic fields, that it produces its own magnetic fields, that electrical currents flow through the organism, and that in all of this we are part of the living process of the entire cosmos."

Becker stresses his conviction that there is much more to the human brain "than the way a computer works," and there is much more to the human body "than you'd assume to have occurred as a result of a chance aggregation of molecules." To those who respond that at this point he's beginning to sound quasi-religious, he replies: "I can't help it. I'm sorry but I have to view it that way. I think medicine should realize that we know next to nothing at present about how living things really work." (We don't even understand yet how to cure the common cold!) He is certain, as a result of his research, that there is some kind of information transfer between a healee and a traditional healer like Wirkus. The healer's awareness of what is going on in the other person's energy fields shows that "information has been moved, and that can only happen when you have a reality, a signal of some kind. My bet is that it is carried by electro-magnetic energy." We are more than a "cellophane bag filled with a mild salt solution," Becker declares. We're not just a biochemical entity. "There is something else!"

Dr. Green agrees with this, and believes that in the transfer of information of which Becker speaks, "consciousness is somehow involved." He admits to not knowing precisely how all of this works yet – "obviously if information is transmitted through some kind of energy it is different from the energy, say, of a light bulb which grows weaker as it extends further away. . . . It's a little more like a letter which arrives just as it was sent. How else can one explain healing at a distance?" Becker's comment on this is to say that if you suppose the existence of a kind of "sixth sense" and say that living organisms are sensitive to magnetic fields and capable of receiving information through them, then you have the beginnings of a theory that could explain not just spiritual healing but also such paranormal phenomena as extra-sensory perception and telepathy.

Significantly, shortly after I first wrote this paragraph, a Cornell University psychologist, Daryl Bem, told the 1993 annual meeting of the American Association for the Advancement of Science that he now has evidence that extra-sensory perception actually exists. He reported that a statistical review of nearly forty studies had provided him with convincing and repeatable results. Bem said his work, done with his late colleague, Charles Honorton of the University of Edinburgh, avoided the flaws of earlier studies. He is certain "we're seeing a genuine scientific anomaly here."[8]

Becker has issued a radical call to the scientific community to expand and deepen its analysis of what is going on in the healer phenomenon, because "the next step, not just in medicine but in understanding all living things and knowing who and what we are in relation to the universe, depends upon it." But what do medical doctors make of the bioenergy approach of such healers as Mietek Wirkus and the views of such scientists as Green and Becker?

I met Dr. Ursula Thunberg, a child psychiatrist with the Jewish Board of Family and Children Services in New York, while I attended a day-long workshop featuring Mietek and Margaret

Wirkus in London. Thunberg has been trained in bioenergy healing at the Wirkus Bioenergy Foundation in Bethesda. She says she found the studies as technical and systematic as anything she faced at medical school. She is convinced that healers are "aware of an aspect of life that's very natural and that follows specific laws." It must follow natural laws, she argues, even though we don't know exactly what they are yet, because "you do it and you get results." Thunberg says that because bioenergy lies outside most people's normal sensory and visual range, little has been said about it until now by doctors and scientists. But, with the new research, its existence is not in doubt, she says. "We are only lacking a new paradigm at this point to organize the data into a frame of reference that is intellectually or scientifically acceptable to us." In her view, recognition by conventional medicine that the bioenergy dimension exists and is part of the healing process is "just around the corner."

Another medical doctor who endorses this approach is Irene Seeland. Dr. Seeland notes that self-healing is a natural part of life and that bioenergy "strengthens and enhances the body's ability to attain wholeness." She deplores those who try to put down and disparage mainstream modern medicine because she knows it can accomplish many good and important things. But, she adds, "Unfortunately, we can't screen out all the side effects [for example, of chemotherapy, radiation, or certain powerful drugs] and the poor body is often devastated by these, with the result that natural healing is hindered. That doesn't happen with bioenergy because it's natural and authentic."[9]

Margaret Wirkus, who has a better command of English than her husband and often acts as his interpreter when being interviewed by the media or medical researchers, says modern medicine too often forgets that healing is ultimately an art and not merely a matter of technology. She cites the maxim of Chinese healing that the human organism is not a "dead body" but a complex vortex of living energy that exists on many levels – some of which we can't see. "The more narrow our focus is, and the more purely technical it is, the less humanistic it becomes," she says. That, precisely, is the problem faced by hi-tech medical care today. The bioenergy proponents believe they have discovered a way to challenge and overcome this defect. As Dr. Becker puts it, "We need to move medicine away from the idea of 'you come to me and I'll heal you' to what it should be; i.e., 'you come to me and I will help you heal yourself.'"

The most carefully documented results of bioenergy healing that I have seen personally were presented at the Doctor-Healer Conference in London in 1992 by a former colleague of Wirkus from Warsaw, Poland. Stefania Szantyr-Powolny, M.D., who, in addition to being a doctor has been practising bioenergy healing for twelve years, said that bioenergy therapy began to be accepted in Poland around 1978 and was given official approval as a supplement to conventional medicine in 1982. Since then she has been dividing her time between the Medical Scientific Institute in Warsaw and the bioenergy section of a Polish institute known as the Psychotronic Society, which was formed in the early 1980s to organize training and examine the abilities of bioenergy healers.

Part of Dr. Szantyr-Powolny's practice has included the clinic of the Society for Deaf Children in Warsaw, a clinic in which Mietek Wirkus also spent much of his time before emigrating to the United States. Describing the team approach used at the clinic, she said that it was the best example of co-operation between medical staff and healers she has ever encountered. Specialists examined and treated the children, using all the latest technology, and then referred them for bioenergy treatment. After several sessions of therapy, the children were tested with audiometers and other relevant devices. In this way, the specialists were able to make objective assessments of the results.

The doctor then described the case histories of children of various ages and with a wide range of diagnoses. The slides and audiograms of their before and after tests revealed some major, well-nigh miraculous improvements. There was the case of a six-year-old girl who was born deaf. Five months after the doctor began her bioenergy treatments, the child had gained near-normal levels of hearing. Another case involved a young man whose hearing had been almost totally destroyed by excessive amounts of streptomycin administered when he was only two years old. She said, "On his fourth visit for bioenergy therapy I was truly moved when he came in and told me, 'Doctor, I can hear again! I can hear water running in the bathroom; I can hear my mother making dinner; I can hear dogs barking.' Could anything be more satisfying and rewarding?"

The most striking thing in many of these cases is that "the improvement of the hearing is connected with the perception of the high tones," she commented. "This means that we are improving the inner ear. Conventional medicine was completely helpless in such cases." She added that with the specialists she had come to the tentative conclusion that part of the answer to what was happening might lie in the possibility that the biotherapy was prompting the development of the central nervous system. But exact explanations remain elusive still.

The final word must go to Mietek and Margaret Wirkus. They know from long experience that people have been and are being healed through Mietek's and other healers' bioenergy therapy. They explain, "What is of greatest importance is the healee's will to live. The bioenergy then supplies renewed energy for the body to heal itself. It's not a case of this type of healing helping some problems and not being appropriate for others. It stimulates the body's own mechanisms for healing itself – the immune system and other systems – and so it is a help in all fields and at all levels of the organism – mental, emotional, and physical. Once people get even one treatment, they say it's as if the clouds have moved away and their life feels as though it is taking on colour again."

I had just completed this chapter in its final form when I obtained a copy of Bill Moyers' book *Healing and the Mind*, the companion to the five-part PBS television series of the same name.[10] For me, the most exciting chapter was the lengthy interview with one of the world's leading authorities on brain biochemistry, Dr. Candace Pert, visiting professor at the Center for Molecular and Behavioral Neuroscience at Rutgers University. (Pert discovered the opiate receptor and other peptide receptors in the brain and in the body, thus explaining the way chemicals travel between mind and body.)

In the chapter "The Chemical Communications," Pert talks about the human organism as a mind-spirit-body unity and about how "information is flowing" among these aspects continually.[11] The messenger molecules are called neuropeptides. The mind, she points out, is not just located above the neck but exists in every living cell because of these messengers. She then goes on to discuss with Moyers the conviction she and other neuroscientists have that the ultimate mystery here, how the various parts of our body "spontaneously" receive and transmit messages of all kinds, will only be solved in terms of "a form of energy" of some type as yet not fully known: "Clearly there's another form of energy that we have not yet understood. For example, there's a form of energy that appears to leave the body when the body dies." Pert goes on to say she would call this energy "spirit" except that scientists ever since Descartes have felt they have to avoid such a term. But, she admits, the traditional habit of thinking of the organism as just a machine (reductionism) leaves too many phenomena unexplained. She makes it absolutely clear that the idea that the healing process can be explained in terms of chemical and electrical processes without "invoking some other energy" no longer makes any sense to her. In her view, the only way forward will involve "a realm we don't understand at all yet"; an external energy belonging to the "realm of spirit and soul." That's precisely what this chapter has been all about.

11

The London Conference on Healing and Energy Medicine, 1992

"Medicine, 300 years ago, made a decision to go with a chemical-mechanical view of the body. The biochemical model is correct but incomplete. Now that we can measure subtle, electro-magnetic fields, the model or paradigm must change. I believe energy-field medicine is the wave of the future . . . and it was the laying-on of hands that brought us here."

– Valerie Hunt, Ed.D., neurophysiologist and researcher in Energy Medicine, Professor Emeritus, UCLA

∼ Doctor-Healer Teams in Britain

During my four years in Britain as a student and on my frequent visits since as a journalist, I have had the great privilege of observing most aspects of healing practised there. This experience has been an enormous help in trying to assess the validity of spiritual healing today. One of the chief reasons for this is that in Britain both the medical profession and the various healing organizations, including the Christian Church, have always been more flexible and more willing to experiment than their counterparts in North America. They are far ahead of us as a result.

When I learned that in the fall of 1992 there was to be an unprecedented international gathering in London of doctors, other health-care professionals who were either healers themselves or working with healers, and clergy, non-medical healers, researchers, and other interested scientists, I decided to attend. The conference, from October 2 to 4, was held at a private American institution, Regent's College, in central London. The famous Regent's Park rose garden, with its manicured shrubbery, its magnificent walks, waterfall, and lush, panoramic display of roses of every colour and variety, lay just across the street from the college's doors. Approximately two hundred delegates attended, coming from Britain, the United States, Canada, and more than a dozen other countries, including Bulgaria, Poland, and Russia. The hosting body was Britain's Doctor-Healer Network. (Incidentally, I learned at the conference that there has been a doctor-healer network in Bulgaria and in one or two other former eastern-bloc countries for many decades. In Bulgaria, it was an underground, clandestine organization until the liberation from Communist rule in 1989.)

The chief organizers of the complex, tightly-scheduled conference were Dr. Dan Benor, whom I had first met in London a year previously, and his wife, Rita, who is a registered nurse and a healer. I want to share some of my impressions from this gathering because, in the first place, there was scant media coverage of the affair – those responsible for the conference unfortunately knew almost as little about how the media work as many of the religious groups I have encountered over the years – and second, because the conference gave me an opportunity to take a closer look at how some of the insights into healing already reported here are actually being applied by working physicians in their own practices or, as they put it in Britain, their surgeries.

As already briefly described, the Doctor-Healer Network, with its five regional groups in southern England, is made up of general physicians who, most often, practise conventional medicine but have one or more healers working in partnership with them. However, a few doctors had discovered their own healing abilities and so shared in the laying-on of hands or other energy-medicine activities. The conference gave me the opportunity to hear first-hand accounts from both sides of how this remarkable partnership works in day-to-day clinical practice.

Before introducing you to a few of the doctors and their healer colleagues, I should make a couple of general observations. All of the doctors, without exception, said they believed that "something objective happens" when healers are practising their skills. Most of them agreed that some kind of energy interaction takes place (some explained it as an "information exchange"); a few remained undecided about the nature of the actual healing process in that they had no theory. However, what they all said was that more people were getting well and more people were staying well since the healers had joined their staff or their surgeries.

Dr. Rindert van Z. Bakker, who was born in Holland, raised in South Africa, and has been a doctor in Sevenoaks, England, since 1975, says he first became interested in complementary forms of medicine some eight or nine years ago. He works in a modern, highly organized surgery, together with three other doctors, two healers, a nurse, and an administrator, and offers a range of services to his patients – from acupuncture, homeopathy, massage, hypnotherapy, and spiritual healing to conventional medicine – and all of it paid for by Britain's National Health Service. (In other words, the non-medical healing is also funded by the public health insurance scheme.) In addition to the services cited above, the Sevenoaks surgery runs sixteen health-promotion clinics in the surrounding villages and hamlets.

Bakker first became interested in spiritual healing in 1990 when a long-term cancer patient, whose treatment he had been supervising, unexpectedly began to recover. He discovered the woman had been treated several times by a healer in Bristol. He made arrangements to meet the healer, Hilary Morgan, and was so impressed by her work he asked her to join the Sevenoaks health team. There, he was so taken with her skills that the surgery hired another healer to work with one of the other doctors a short time afterwards.

Bakker, a tallish man in his early fifties, who now gives courses on the use of healers in general practice to other doctors in Britain, believes complementary therapies should be available to any patient who requires them. It's not that he has in any way abandoned conventional medicine; but that he has not always found it appropriate or adequate in treating the vast sweep of human ailments his patients bring him. Once a week he meets for part of the afternoon with Hilary Morgan to go over reports on the various patients she is seeing, to consult with her about which new patients she feels healing could benefit most, and in general to supervise her work. He told the conference that because the healer can spend much more time with patients than he can, he often learns a great deal more about their conditions from her than from his own interviews. Bakker says, "The results she obtains are occasionally dramatic and, interestingly, the problems she ends up dealing with are not necessarily those the patient came to see the doctor about originally at all."

Morgan, who saw about five hundred patients at the Sevenoaks surgery last year, has access to a patient's file or "notes" provided she has the person's permission and that she signs the file to indicate that she has seen it. She told the conference that all patients seen by her at the Sevenoaks surgery are "doctor-generated"; that is, they have been referred to her by a doctor, and have not walked in off the street. Sometimes she does emergency healing, where some trauma or injury can be soothed by the laying-on of hands; she treats a number of cancer patients, some of them for chronic pain; and she works extensively with pregnant women, particularly those experiencing a lot of nausea. In her first few months at Sevenoaks, she says, she met with "a certain resistance" from one or two of the other health professionals at the clinic who were not as open-minded as Bakker. Today, however, she has the kind of working relationship with everyone there that was an "impossible dream" when she first discovered her "calling" to be a healer in the late 1970s.

Dr. Craig Brown is a general practitioner with a busy practice in a town called Rustington, on the south coast of England. Now in his early forties, Brown has been researching spiritual healing for more than seven years, and he has been seeing patients in his surgery in partnership with a healer, Del Ralph, for five years. In all, there are twelve thousand patients in his care. Brown told the conference that his experience in working with healers and in researching the spiritual dimension of his patients' lives have convinced him that the future of medicine lies in a greater appreciation of the spiritual forces at work in and around us all. "We can bring about a transformative change by looking at the spiritual level of people's lives," he declared.

Brown said he usually spends about ten minutes with each patient – the national average in Britain is reported to be seven minutes – and that he uses the classical medical approach. However, in addition, for several years he has silently made "a spiritual diagnosis" of each patient, which he records in a diary. In each case he asks himself, What, in briefest form, is the spiritual problem this person faces right now? The second question – for himself – was, Can these problems be classified? He then draws up a simple list of three main types of inner difficulty faced: negative emotions, for example, of guilt, worry, rage, and depression; major challenges such as accidents, illness, bereavement, old age, and death; life changes such as, puberty, marriage, vicissitudes to do with employment, menopause.

In addition to treating any obvious physical symptoms or

diseases in the conventional manner, he endeavours not just to identify the patient's main spiritual problem but then to bring to bear the opposite qualities – for example, hope instead of despair, confidence instead of anxiety – through his own advice and through the counselling and laying-on of hands by the healer. Brown asks all his patients to assess their quality of life through the use of a detailed questionnaire he has designed for the purpose, both at the outset of their treatment and also when they decide they have been restored to health. The contrast between the two, he says, is the ultimate test of whether significant healing has taken place.

Brown impressed me as being a dedicated, down-to-earth physician who knows the truth of his convictions from having tried them out. He is clearly a man who is convinced of the power of non-medical techniques to heal, but as a scientist he makes every possible effort to systematize and objectify the process. He makes no particular profession of religious faith, but he says he believes there is a "light" or energy within each person that has its source in "God or the cosmos." He adds, "So, I look for that light in every patient I see in my surgery. At the end of the day, together with my staff, I have a brief meditation where I try to send that light out to all the patients we have treated that day." Some critics might be tempted to dismiss this kind of approach as New Age quackery, but, as he described it, it really is an act of prayer. There are thousands of people in North America, if not millions, who would give a lot for a physician who cared that personally and that much.

Lorraine Ham, for ten years a member of Britain's National Federation of Spiritual Healers, integrates relaxation, breathing techniques, creative visualization, meditation, and positive thinking with the laying-on of hands in a holistic approach. She works as a healer at a clinic in Ottley, Yorkshire, with eight doctors and four nurses. In addition, she and another woman healer visit regularly in local hospitals. Ham says that when she was first hired by the team of physicians at Ottley they only sent her the most difficult cases – "their failures" – a lot of whom were taking several long-term medications and suffering from multiple psychological problems. All eight doctors still refer this type of patient to her, but now they also send her the less seriously ill. For example, before prescribing tranquilizers to patients, the doctors first send them to her for a course of hypnosis and spiritual healing. She works to change a patient's thinking patterns and usually makes suggestions about improving lifestyle, the environment of the person's life, and the overall direction he or she is taking.

In the case of those who are terminally ill, Ham says it is important to make a distinction between a cure and healing. Healing in this sense is deeper and has to do with the whole person, especially their inner selves. She offers the dying a "healing into death," which helps the patient let go of fears and heals their spirit. "It helps the family and friends as well; often they find healing of spirit from this process as they see the change in their loved one."

The biggest change brought about by the use of spiritual healing, according to Ham, is often in the realm of the patient's emotions and in his or her level of self-understanding. "It's complementary to what the doctors do, not an alternative," she stresses. "It gives the patient an option. It gives the doctor an option as well." She points out that if she had a diseased appendix she would want a competent doctor to take it out. At the same time, at the cancer clinic which Ham visits regularly, there are many patients with conditions for which conventional medicine, she says, has little to offer. Since she views disease basically as "stuck energy," she uses every technique from the laying-on of hands to visualization, yoga, breathing, laughter, dance – anything to get the body and soul moving – "in order to change the energies."

At times, she says, you can literally smell the fear and feel the panic in certain hospital wards she visits. "In Britain anyway, we're taught to have a stiff upper lip and to suppress our emotions to the point where many patients facing painful therapies or terminal prognoses are lying there paralysed by terror and unable to get release. The nurses often worry about these folk. They want to help but they can't reach them. Often, in those cases, a healer can help unblock all this emotional energy and ease the pain."

Ham went on to tell a touching story of a very small, very elderly Polish man in the cancer ward who wasn't responding to any attempt to break through his wall of sadness, denial, and isolation. She pulled a chair up beside his bed, asked if she could hold his hand, and then just sat with him as she willed energy to flow into his frail body. In a while, she noticed tears glistening in his eyes and she asked him gently what he was thinking about. He told her he was thinking of his grandmother who had been such a special person in his life as a boy growing up in Poland. Shyly, he whispered, "Can I tell you why I'm crying? I've had this strange awareness that my grandmother has been here in the hospital room with me these past few days, and now I've just been told I'm being sent to a hospice. I'm afraid she won't go with me when I leave here and I'll be all alone, waiting to die." The healer quietly assured him his grandmother would go with him, travelling in the ambulance, and that he could rest in the confidence that she'd never let him die alone. The man's face was suddenly illumined as though from some inner light. He smiled for the first time in weeks as he said, "Now I'm ready for anything. You know, I never told you or anyone else here before but my grandmother was a healer, too."

Spiritual healing can be preventative, the Yorkshire healer believes. She has found it of enormous benefit to people about to face any trauma, from medical examinations and serious tests to surgery. When spiritual healing has taken place before surgery, there is less trauma and less pain after the operation. Listening to her and talking with her later, I was once again impressed by the high calibre of people who are healers in Britain. I was struck by her humility, her sanity and reasonableness, and her quiet confidence that this was an art and a skill every bit as valid as a doctor's or other health-care professional's. She made no extravagant claims and gave no hint of possessing some kind of mystical powers that set her apart from the rest of us. In fact, she made a point of describing how doctors and nurses unwittingly do a great deal of non-medical healing through their general manner and approach to patients: "A lot of what healers do is done by any good nurse or good doctor without putting a name to it. Spiritual healers, I believe, make this unseen healing visible and, often, possible on an even deeper scale."

The final word on Lorraine Ham, however, must go to the chief doctor at the Ottley clinic. In assessing her work after her first year as part of the team, he told her, "My problem is that you're not quantifiable. But the bottom line is that the overall results are better than before you came. More people are getting well and they're doing it faster!"

These people are only a few out of a diverse cast of doctors and healers who at one point or another shared their experiences and approaches at the London conference. Also at the conference was a neuropsychiatrist, Dr. Leonhard Hochenegg, from Hall, in Tirol, Austria, who now works primarily as a healer and who has written several books on his holistic theories. There was an American clinical psychologist, Sharon Wendt, Ph.D., who is the founder of the holistic Wellness Center in Indiana. Dr. Wendt specializes in psychoneuroimmunology, subtle energies, and healing. Most of her present work is with cancer patients. She calls her approach "Radiant Heart Therapy." It involves healing the heart chakra through subtle energy and visualization. Wendt is currently writing a book, *The Joy of Healing*, about her experiences in working with those who have cancer. And there was a consulting psychiatrist, Dr. Brenda Davies, from a private practice in Harrow, Middlesex, who has been aware she was a healer since she was young girl. All in all, the conference was a remarkable experience for anyone interested in knowing what some doctors think about spiritual healing. I met more than a dozen who practise it themselves and many more who are now working alongside healers and who wonder aloud why they didn't begin to do so a lot sooner.

~ The Researchers

The work of some of the key people who attended the conference to share their research, most notably Dr. Bernard Grad and Dr. Daniel Benor, has already been described in considerable detail.

Here, I will talk about just one researcher who stood out from the rest. Undoubtedly the most colourful and most dynamic speaker of the entire event was the professor emeritus from UCLA with whose quote I began this chapter, Dr. Valerie Hunt. With vigour and enthusiasm far greater than one might expect from someone of her age (she is over seventy), Hunt reported first on her own remarkable experiences as a healer and then spent three lectures outlining her own research and that of others at the Noetic Science Institute in San Francisco. She says the latest studies lead her to believe that the kind of intuitive or instinctual knowledge healers have of what is wrong with a person and how to go about the healing process will one day be a "standard form of getting and sending information." She told the conference that she agrees with Dr. Robert Becker when he says that energy-field communication – the ability to "read" the fields around another's body – is a primary form of informational transaction. "The mind is the most complex information-decoder in the world, and a healer, by using different kinds of levels of awareness, can directly interpret what is going on in the body of the healee," Hunt says. I have not seen her published results, but she claims to have been able to measure the vibrational levels of the fields both of healers and of healees with instruments capable of detecting 200,000 cycles per second. By this method, she has been able to prove that "when the vibrations of one's energy field are low there is always disease."

Dr. Hunt holds that official acceptance of subtle energies and Energy Medicine is just around the corner for Western medical science and says it will follow the inevitable three-step pattern of all great innovative ideas. First, it will be ridiculed, then it will be tolerated, and finally it will be held as self-evident truth by everybody.

More striking than anything she said, however, were videos she showed us that illustrated the auras or energy fields around humans, animals, and supposedly inanimate objects – a running stream, waves on the shore, trees, and finally the food we eat. Using a technique that she called "computer-enhanced" photography, her lab had filmed a woman sitting alone and then interacting with a child of four or five. You could clearly see the energy radiating from each of them, particularly from their heads. The way the flow increased markedly once the adult and child began to relate to each other was most striking. Similarly, in a video of a man walking with a dog by the seashore, when the dog came close, wagging his tail and looking for the stick to be thrown, the auras of both the man and the dog flared out with increased intensity. What's more, you could see an interchange of energy taking place as the predominant colours in the aura of each began to show up in the auras of the other. The Kirlians had adumbrated this by photographing energy exchanges between people and plants.[1] I had no way at that point of validating Hunt's technology or treatment of the video. But, accepting it at face value, the video was an amazing illustration of the actual play of energies about the human body and the whole of nature. Like the results of Kirlian photography, it was visual evidence that subtle energies are real and not just a figment of imagination.

I2

Prayer

"More things are wrought by prayer than this world dreams of."
  – Alfred, Lord Tennyson, "The Passing of Arthur," *Idylls of the King*

                              "You are here to kneel
Where prayer has been valid. And prayer is more
Than an order of words, the conscious occupation
Of the praying mind, or the sound of the voice praying."
  – T. S. Eliot, "Little Gidding," *Four Quartets*

W hen we become sick – particularly if the disease is life-threatening – or when someone very close to us falls seriously ill in body, mind, or spirit, most of us find ourselves praying almost by instinct. We may be virtually inarticulate in this, we may even be unaware that we are praying, but we resort to prayer nonetheless. As Paul put it on one occasion, we often don't know what or how to pray, but prayer goes on within us all the same "with inexpressible cries." Prayers for the sick have been a part of religious rites and ceremonies from the dawn of time. Many centuries before the birth of Christ, the ancient Greeks, as well as the Egyptians, slept and prayed in temples dedicated to healing. Socrates, just before his death, remembered he owed a cockerel to Asklepios, the god of healing, because of his gratitude for health restored. The Bible and the sacred literature of most of the major religions of the world are filled with admonitions to pray and with actual prayers for those who are ill. Most of the Christian denominations – notably the Anglican, Roman Catholic, Eastern Orthodox, and Pentecostal churches – have special services or prayers for the sick. So do aboriginal peoples everywhere.

Few aspects of religion are more practised (and talked about in religious circles) and yet less understood than prayer. Sceptics, agnostics, and atheists tend to view all praying as a waste of time, a form of talking to oneself. In their opinion, to indulge in prayer is to resort to magic or a kind of infantile dependency on a heavenly parent-substitute. Any benefit derived therefrom, they argue, is the kind which comes with any positive form of auto-suggestion. These arguments are set forth completely without any evidence or further elaboration. The folly of praying is held to be self-evident.

To be wholly fair, given the way prayer is depicted and abused – athletes who use prayer as part of their win-at-any-cost ethos, airplane crash survivors who claim their emergence intact while others perished is evidence of "answered prayers," or lottery winners who say they prayed for their number to come up – one can't really blame those who remain cynical. But just that something is abused or distorted beyond recognition is not a valid reason to question its authenticity. The fact that no word in the English language is more perverted or exploited than the word "love" is no proof, logical or other, that the reality signified by love does not exist.

A more serious problem has to be faced, though, when it comes to praying for the sick. You can believe, as I do, that prayer is a conversation with God, or, as I prefer to put it, a tuning into or turning of one's inner eye towards the very Source and Ground of all Being. You can even accept part of the non-believer's argument that prayer is of help mainly to oneself – not that it's merely auto-suggestion, but that since God doesn't need our prayers, they may be chiefly for our own good. Being spiritual beings, we *need* to pour out our deepest longings, hopes, and fears in the presence of the ultimate reality we know as God. Similarly, those who feel moved to worship God are not, presumably, doing this because God needs it (as if any god worthy of the name would be obsessed with the need to be adored) but because human beings profoundly need to direct and tune all their other loyalties, plans, priorities and purposes in and before God.

The problem arises when you or a loved one are seriously ill and you begin to pray: O God, please make me (him, her, or them) well again, according to your will. The tone, not to mention the feeling behind it, suggests we first have to get God's attention, as it were, and then begin badgering and cajoling Him to intervene in a special way on our behalf. Prayer thus becomes a form of special pleading, a pious attempt to twist the arm of the Ultimate Power. There is an assumption here that God plays favourites, that those who know the right prayers or who manage the correct amount of fervour or faith will succeed where the great masses who are sick around the globe, including millions of innocent babies and children, lack this special kind of health-care insurance and so are on their own.

But, in the context of all that we have been looking at, a rather different, much more sensible approach begins to open up. Suppose for a moment that there are natural laws governing the way prayer works, that it behaves in exactly the way other energies and forces in the cosmos do; that is, according to the laws of its own nature and the nature of those aspects of reality it affects most directly. We know that there are wavelengths of both sight and sound that are far too short and that vibrate at too high an intensity for us to see or hear. The light of an x-ray machine or an infrared beam are more, not less, powerful because of their short wavelength. The sounds and images of radio and television fill the air all around us and their effects are pervasive and potent beyond description. Yet, they flow by us invisibly, inaudibly, and by a process very few of us comprehend.

Suppose there is energy released by the act of praying and that this energy is akin to other unseen or unheard energies. We have already seen that the kind of subtle energy kindled or directed by a healer's mind, through his hands or sometimes at a distance, does have verifiable, biophysical effects. It seems to me not impossible nor even improbable that a similar mechanism is involved in praying. By the act of visualizing the sick person becoming whole in body and soul, by the act of linking them with God through prayer, we may well be directing a flow of high-intensity healing energy towards the person who is ill or injured. This flow, in turn, has the capacity to boost or kick-start the person's innate capacity for self-healing.

Since, for a believer – of whatever stripe – all of life comes ultimately from God, such a view of prayer in no way minimizes its spirituality or its links with final transcendence. The whole of nature, as contemporary thinkers such as ecological philosopher Fr. Thomas Berry have forcefully reminded us, is deeply spiritual, is a revelation of the divine. The fact that it operates according to immutable laws in no way diminishes that truth. Thus, if one of two people with similar diseases requested prayer, as well as praying for him- or herself, while the other would have none of this, it would not be a case of asking God to play favourites. If one patient refuses all drugs while another benefits from whatever the doctors prescribe, nobody would dream of calling it favouritism if the first did poorly while the second recovered quickly. The use of antibiotics since we have discovered how they can kill bacteria is not favouritism. The same is true of nutritional advances. In the same way, availing oneself of prayer energy while getting the best in medical care is really a matter of bringing to bear all available resources, seen and unseen.

Not nearly enough research into the energy of prayer has been done, but in case anyone feels that in discussing prayer I have abandoned objectivity in favour of subjective theologizing, it's important to point out that an increasing number of scientists have begun to devise and carry out specific experiments in this field. In one of the most rigidly controlled studies ever done on the effects of prayer, cardiologist Dr. Randolph Byrd, formerly a professor at the University of California, has demonstrated that prayer "works" and can indeed play a powerful role in healing. Using double-blind controls and a group of 393 coronary care patients at San Francisco General Hospital, Byrd randomly divided them into two groups. One group (192 patients) was prayed for by home prayer-groups and the other (201 patients) was not. In all other ways, they were all treated in the normal manner by the hospital staff. Dr. Larry Dossey in his book *Recovering the Soul: A Scientific and Spiritual Search* stresses the rigid criteria Byrd employed, describing his methods as "the most rigid that can be used in clinical studies in medicine, meaning that it was a randomized, prospective, double-blind experiment in which neither the patients, nurses, nor doctors knew which group the patients were in."[1]

Byrd recruited both Roman Catholic and Protestant groups from across the United States to pray for the members of the first group. They were given the patients' names with a little information about their condition and were asked to pray for them daily – with no instructions on how to carry this out. "Each person prayed for many different patients," Byrd explains. "It meant that each person in the experiment had between five and seven people praying for him or her."

The results of this ten-month study were quite remarkable. The prayed-for patients differed from the others in several striking ways: they were five times less likely than the control group to need antibiotics (three compared with sixteen); they were three times less likely to develop pulmonary edema, a condition where the lungs fill with fluid as the heart fails to pump strongly enough (six compared with eighteen); none of them needed endotracheal intubation (an artificial airway inserted into the throat and attached to a mechanical ventilator), while twelve in the control group had to have ventilatory support; and fewer patients in the prayed-for group died during the study, although the divergence here was not statistically significant.

Dr. Dossey comments, and I agree, "If the technique studied [prayer] had been a new drug or a surgical procedure . . . it would almost certainly have been heralded as some kind of 'breakthrough.'" He goes on to say that even hard-boiled sceptics have been impressed by Byrd's findings. He cites one doctor, William Nolan, who has written a book "debunking faith healing," who admits Byrd's study sounds very persuasive. Nolan has commented wryly, "Maybe we doctors should be writing on our order sheets, 'Pray three times a day.' If it works, it works."

Dossey believes that this and other similar studies suggest there is something about the activity of the mind that allows it to intervene in the course of distant events. In Byrd's study, the distance of the people praying varied considerably but seemed in no way to influence the results. This would seem to suggest that if there is a subtle energy involved in prayer it is quite different from understood energetic forces, which grow predictably and inexorably weaker as they travel from the source.[2]

When it comes to understanding the precise nature of these subtle energies, a great deal of mystery still remains. But that alone should not daunt us unduly. Modern medicine, when its expositors are completely candid, is beset by vast mysteries. With every advance comes an awareness of how little of biophysics has been explored. When it comes to how much modern medicine actually knows (as a journalist friend of mine is sometimes wont to say), "There's less there than meets the eye."

Byrd's study is by no means unique. I have come across several earlier research projects concerning prayer, offering firm evidence of objective effects. And the latest project deserves a brief description here. The author of the study – an as yet unpublished doctoral thesis – is Dr. Seán Ó'Laoire, a Roman Catholic priest who has a parish in San Francisco. The research project, "An Experimental Study of the Effects of Intercessory Prayer-at-a-distance on Self-esteem, Anxiety and Depression," was undertaken at the Institute of Transpersonal Psychology, Palo Alto, California.[3]

This was a controlled, randomized, double-blind study, using the very latest in approved, objective testing for mood, self-esteem, anxiety, depression, and other indicators of psychological health. Ó'Laoire used 496 adult volunteers; of these, 90 volunteered to be the "agents" or the ones who would do the praying, and the "subjects" were divided – without being told who was who – into a control group of 147 and a group of 259 who would be prayed for. (They were told that if the experiment showed objective results obtained by prayer, then those not prayed for, the control group, would be prayed for subsequently.)

The agents were given photos and the names of their subjects, and they agreed to pray for them for fifteen minutes daily for a period of twelve weeks. They also agreed to keep a "prayer diary," detailing the record of their prayer activity. All 496 participants were given five objective, standard psychological tests before the twelve-week period began, and five when the experiment was over. These included the Coopersmith Self-Esteem Inventory and the Beck Depression Inventory. The final results demonstrated "significant improvement" in the subjects in all the categories tested: the amount of self-esteem, the levels of both state and trait anxiety, the amount of depression, and the extent of mood disorders in general. Subjective testing showed there was improvement, as well, in how the subjects felt about their relationships, creative expression, spirituality, and general physical, emotional, and intellectual well-being.

There was, of course, much more to the study than I can possibly go into here, but one other phenomenon deserves mention.

Although the ninety people who offered to be the agents, or the ones who prayed for the rest, offered themselves randomly, they proved to be different in some respects from those who opted to be prayed for. They were more likely to believe in the power of prayer, and were more likely to be church-goers. They also had higher self-esteem, fewer mood disturbances, and lower levels of anxiety and depression than the subjects and controls. Ó'Laoire comments, "For whatever reasons, the agents looked much more like self-actualized people than the subjects." Also interesting is the fact that the agents also showed improvement during the twelve-week experiment – indeed, their improvement was more pronounced. "Over the course of the study the agents' self-perception of improvement in spiritual health, relationships and creative expression was significantly better than that of the subjects," Ó'Laoire writes.

It is appropriate here to mention briefly the topic of meditation. In my experience, the majority of people in the West are put off by the entire concept. Perhaps it smacks too much of New Age trendiness and conjures up visions of sitting cross-legged on a carpet intoning an incomprehensible word or phrase for hours on end. But this, of course, is a misunderstanding of meditation. Meditation is, in a way, something we all do many times during the day whenever we give our mental attention to one thought or series of thoughts and mull it (them) over for a few moments. In the more technical sense, it is a deliberate entering into stillness and inner silence for a set period. It can be done anywhere at any time. It is what Jesus was talking about when he said one should enter into one's closet – that is, one's innermost self – when praying.

Those who have practised meditation over the centuries have left us many schools and techniques that are aimed at helping the individual clear his or her mind of its ongoing, often crazy chatter. Looking steadily at a burning candle or at some religious object, such as a crucifix or a statue of the Virgin Mary, can help blot out wayward thoughts. That, of course, is the point of slowly reciting a mantra, some special word; for example, "*maranatha*" (Aramaic for "come Lord") or "amen" (from the Hebrew "so be it") or, in the case of Transcendental Meditation (TM), the Sanscrit name of a Hindu deity. You simply focus your mind by repeating the word or phrase for fifteen or twenty minutes twice a day. Whenever your mind wanders, you simply and gently bring it back to the mantra.[4]

Scientific studies done with experienced meditators have now established beyond any reasonable doubt that regular meditation has measurable and quite specific results. Dr. Herbert Benson's brief book *The Relaxation Response* is probably the classic work on meditation.[5] He writes that, as one meditates in this manner, there is an overall awareness of relaxation and a feeling of increasing well-being. Breathing slows down, the heart-rate also slows perceptibly, blood pressure drops, and there is an increased output of creative, healing Alpha waves by the brain. Indeed, experiments with yogis in meditation have verified their ability to slow all of their vital functions to the point of near-total arrest.

Significantly, as Benson abundantly proves, the physiological benefits of meditation have little, if any, relation to the actual mantra used. One could repeat the word Pepsicola, or the phrase *mamma mia* (the *m* sound is particularly recommended), and achieve the same effects. You don't have to go to some highly publicized organization such as TM, take part in a Hindu-based initiation rite, and pay a fee for an allegedly unique mantra. I meditate with the well-known word "amen" as a focus word, but I dislike sitting motionless in the traditional style of meditation. As I enjoy the quiet of natural surroundings, I prefer instead to go for a long walk in the country and meditate, or let my mind go "in the silence dancing" as John (Dom Gregory) Main, the author of several books on Christian meditation, calls it.[6] The point here is that every healer I have met or read about uses some form of relaxed stillness or meditation in the healing process. As I alluded earlier, some researchers have called Therapeutic Touch a "healing meditation." In this stillness, they may visualize the healee becoming well and whole or they may consciously summon up healing energy and direct it to the person in need. Monitoring of healers

and healees at the time of treatment with an electroencephalo-
gram (EEG) has shown that there are changes in the brainwave
patterns of both – again with a predominance of Alpha waves.

The American healer Agnes Sanford, whom we have already
met and whose healing successes are well-documented, believed
firmly in meditation as the stage in which the healer realizes the
presence of God and affirms contact with that Power. Quoting the
Hebrew Bible (or Old Testament), she reminds us of the familiar
words, "Be still and know that I am God." First one has to concentrate or meditate in quietness upon the reality that sustains and
undergirds all of life. She then says that having contacted the
source of power you have to "turn it on." She advises believers to
ask simply, "Heavenly Father, please increase in me Your life-
giving power." Those who don't feel comfortable with that can say,
"Whoever you are, whatever you are, come into me now!" She
then affirms that this has indeed happened with a brief prayer of
thanks, and proceeds to direct that healing energy to the healee.
By meditating or thinking upon the fact that we are part of God
and that divine life is running through us at all times, we can speed
up the natural healing forces either of our own or of other people's
bodies. As Sanford puts it, "One does not need to be a saint or a scientist in order to do this."[7]

Not all prayers or thoughts directed towards another's healing,
whether close at hand or at a distance, are answered the way we
think they should be. But this should surprise nobody. This is not
some form of magic where you perform certain rituals and specific
results are then supposed to be inevitable. The biggest difficulty
facing both medical and non-medical healing is that human
beings are very complex creatures. There are so many factors at
work in every illness or trauma that guarantees of total recovery
can rarely be given either by conventional medicine or by traditional healers. What's more, all physical healing is doomed to ultimate defeat because of our mortality. Though Western society
often acts as though death is the ultimate insult and imposition, an
unpleasantness our hi-tech medicine ought somehow to prevent,
we know we all have to die eventually. There will come a time in

everyone's life when the proper healing prayer or intervention will fittingly be made in the "voice" of that ancient Christian prayer: that "at the last" there may be "a perfect end." It's because of this basic sense that the final mystery of our lives is hidden in the will or mind of God – or the cosmic spirit, if you prefer – that most Christian prayer for healing is quantified by the condition "according to Thy Will." This is not doubt or fatalism masking itself as piety. It's a quiet recognition that in the last analysis we are in the hands of God.[8]

13

Traditional Healing in China

"Acupuncture . . . has startling implications for the future of medicine. However, the aspect of oriental medicine that has the potential to truly rock the Western world is Qigong."

"Western rational science and the culture it has created is . . . the only cultural system that has completely forgotten its energy cultivation tradition."

– Roger Jahnke, OMD[1]

As Western medicine moves little by little towards a new paradigm of the human organism, one in which the body is seen less as a kind of biochemical machine and more as a resonating energy field, there is, as we have seen, a renewed interest in all forms of traditional healing. Many methods and concepts of therapy in other cultures that were once viewed as mere superstition and magic are being re-examined and validated. To quote one Western master and practitioner of the Chinese art of Qigong (pronounced chee gong), Dr. Roger Jahnke: "As western science digs itself out from under its 'seeing is believing' blindness, what occurs is a profound validation of ideas and traditions that were being called 'mysterious,' 'savage,' 'unscientific,' and 'primitive,' as little as a decade ago."[2]

The truth of this remark can be seen immediately when one considers the great reluctance of Western doctors at one time to take acupuncture and related approaches seriously. Today, however, it and similar therapies such as shiatsu are widely taught and used successfully for certain ailments – for example, muscular spasms, lower back pain, neuralgia, arthritis, and functional gastric complaints – by many Western doctors. In the book *Healing and the Mind*, the companion volume to the PBS TV series by the same name, Bill Moyers describes watching brain surgery in a hospital in Beijing. Everything about the operation was the same as it would be in a Western hospital except that there were six thin needles protruding from the patient's forehead, calves, and ankles. They were being used to block her pain. She had been given a mild sedative and a narcotic – but less than half the amount Western doctors would have used. Because the woman remained awake through the operation, she was able to co-operate with the surgeons and help them in their three-hour task.[3] Incidentally, while Moyers and his team were filming in China, the International Traditional Medicine Congress, with seven hundred doctors and scholars attending from forty different countries, was meeting in Beijing. They proclaimed October 22 as World Traditional Medicine Day and made a statement announcing that traditional

Chinese medicine is "by no means inferior to synthetic drugs and antibiotics."[4]

Since it is now so widely known and has been the subject of so many books, articles, and films, we do not need to discuss acupuncture here at any length. But, inasmuch as it is based upon principles similar to Qigong and is a variation of the practice of laying-on of hands, it is evidence not to be ignored. The theory is that there is a vital energy running through and around the human organism, which follows specific meridians or channels and whose flow can be affected directly by exceedingly thin needles inserted into precise points on the skin. The practice, which is at least five thousand years old, is believed to have originated in the observation that certain injuries to specific parts of the body, say by a cut or blow from a weapon or a puncture from a bone fish hook, often produced surprising cures for painful or diseased conditions in other parts. As these observations accumulated over generations, it was noticed that the size or depth of the cut made little difference; it was the exact location that counted. Eventually, elaborate charts were made of the human body showing the twelve chief meridians and mapping out some two thousand acupuncture points. (Incidentally, it was believed that the major meridians met in the hands; hence the sensitivity and capacity of the human hand for diagnosing illness and imparting healing.) It was, and is, believed that these acupuncture points, by affecting the autonomic (involuntary) nervous system, can be used to stimulate and balance the free flow of energy (*chi*) throughout the body, thus promoting health. It's not just a matter of sticking needles in dispassionately. The acupuncturist must use his or her own *chi* – sensing it in the hand and fingers – as the needle is inserted, and must feel the responding *chi* in the patient as well. Done in this manner, there is no sensation of pain whatever.

Some years ago, when I was suffering from a severe, crippling back pain, which was not responding to lengthy, conventional medical care, a visiting doctor, a colleague of my brother, volunteered to try acupuncture on me. There was no feeling as he took a long, fine needle between his thumb and forefinger and, twirling it as he pricked my skin, inserted it – to my complete surprise – in my right eyebrow. He took two more needles and, with the same delicate motion, inserted them at least half an inch into the tense muscles of my lower back. The relief was almost instantaneous, and I was soon able to walk without either a marked limp or acute pain. Whether it was just that I was credulous and suggestible or that he had managed to prod my body into healing itself I can not say with absolute certainty. But something happened for which I was extremely grateful. I have never had back pain in anything like the same intensity since.[5]

The current interest of Western doctors and researchers in Qigong healing, which has been practised for many centuries in China, has put it at the leading edge of the new medicine. Jahnke – who has written a book about Qigong, *The Most Profound Medicine*, and both practises and teaches various techniques of Chinese medicine at the Health Action Clinic in Santa Barbara, California – writes, "We can't say yet that Qigong has caused a revolution in western science and medicine. It is, however, a very primary player in a far-reaching, cross-disciplinary transformation that is taking place." Jahnke believes this "profound and dramatic" transformation is "akin to that of the 16th century when the work of Newton and Galileo utterly transformed how we saw the world."[6]

The technique, according to Kenneth Cohen, a Qigong master and author of more than one hundred journal articles on Chinese medicine and related topics, goes back at least to the Sung Dynasty (960-1279 A.D.), where it was called *buqi*, "spreading the Qi." Other authorities on Chinese medicine say that it's much older, going back some three to four thousand years. What is interesting for our purposes is that it has been undergoing a vast revival in China ever since the early 1950s. Recent visitors to China report that "everywhere, in the parks, athletic fields and even on the streets, people were practising Tai Chi and Qigong."[7] Most of China's major hospitals today have both Qigong research units and also treatment centres. It is used in treating a wide range of

ailments from arthritis, cancer, and hypertension to gastrointestinal problems, headaches, and insomnia. According to recent statistics prepared by these Qigong research units, what is called
"external Qigong" – which I'll explain in a moment – has better
results than acupuncture. The two approaches are used to treat the
same kinds of diseases, but the rate of recurrence is greater with
acupuncture than with Qigong, the researchers say. Dr. Elmer
Green, author of the book *Beyond Feedback*, and, as we have seen
earlier, a leading researcher into non-medical healing, has experimented extensively with Qigong healing and has said, "We have
concluded from our work with hundreds of patients that anything
you can accomplish with an acupuncture needle you can do with
your own mind."[8]

Delegates to the Fifth International Congress of Chinese Medicine and the First International Congress of Qigong at the University of California, Berkeley, in June 1990, were given documented
results of fully controlled, scientific experiments done in North
America (at the School of Chinese Medicine, in Oakland), as well
as in China, where Qigong was applied to various kinds of cancer,
severe headaches, and other ailments. In one American study,
among ninety-two cases of breast cancer treated with Qigong,
82.2 per cent had favourable results and 17.6 per cent had no
results.[9] At one school of Chinese medicine in Oakland, California, among forty-nine patients with dizziness and headaches, 98
per cent recovered after practising a form of Qigong meditation.

The Chinese sign or word for energy is translated into English in
various ways. The chief of these is Chi or Qi, which are pronounced the same way (chee). At its very simplest, it is the life-
force or vital life-energy pervading every living organism. It is very
much like an extremely subtle form of electricity, and extends
throughout the universe. In Taoist literature, the Chinese character for Qi reportedly means "the formless fire of life." It corre-
sponds, in a way, both to oxygen as the basic necessity of life and to
the bioelectricity by which we live and move and think. There are
in Chinese thought two kinds of Qi or Chi: that which can be
acquired from proper food and clean air (in the latter case, it's not

simply oxygen but an energetic or vital portion of it which one can learn to absorb selectively and use), and that which is inborn or original to us – our basic constitution, which comes to us from our parents and as a "gift" from the cosmos itself. In essence, the concept differs little from the orgone theory of Wilhelm Reich or the various other life-energy beliefs we have encountered, from the Hindu idea of *prana* to the *logos* of the Stoics, or the "light which gives light to every person who comes into the world" in the prologue to John's Gospel.

The practice and philosophy of Qigong is basically concerned with how to cultivate and maintain this energy, Qi, at its optimum balance and level in the overall system. Stated more technically, it's the practice of "activating, refining and circulating the human bioelectrical field."[10] It has been called acupuncture without needles. The rationale behind it is that since the bioelectrical field maintains and supports the functions of the various tissues and organs, including the whole of the immune system, Qigong can have a very profound affect on overall health. There is a Chinese saying, "The mind directs the Qi, the Qi directs the blood." This is similar to the belief of the healers we have already described that the energy they send forth has "an intelligence of its own."

The stance and the arm and hand motions of Qigong doctors and other practitioners using the external Qigong approach is very like those of Mietek Wirkus and other bioenergy healers. According to Kenneth Cohen, by trial and error over the centuries, Chinese doctors have discovered the healing effects of certain hand gestures – waving, circling, pushing, and pulling – done at a short distance from the patient's body but directly affecting his or her energy field. It is really a kind of laying-on of hands at a distance. In other ways, it closely resembles Dolores Krieger's Therapeutic Touch. Jahnke argues, however, that Qigong demands a much more systematic form of training for the healer to increase his power to project Qi, "plus a more sophisticated method of diagnosis and treatment according to the principles of traditional Chinese medicine."[11]

Qi, or vital life-energy, is central not just to acupuncture and

Qigong but to every form of Chinese medicine (and to most oriental martial arts as well). According to the theory, when Qi becomes too congested or stuck in the body, illness results. Similarly, when Qi is either depleted or overabundant (in both acupuncture and Qigong an excess of energy is believed to be as bad as too little), the basic balance essential to health is upset and disease follows. The practitioner – and here is where it becomes more difficult for the Western-trained mind to grasp – eventually becomes highly skilled at doing what is in fact a "non-touch assessment" of the patient, scanning the energy field for imbalances and intuitively knowing where to project Qi to set it right. It should be noted in passing that this kind of "intuitive diagnosis" has always been a mark of certain traditional healers in the West and even with some Christian healers, like Godfrey Mowatt. (I have recently met several doctors from Bulgaria and other former eastern-bloc countries who use this form of diagnosis regularly in their otherwise conventional practices. A considerable body of literature, including books and scientific papers, is already growing up at this new frontier for medicine. Several British doctors who were at the London Conference on Healing and Energy Medicine in 1992 are currently experimenting with intuitive or scanning-type diagnosis as well as using more conventional techniques and laboratory tests.) Scientists such as Dr. Robert Becker and Dr. Elmer Green believe that in such diagnosis what is actually taking place is some form of transfer of information, consciously or unconsciously, from the sick person to the healer.

This is far from being as far-fetched or exotic as it might at first seem. The human organism is an astonishingly complex nexus of information transference. Our immune system itself is not simply directed by signals from the brain via the central nervous network, various glands and hormones, and so on. In many ways human consciousness pervades the whole body and every cell receives and transmits information continuously.[12] Indeed, in modern physics, where matter is no longer seen as particles of matter but as a "dance of energy," and the whole cosmos is believed to be composed of dynamic relationships of energy, some physicists have suggested that to the traditional elements of space, time, and matter there must now be added a fourth component, information. Like the DNA that controls and directs the unfolding of cells and hence of life, the teeming energy which is the ground of all else is in one of its basic aspects an infinite flow of information. There has only to be a receptor, or interpreter, for communication to take place. The healer, in Qigong and other traditional forms of healing, may function as this interpreter.

According to Jahnke and Cohen, the Qi that is then sent in response to what has been learned by scanning the healee issues from the hands of the healer directly into the field and body of the healee. The healers make themselves aware of the energy, and the energy seems, as noted, to have its own intelligence. It knows what to do; that is, whatever else it is, it is a kind of coded information to the healing systems of the sick person. As the circulation of the person's energy improves, the typical subjective signs are feelings of warmth, tingling, weight in the affected parts, and a general sense of "expansiveness" or increased vitality.

In case anyone thinks we're dealing here simply with subjectivity, however, let me point out that there are now many carefully conducted research projects that demonstrate the objective effectiveness of external Qigong. These were begun in the 1950s, when the Chinese government, eager to combine the best of Western medicine and indigenous practices, ordered a series of explorations to see what worked best. Experiments done on gastrointestinal cancer patients, for example, found that when chemotherapy and radiation therapy were combined with Qigong the patients fared much better than when treated by the Western methods alone.[13] The editor of the newsletter of the International Society for the Study of Subtle Energies and Energy Medicine, Dr. Carol J. Schneider, wrote upon her return from China in 1992 that in Shanghai she observed Qigong exercises being done for hypertension and examined data showing how well the patients in the experiment were doing in controlling their own blood pressure. She also visited another research project at a hospital where one hundred cancer patients were taking part in government-funded tests. Schneider says, "We found evidence of interest in Qigong all around us."[14]

At the very heart of traditional Chinese medicine is the conviction that the truly great physician is the one who teaches people how to heal themselves. As the most effective medicine actually resides within each of us, the task is to turn it on or awaken it into full being. In its most basic form, Qigong is about patient empowerment. It is practised through regular exercises which emphasize very slow, deep breathing that pushes the diaphragm downwards: "The lower lobes of the lungs are pulled down, allowing more efficient oxygen/carbon dioxide exchange. The abdomen and lower back gently contract. These opening and closing movements increase the elasticity of lung tissues and have a massaging effect on the internal organs."[15]

As the breathing is slowed down, it becomes deeper and finer and gradually induces relaxation with its attendant stress reduction and sense of both mental and physical calm. As one inhales or ingests the Qi around and in the air, the mind focuses on the area for which healing is desired and gently directs the energy or "circulates the light" to that point. Cohen says that by practice one learns to "regulate normally unconscious processes, including the subjective sense of vitality and life energy." This results in better peripheral blood circulation and in the "classical subjective signs" of successful Qigong, "warmth, weight, vibration and expansiveness." Significantly, as Cohen notes, these are also medical indicators of vasodilation and improved circulation. Because some Western autogenic (self-directed) relaxation exercises and biofeedback techniques begin by having the subject conjure up feelings of warmth and heaviness (that is, the results of Qigong) in order to become relaxed and eliminate stress, Cohen says both training in autogenic relaxation and biofeedback can be thought of as Western forms of Qigong. Cohen writes that through Qigong practices, "we change the body's underlying electrical programming and the ease and accuracy of electrical signals reaching the various tissues."

According to Qigong teaching, there are certain places in the body itself where Qi is stored, and these can be drawn upon for self-healing. The most important are called the zang, those internal organs classified under the heading of yin – the holding, receiving, storing organs – including the liver, spleen, heart, lungs, and kidneys. These all "overflow" into the yang organs – the gall bladder, small and large intestine, stomach, and bladder – which transmit fluids. There are also three "storage batteries," the Dan Tian or "fields of elixir." Practitioners say that one directs awareness there and symbolically or imaginatively plants there the elixir of long life, health, and wisdom. One Dan Tian (the principal one) lies in the pelvic area just below the navel, one is at the heart, and the other is between the eyebrows. Significantly, these coincide with three of the *chakras* – sources or "wheels of energy" – in Hindu thought. The aim is to fill mentally these various "batteries" and energy fields in order to repair any body damage and improve overall well-being and prospects for a long and happy life.

Because this entire approach to healing requires no special machines, technology, buildings, clothing, or other costly accoutrements, it's small wonder more and more Western medical establishments are beginning to show an interest. As Jahnke points out, "Cultivating one's own life force has no cost, it requires no prescription, it is always with you, you need no membership. . . . It's extremely low impact but can be completely aerobic, you do not need a diagnosis and doing it for fun during health is preferable to doping it after one is sick to cure a . . . problem." He cites the $600 billion spent on medical products and services in the United States in 1989 alone, and adds, "It is startling we could have the most profound medicine within us and somehow forget to use it."

The leading Canadian practitioner of Qigong, Dr. Steven Aung, a family physician in Edmonton, Alberta, agrees with this assessment. Aung was born in China but raised in Burma where, at the age of seven, he first encountered Qigong and the practice of deep meditation. He now teaches courses in both acupuncture and Qigong at the University of Alberta and has given lectures on the latter to doctors in several Canadian cities. Aung told me he is fully convinced that the time has come to make Qigong much more widely known. "It's not good enough any more just to give people pills and needles. They need to be put in touch with their own life energy," he said. He is currently writing a book to make Qigong more readily accessible to Western modes of understanding.

The remarkable thing is that Qigong aims at realizing and maintaining vibrant bodily health but its essence is deeply spiritual. As Dr. David Eisenberg, author of *Encounters With Qi*, has said, "In Chinese medicine, the medical masters . . . were also the spiritual leaders. They never split the two."[16] Behind belief in the cultivation of the body's vital energy lies the conviction that the cosmos, like the individual, is moved by spiritual forces. The path to true wholeness involves an evolution of one's innermost self or a refinement of the spirit, which is sometimes referred to as "refining the body of pure energy." There is a holistic understanding here that Western medicine is only now beginning to realize it has lost and must recover.

A final note. I would like to cite some further evidence that Qigong theory is based upon impressive objective data. There are solid reasons why many highly respected research organizations are presently spending substantial budgets on Qigong-related research. At the Qigong conference held at Berkeley in June 1990, there were several Qigong masters from China, lecturing and delivering learned papers. These included Dr. Zuyan Lu of the Beijing Institute of High Energy Physics. Dr. Lu reported on the external Qigong abilities of a certain Dr. Yan Xin. In an experiment entitled "The Effect of Qi on the Half-life of the Radioactive Isotope Americium-241," Dr. Xin was able to alter the rate of decay of the isotope. Since it is a scientific fact that radioactive substances each have a constant decay rate (which can't be affected or changed by chemical or physical factors), such a bizarre result is a major challenge to the standard paradigm of scientific thought. At the conference, forty papers were presented, ten of which dealt with the sending of Qi to others with the intention of healing.[17]

At the First World Conference for the Academic Exchange of

Medical Qigong held in 1988, 128 research papers were presented. Of these, nearly fifty were on topics related to the matter of Qi emission. Those wishing further information should read Harvard Professor David Eisenberg's provocative book *Encounters With Qi*. Those who haven't already seen it should keep an eye out for the television rebroadcasting in Canada of a documentary on healing produced for Britain's ITV by Yorkshire TV. First shown in Canada on CBC's Newsworld, on February 3, 1991, it shows Chinese practitioners of Qigong in action and includes interviews with Dr. Daniel Benor (leader of the Doctor-Healer Network in the U.K.) and several non-medical healers using some of the other methods described in this enquiry. A number of British doctors included in the film speak out positively about the "healing phenomenon," most notably Dr. John Dawson, an official of the British Medical Society. All of the doctors agree with a position we have already seen presented by other authorities: "We're on the verge of some kind of breakthrough. We're at the edge of discovery about the energy of the body – it's something that will be of the magnitude of Harvey's discoveries regarding blood circulation."

14

The Challenges

"As a scientist, I believe we're going to understand everything one day, but this understanding will require bringing in a realm we don't understand at all yet. We're going to have to bring in that extra-energy realm, the realm of spirit and soul that Descartes kicked out of Western scientific thought."

– Professor Candace Pert, The Center for Molecular and Behavioral Neuroscience, Rutgers University.[1]

∽ The Challenge to Modern Medicine

Modern medicine is at a crossroads. For more than three hundred years, ever since the theories propounded by Descartes and then Newton were widely adopted, the mechanistic or biochemical paradigm for the human organism has been the basic model followed, often with near-miraculous results. The average human lifespan in affluent countries has been dramatically increased chiefly because of improved hygiene and nutrition and control of childhood infectious diseases. For the most part, diseases once dreaded as inexorable scourges have either been eliminated or reduced to easily treatable, occasional phenomena. In short, the successes and the general progress have been in many respects quite dazzling. New knowledge, combined with the advances in medical technology of the past few decades, mean that the modern doctor can now treat a foetus in the womb, do microsurgery on the human brain, or replace a vital organ in one patient with an organ taken from somebody else.

It hasn't all been a success story, of course. For forty years, cancer has been a major target of research in the United States, Canada, and elsewhere. We spend $70 million annually to fight it in this country. In the United States, the National Cancer Institute has a yearly budget of $1.6 billion for research. Yet, not only has there been no cure found but – and this is the most daunting aspect of all – the general cancer rate has continued to rise. Mortality rates for children with cancer have been substantially cut, but they account for only a small percentage of cancer incidence. As far as older age groups are concerned, science has largely failed to make a breakthrough. As the journal *Chronic Diseases in Canada* reported in February 1993, the cancer war is one we're actually losing. The magazine said it was time for a whole new approach. The worldwide AIDS epidemic has yet to be met with an effective vaccine or cure, and there are plenty of other incurable illnesses, new and old, we could mention.

Unavoidably, however, given the undeniable, massive progress in most fields, considerable hubris has resulted. Those who have compared the modern medical élite with the gods of a new religion or, at the very least, as its priests, have a valid point. For the first time in history, the health of the individual is monopolized in a purely mechanistic, materialistic fashion by a professional "priesthood" all similarly trained, and organized as tightly as any trade union. Western medical science has completely superseded or suppressed all other castes of healers and all other modes and dimensions of healing. The spiritual component, even where it is recognized, has been pushed to the periphery. The prevailing medical attitude has been – at least in the perception of the majority – you come to us and we'll not only tell you what's wrong but we'll do all that needs to be done to heal you.

Some serious problems arise out of this specialization, resulting in what can only be called a major crisis. In the first place, the very success of Western medicine has created a nightmare. Encouraging the public to run to doctors or clinics every time there is an ache or pain and to expect a pill, potion, or procedure for every ailment, no matter what its nature or origin, has produced in almost every industrialized country an economic burden of alarming proportions. The total bill for medical products and services in the United States in 1989 came to an astounding $600 billion dollars. There is little need to say more about this. One can read about it almost daily in the press.

The greatly extended lifespan of the citizens of these same countries has further exacerbated this health-care cost crisis. As people live longer, they have vastly more need of medical services and actually run up a greater list of costs in the final six months of life than in all the rest of their days put together. Canada is a prime example. By the year 2021, there will be more than six million people in Canada – nearly one in five – who are over the age of sixty-five. That's exactly twice as many seniors as there are today. As the *Globe and Mail's* health reporter wrote on May 1, 1992, "The implications are staggering for Canada's universal access, publicly financed health-care system. The elderly already consume a disproportionate share of medical dollars, and that share is rising." Consider the fact that in 1989, those over seventy-five – *who were less than 5 per cent of the population* – took up more than one-third of all hospital days in Canada. The reporter added that many believe that the problem is not so much the number of elderly but the fact that "they are overdoctored, overmedicated and overhospitalized." This problem is already chronic and getting worse, not just in Canada but in the United States, Britain, and a host of other countries. Quoted in the same article, Keith Anderson, the manager of two extended-care homes in Vancouver, says that unless drastic changes are made "economic reality" will force an abandonment of current ways of looking at the health-care needs of the elderly. He says, "What we need is high-touch, not high-tech."

The funding nightmare might be made more tolerable or be overcome somehow if increased longevity meant increased quality of life. But the distressing truth is that the medical wizardry that can give such brilliant results has at times also produced the phenomenon now known as "medical captivity." People can be kept alive on machines and drugs like the proverbial fly on a pin. They aren't living in any meaningful sense of the word, and yet they aren't permitted to die. They are suspended between living and non-living, a burden to themselves, their loved ones, and the generations crowding behind.

The over-reliance on medications of every conceivable kind – encouraged not just by the public's desire for a "quick fix" for every want or need, but also by pressure, in the form of advertising, from the enormously powerful international drug manufacturers upon doctors and ordinary citizens alike – has led to a whole series of unforeseen disasters. While the patient's sense of responsibility for his or her own health has been severely weakened, many of the viruses and bacteria which the drugs are designed to fight have been unwittingly strengthened. In a recent front page story, "How Bugs Outwit Drugs," the *Globe and Mail* pointed out that the golden age of antibiotics, which began with the discovery of penicillin, appears to be over. Bacteria are "bouncing back with a vengeance" as new and much hardier strains, which have outsmarted penicillin and its counterparts, are taking over. Some of these superbacteria "literally chew penicillin up and spit it out," the article said.[2] Tuberculosis, once all but beaten in North America, is making a frightening comeback in major American cities. Many strains of venereal disease are now immune to the once-standard shots or doses of this or that wonder-drug.

The response of medical science and the pharmaceutical companies, predictably, is to search for ever-more-potent drugs to deal with these bacterial mutations. But drugs that are so much more powerful carry with them more numerous and more damaging side effects than do their predecessors. The costs, of course, escalate exponentially. The article in the *Globe and Mail* noted that today "a course of treatment for a skin or ear infection can cost as much as $100 compared with a few dollars for the original antibiotics." What's more, there is no foreseeable end to this cycle. The super-drugs will simply result in super-superbugs in a few years' time. The number of bacteria completely immune to regular forms of treatment is rising at an alarming rate. The problem tragically, is at its worst in hospitals where the mixture of hordes of sick people and a kaleidoscope of antibiotics provides a lush breeding-ground for drug-resistant strains. There's a lot more than humour to the saying that a hospital is no place to be if you're sick! A patient who enters an acute-care hospital facility in Canada today reportedly runs a 5 to 10 per cent chance of picking up an infection there. It could prove fatal.

There is more, much more. There are indeed, thank God, many wonderful, dedicated doctors who understand the art as well as the science of healing. But, increasingly, as the report which I quoted in the introduction about the sixty-one million Americans who use unconventional therapies amply illustrates, the general public has grown disenchanted with the impersonal, hi-tech feel of much current medical care. The emphasis is so much on disease or pathology that you sometimes wonder what doctors are ever taught about preventative medicine and actual health itself. It's very easy in today's hospitals and clinics to feel like a piece of meat or as just one more subject for detached analysis by experts in white coats. The tunnel vision of the biochemical model too often strips the patient not just of dignity but of his or her full humanity. I know from personal experience that family members visiting a hospital patient often have unbelievable difficulty finding anyone to talk to them about the patient's condition or concerns. When they finally manage to corner somebody, frequently they are told that only Dr. Y can speak about the person in question. Unfortunately, Dr. Y is busy in the operating room, is teaching, or has left for the day.

Not just that. Far too often conventional medicine misses whole areas and horizons of healing which bear intimately upon the recovery and well-being of the sick. Nine times out of ten, the specialist hasn't the slightest interest in what is going on in the life of the person being treated – even though it may be crucial to what made him or her ill in the first place. A woman who had recently been through a long, costly, and unsuccessful "work-up" by a fertility specialist wrote to tell me about her frustration and deep hurt. She had been finding the process more and more spiritually and emotionally draining, but when she attempted to broach this with the doctor he became cold and authoritarian. The not-so-subtle message was, don't bother me with that; I'm an obstetrician and not a psychiatrist. Anything other than your fertility is not my problem. One day he told her quite bluntly, "Look, if you can't handle this, the secretary will make an appointment for you to see Dr. ———. He's the psychologist on staff here."

It's precisely this cutting up of people into dozens of pieces, each belonging to some specialty or other, that has caused so many today to feel cheated in their quest for healing. They may be laypersons, but they understand intuitively the truth that health has to do with total wholeness. The present outpouring of books and the rapidly increasing number of groups dedicated to holistic healing is anything but accidental. They are the direct result of massive, popular frustration and dissatisfaction with the truncated and too-often dehumanized approach of conventional medical science.

Some medical critics glibly and patronizingly suggest that this is a herd-like reaction or New Age fad largely supported by the uneducated masses. Unfortunately for this theory, all the facts point in another direction. We have already seen that the February 28, 1993, issue of the *New England Journal of Medicine* stated unequivocally how surprised researchers were to discover that the higher the education of the persons polled the more likely they were to have sought out some unconventional therapy. Researchers at the University of Pennsylvania Cancer Center interviewed three hundred patients who were there for chemotherapy and other mainstream medical treatments. They next surveyed another three hundred cancer patients they defined as being "treated by purveyors of quack and fraudulent remedies." They then asked the question, What characterizes these people who go to quacks? They assumed the basic factor here would be education. Well, it was, but not in the way they expected. Those who preferred natural or spiritual healing were more educated than the others; in fact, were twice as likely to have gone to college. Indeed, the researchers found that one in five of those who went to what researchers were calling "quacks" had a master's degree or a doctorate. Of the first group of three hundred, those who said they preferred conventional medicine alone, 60 per cent had never gone beyond high school.[3]

When they were asked by the researchers why they went to "quacks," the patients replied that they wanted something medicine wasn't offering them. They said they wanted to restore their immune systems, because we know that people with strong immune systems don't get cancer. We've got enough sense to know that because of our education. They noted as well that conventional medicine is really the science of replacing bodily functions rather than the science of *restoring* them.

As you might expect, there is a lot of resistance to any form of complementary or alternative healing from the majority of Western doctors. No hierarchy likes to have its dogmas questioned by lay members. Yet, as with the Roman Catholic Church, for example, or indeed all major faiths today, there is a progressive movement going on in the medical establishment. As we have seen, there are doctors and medical institutions willing to open themselves to new or ancient insights and paradigms of healing while keeping a firm hold on the solid achievements of conventional medicine. Without question, a willingness to work with traditional healers or healing techniques has been of tremendous help to doctors conscientiously trying to meet the total needs of the total person in their practice. It would be ideal if all or most doctors themselves developed the laying-on of hands as part of their strategy in the fight against sickness. Failing that, the setting up in North America of doctor-healer teams like those in Britain and the further encouragement of the kind of co-operation seen in the Therapeutic Touch movement among professional nurses could widen the use of healers while preserving the necessary safeguards and supervision. Co-operation with healers could save doctors time and expenditures while at the same time humanizing their practices through closer contact with many of their more seriously ill patients. Having experienced surgery myself, I know what a difference it could make if there were a healer available in the waiting area outside the surgery doors – to calm, reassure, and "bless" the patient before the operation – and also in the recovery room. And, not least of all, the economic benefits to patients and to the entire health-care system would be tremendous.

One final point. For even the most sceptical, there has been, I believe, enough solid evidence and argument set forth in these pages to warrant at the very least a new commitment by government and the medical establishment alike to put far more money – or, indeed, any money – into the research and testing of spiritual healing. At present in Canada, for example, while $70 million is spent annually on conventional cancer research – in a war we're losing – next to nothing is being spent to examine the claims for non-medical therapies. The situation is only slightly better in Britain. Scientists in the United States in some of the republics of the former Soviet Union, and in China, are experimenting with these therapies, with some exciting results. Yet, funding is still very sporadic and miserly even where such non-medical healing is taken seriously. The real challenge to medical science, especially if it mistakenly continues with its overall sceptical posture, is to dare to do the necessary experiments and tests. Nobody is asking for a leap of faith, but it's high time for those who say they live by an empirical, open-minded scientific approach to evidence to put some money and effort into the kind of research that is required. Those doctors and others who are not convinced of the reality of non-medical healing must be asked what it would take to convince them, and when are they prepared to begin the tests?

∽ The Challenge to the Churches

A recent news clipping on my desk tells how more than a thousand people, *most of them under thirty years of age*, leave the churches every week in England. In the decade 1979 to 1989, Anglican congregations dropped by about 10 per cent, Methodist by 11 per cent, Roman Catholic by 14 per cent, and United Reformed by 18 per cent. The statistics for North America are similar. There are many reasons for this steady decline of what used to be called the major denominations. None has played a greater role than their failure to identify and meet the spiritual longings and questions of modern men and women, especially those of the generation born in the late 1940s to early 1960s. Religion simply holds little interest or relevance for an increasingly large majority of people. Yet, distressing signs and symptoms of a spiritual vacuum and widespread spiritual malaise are everywhere around us. Physicians are aware of what Carl Jung noted long ago, that the majority of their patients are suffering from what are basically non-medical problems. Their very real aches and pains often are masking or flowing from a troubled spirit.

All faiths need to ask themselves what are the ramifications of this thirst of our community for holistic healing? All the major faiths have a long tradition of healing at their core. Christianity, as we have seen, began with a Master who was a healer. It was, particularly in its earliest years, a healing movement. And it has the wholeness or healing of the total person – body, mind, and spirit – at the centre of all its basic doctrine, worship, and out-reach. The problem is that this key concern has at times been wholly eclipsed or forgotten. There has been plenty of talk about sin and forgiveness, about love of neighbour and about the plight of the poor and downtrodden. Courageous and costly positions have been taken on contentious matters, such as aboriginal rights versus oil and hydroelectric companies in the Canadian North or racism in South Africa. But there has been little or no attempt to bring a holistic approach to bear. Some churches seem utterly preoccupied with social-justice issues to the almost complete dis-regard of people's need and search for spiritual reality and comfort. The matter of their physical and emotional health is entirely left to the medical professionals or to the wide range of secular recov-ery and self-help groups that constitute such a growth industry in these unsettled times.

The conclusion, which to me seems inescapable, which seems to cry out loud in the light of this investigation, is that, if the Christian churches could somehow recover the awareness that healing in the fullest sense of the word is really what they are about, they could experience a powerful renaissance or renewal. It's not just that they would grow or become a major influence in our culture once again (because simply bigger or fuller churches would prove very little, and the last thing we need is a return to any form of Christian triumphalism) but that the benefits flowing to those being ministered to would be incalculable.

The biggest differences would make themselves felt in commu-nication and in the sacraments and forms of worship.

• *Communication.* As someone who has spent a lifetime trying to communicate ideas, I am as aware as anyone that most religious language, and more important, the concepts and general outlook behind it, belong to a wholly different epoch. By re-examining all of them, and by using paradigms and vocabulary concerned with the healing process and with human aspirations for wholeness, the churches could find fresh, truly effective means of communicating with people. Instead of talking about people being "saved" or

"born again," instead of going on about salvation, holiness, sancti-
fication, or atonement, there could be a return to the truths underlying these archaic terms.

If the effort were made, it would be discovered that what is ultimately at stake is the total health of the total person. Even something as central as the significance of the death of Jesus Christ
(what preachers mean when they talk about "the cross") needs to
be freshly understood in the light of the verse in Isaiah regarding
the Suffering Servant. The verse has always been held by Christians to be a prophetic reference to Christ. It says simply, "And
with his stripes [the wounds suffered in a flogging] we are healed."
In other words, the imagery needs to change from that of a court-
room, where we as guilty sinners have been sentenced to death
only to have Christ take our place and die sacrificially on our
behalf – a construct much loved by fundamentalist Christians – to
that of a sickroom, where those afflicted with illness are waiting
and hoping to be restored to health. Christ identified with our
pain. He suffered to reveal the depth of God's love and forgiveness
so that we might know spiritual and bodily health.

• *Sacraments and Worship.* It's not just a matter of changing the
thinking and language of the churches, however. There needs to
be a reappraisal of every aspect of each church's life. The exciting
truth is that underneath so much that has become staid, routine,
and either dull or so encrusted with tradition that its original purpose can no longer be discerned, there is an unlimited wealth of
healing imagery and power. The sacraments are a strong case in
point. I have always thought it a tragedy that in baptism, where the
emphasis should be on the health-giving energy of the primal
breath of God, the Holy Spirit, that the talk of sin and "regeneration" drowns all this out. In the Anglican service, for example
(where infant baptism is the norm), there is serious talk about the
infant's commitment to "fight manfully under his [Christ's] banner
against the world, the flesh, and the devil," and very little if any
mention of the wholeness of body, mind, and spirit that is God's
loving intention for every child. Baptism, at whatever age, is about

an awakening to the fact that we are essentially spiritual by nature. It is the time we receive the new energy which is both released and required by a new birth.

Healing is also central to the sacrament of the Eucharist or Holy Communion. When I was active in a parish ministry, it always moved me to pass along the rows of outstretched hands, the hands of old and young, of the troubled and the afflicted, as well as of the hale and hearty, and to say the powerful words, "May the body of our Lord Jesus Christ *preserve your body and soul unto everlasting life.*" Similarly with the wine, "May the blood . . . preserve your body and soul unto everlasting life." These deeply symbolic, sacramental elements of bread and wine are intended to bring healing that is physical, emotional, and spiritual. That is what is meant by "preserve your body and soul." The sacraments are administered in the context of prayer, of being assured of forgiveness, and of being surrounded by a loving community. When the healing significance of what is being done is fully appreciated by all the participants, I believe that we can enter into the enormous, unseen radiating power that works for the total well-being not just of those present but of those at a distance for whom prayer is made. One does not have to be a mystic to know the truth of T. S. Eliot's phrase about sensing the energy present when one "kneels where prayer has been valid." But people coming to church need to know and also to feel that the entire process, from the affirmations of the hymns and prayers to the renewed ability to see oneself and the world around in a more loving, positive way as a result of the sermon, is aimed at strengthening and renewing the life of every person there. The entire enterprise is supposed to be about recharging the batteries of each participant so that he or she can courageously and with joy go forth to live a fuller, more abundant life. If that were the criterion by which every part of every service were to be guided and judged – from the singing and other music to the prayers and the choice of readings – worship would always be a therapeutic experience and not a dutiful chore, or worse.

One of the great tragedies of current religious life, in my view, is that in most circles, at least in North America, when you mention healing services, the immediate reaction is to think of television healers, with all the excesses, scams, and outright intellectual insults associated with them. But it should by now be evident that the television healers and their imitators in those denominations more noted for enthusiasm or zeal than for sound scholarship are not the models I have in mind.

All over Canada and the United States, the recovery of the ministry of healing is going on quietly, with no fanfare of any kind. More and more Anglican, Roman Catholic, and United churches in particular are bringing healing into the open once again. In some Anglican churches I have visited, a Holy Communion and healing service is held monthly on a Sunday. In one parish where I spoke recently, during the reception of Holy Communion the senior priest and a senior lay reader stood at the front of the church. As people went up to receive the bread and wine, some went first to speak briefly to one of the two healers – for this turned out to be their role – and to receive the laying-on of hands. Some came on behalf of others, some for themselves. According to the priest in charge, the needs of the people varied from specific illnesses to problems of difficult relationships, grief, or loneliness. I can only make the subjective observation that something seemed to be happening. The sense of energy and of belonging to each other was quite palpable.

Most churches, however, prefer to hold the healing service on a weekday. At the lovely Episcopal Church of St. Martin, in Pompano Beach, Florida, there is a weekly mid-morning Communion and healing service every Thursday, which my wife and I often attend while on vacation. Those wishing prayer and the laying-on of hands for a particular reason or person simply remain at the altar rail after receiving Communion. The priests then come along and ask quietly if there is a special concern. You can either indicate no or whisper a request. In either case, the priest usually places his hands lightly upon the person's head and prays for them and those they love. Any clergy wishing to hold healing services of this type can contact the major bookrooms of their own denominations for books of simple instruction or, in the case of Episcopalians

(Anglicans) and Catholics, they only need to make use of the rites already laid down in their official prayerbooks. The Fellowship of the Order of St. Luke is interdenominational and has secretaries in most major centres (for example, at diocesan or synod headquarters) who are willing to give further assistance.

At seven o'clock on a recent Saturday evening, my wife and I found ourselves sitting in a Roman Catholic church in downtown Toronto. Outside, a bleak, November rain was falling. Heavy traffic was bringing a horde of hockey fans to Maple Leaf Gardens or to nearby bars and cinemas. On a corner, a couple of prostitutes were busy trying to solicit customers from the procession of cars which regularly cruise "the track." Inside the vaulted nave of Our Lady of Lourdes parish church, however, something quite different was going on. About 150 members of Toronto's HIV-affected community – people living with AIDS or HIV and their friends and family members – were gathered for a remarkable healing service, one that is the first of its kind in Canada and takes place on the third Saturday of every month. Similar services are held in New York, San Francisco, and other major American cities.

The congregation was made up chiefly – a little over two-thirds – of men of all ages. Most were white, well-dressed, and, apart from a few who were visibly ill, they appeared completely healthy. Nobody seeing them elsewhere could have guessed they were under a virtual death-sentence because of HIV. The service, a eucharistic celebration presided over by three priests, was unadorned and low-key, but not lacking in emotion. The leading priest, Fr. Robert Doran, a Jesuit who teaches at Regis College in the Toronto School of Theology, delivered a very intense and moving homily in which he spoke of a recent spate of deaths in the AIDS-affected community and of several members of the Our Lady of Lourdes group whose deaths he had attended during the month just passed. His text was the words of Jesus on the cross to the penitent thief: "Today you will be with me in paradise." He spoke of the importance of this message of hope and acceptance to those with AIDS. He also told how he was only able to endure the grief he and others ministering to those with AIDS experience daily because, even though members of the community are facing death, so many of them are able to heal relationships and their innermost selves. Doran explained that where such healing has taken place, death is met, not with panic or despair, but with confidence and quiet, courageous joy.

The central drama of the mass came when the priest invited any who wished for healing to come forward. Just over thirty of them, male and female, in some cases accompanied by lovers, friends, or family members, came up and stood below the altar. Some clung to their companions, others stood alone and strangely vulnerable. The three priests and two lay people then moved along the line, placing both hands upon the head of each and praying silently for a few moments. Then, using sacramental oil, blessed for the purpose, they moved back along the line again, anointing the forehead and both palms of each person in the ancient sacrament for the sick. It was obviously a potent symbol of their acceptance by God, of the community's care for them and solidarity with them. The oil symbolized the soothing, healing power of God.

But was it more than symbol? We have seen from our exploration that there are good reasons for believing that it was. Doran believes that this healing service "can include physical healing, such as stopping the progression of the disease or even seroconversion." At the same time, he does not claim magical solutions or encourage false hopes. With God all things are possible, but the real aim of spiritual healing is not the avoidance of death as the ultimate evil but rather the restoration of a healed relationship with ourselves, those around us, and with God or the Source of life itself.

Doran says that the thirst for inner healing and growth in the AIDS-affected community is tremendous. "People need God, they know it, and they want to develop that relationship," he says. Many HIV-infected people feel that "the language of spirituality has been taken away from them" because their churches have rejected them. They're facing "an apparently absurd death" at an early age and, in addressing the ultimate questions of the meaning of life, they have a need to reclaim spiritual language. The jargon of psychology or sociology is not enough for them, according to Doran. The question of God arises sharply and must be answered.

In one of the earliest reports on the healing service at Our Lady of Lourdes, in the *Catholic New Times*, Bob Blouin, a forty-year-old gay Catholic who was diagnosed as HIV-positive in early 1988, tells what coming to the first healing mass at the church meant to him. He had been trying to escape from the agonizing thought that God was punishing him. He had been struggling to come to terms with his Catholicism and a lifetime of feeling that his sexual orientation ostracized him from his Church. At the healing service he felt at home for the first time. He wrote that at first he expected to be "thunderstruck and cured of HIV." Gradually, he realized he was being healed – but on deeper levels than he had dreamed of. He found acceptance, and non-judgement, in fact, the kind of unconditional love that all religions talk about but do not always manifest. Now he says, "Although I wouldn't wish HIV on anyone, I would wish its benefits on everyone. The liberation of having nothing left to lose! . . . Now every day is a bonus. I see and feel and touch and taste the Creator in everything. I weep over the beauty of creation. In facing my own mortality, I'm beginning to live."

∾ The Core of Christianity – and a Giant Paradox

Visitors from around the world who come to North America for the first time, particularly to the United States, have usually been prepared by the media for the consumerism and brash materialism so rampant in the culture. What takes them by surprise is the extraordinary religiosity which comes at them from all around. Radio and television abound with Bible-wielding evangelists of every conceivable kind. American politicians, from the president down, obviously regard God and the American flag as two ways of looking at the same reality. Christianity functions as a sort of civil religion even though the constitution argues for the separation of church and state. In spite of a substantial decline in membership, American and, to a somewhat lesser degree, Canadian churches are well-filled, especially when contrasted with their European counterparts. In both Canada and the United States, the number of people who believe in God, according to the pollsters, comes very close to 90 per cent.

But the irony and the paradox lie in the fact that in spite of all this overt influence of religion – overwhelmingly, albeit perhaps nominally, Christian – it seems to make very little real, substantial difference to national or personal life. There is no evidence to suggest that the United States and Canada are any more ethical and compassionate than countries where commitment to religious faith is less strong. The United States is one of the most crime-ridden, violent countries in the so-called developed world. Canadians, living in one of the most resource-rich and beautiful regions of the globe (Canada was judged to be number one on a United Nations comfort-and-lifestyle index in 1992), seem to have little uniting them at present. Narrow self-interest seems the prevailing creed. In spite of the lip-service to Christian faith and values by the majority of North Americans, the core message of Christianity *for an individual's personal life* seems to have missed the mark almost completely. How else are we to account for the truth that the major problem for North Americans today – apart from the often-cited questions of how to lose weight and where to park one's car – is that of low self-esteem? If there is one theme running through the myriad self-help and recovery groups and the endless tapes, books, and seminars which nurture their growth, it is the deep need of people to discover who and what they are. The traditional faiths, which are supposed to relate one to oneself, one's neighbour, and the entire cosmos, and to give a full sense of what it means to be a human being, have failed to deliver. As I said in *For Christ's Sake*, many people go through the motions of worship in churches because they believe the "water of life" is there somewhere behind the religious façade. It's just that they can't get close enough to drink and be satisfied. In some denominations, they are told so often what miserable, rotten sinners they are that no good news or Gospel ever breaks through.

Ultimately, it is the function of all religions to bring their adherents to that ultimate point of healing where they feel and know themselves to be in harmony with life itself. The ways and means of each religion are different, but in the end the goal is the same. Since I work from a Christian commitment and since that is still the dominant ethos in the Western world, it is important I try to clarify here what this essential healing is in Christian terms. Scholars within the other major faiths must do it for theirs.

Christian leaders talk endlessly, even glibly, about the Gospel. It is widely assumed everyone knows what this means and that it's great significance for everyone is self-evident. Not so. Of course, any Christian, however casual, is aware that the word Gospel means good news. Just what this good news consists of, however, and why it is thought to be both "good" and "news" is a total mystery to most believers. But when one thinks a little, there are historical figures who did experience this "good news" in a remarkable way and had their lives totally turned around as a result. Perhaps by reminding ourselves of them we can get closer to the matter.

Take Martin Luther. He believed in God. In fact, he was a priest of the Roman Catholic Church. But, internally, he was a mass of conflicts, angst, and doubt. The harder he tried to win God's approval – to find and feel himself in total harmony with life – the more he felt unworthy. But one day while reading about the intimate experience of another man who was very much like himself – Paul, in his letter to the Roman Christians – Luther suddenly saw for the first time what Paul was talking about when he wrote that we are justified by faith. Paul, like Luther, had tried everything he knew to be worthy of God's approval, had tried to live a good life, and had been worn out physically and mentally by the struggle. Then it struck him that the God or Ultimate Being and Intelligence who made and sustains the universe is so loving and graciously accepting that He claims us as beloved sons and daughters just as we are.

Both Paul and Luther realized that the entire meaning of Christ's life, death, and resurrection was that humanity is dealing with the kind of God you can trust to the limit because He has gone to the limit for you. What an enormous sense of relief, what an incredible healing of the whole personality. Both of these men realized, when the truth broke in upon them, that they could throw themselves into that infinite ocean of divine love. It was like a frantically struggling, drowning man suddenly finding that by relaxing and trusting his body to the water he can actually be borne up by it and float in safety as he learns to swim. To change the imagery, truly hearing the Gospel means being able to commit oneself to life as an eagle commits itself to the wind. The eagle is never totally passive, but its considerable weight is as nothing once it abandons itself to the potent uprush of the air. John Newton (1725-1807), the author of the well-known hymn "Amazing Grace," has left us his eloquent testimony to this very same experience: "I once was lost, but now am found/was blind but now I see." Newton, a former slaver and hard-drinking sea captain, wrote his own epitaph: "John Newton, clerk, once an infidel and libertine, a servant of slaves in Africa, was by the rich mercy of our Lord and Saviour Jesus Christ preserved, restored, pardoned, and appointed to preach the Faith he had long laboured to destroy."

The point here is not that it's necessary for all to become Christians or believers of other faiths. The core experience, however, the transcendent experience of acceptance by God, or by life itself if one is not a theist, is essential to wholeness or, if you like, to personal salvation.

In my experience, no greater therapy exists in all the world than the consciousness of life – however hard, however complex, however filled with inexplicable events and pain – as something ultimately in the control of an infinitely loving mind and presence. Nothing brings a greater and more authentic sense of personal worth and of belonging, however humbly, to a purpose and design that is vastly beyond ourselves than knowing in our heart of hearts that, "warts and all," we are called and loved by God. That, it seems to me, is indeed good news, and is the start of the great healing known in all religions as "the way of return" or, more simply, as "the way." (The earliest name for the followers of Christ was People of the Way.)

The challenge to the churches, then, from our study of the healing phenomenon, is not just for them to make fuller use of traditional healing rites and to encourage the medical profession towards a more holistic approach to the sick, but to enunciate more clearly in everything they attempt or say the full, healing message of acceptance which the Gospel contains. Many of the illnesses of society and of our world could be healed if this basic, religious experience were more universally known. Those who have truly experienced acceptance, in spite of who and what they are, will be better able to reach out across the gulfs that divide us and bring healing to our world.

~ A Theological Reflection

In researching my book *Life After Death*, I was surprised to find how much the major religious faiths have in common when it comes to that central concern, in spite of all their apparent differences. While pursuing the issues around healing raised in this book, something similar has happened. Investigating the attempts of modern researchers to measure and define the subtle energy or energies involved in healing and looking again at the core teachings of the great religions brought me face to face with an important realization: each religion in its own way is trying to describe the same reality or force. If I am right this not only throws fresh light on the quest for greater inter-faith understanding and co-operation, it also adds one more strand to the fabric of evidence we have been examining for the validity of non-medical healing. As modern quantum physics is already doing, it furthers the possibilities for reconciliation between religion and science as well.

In the case of Judaism and Christianity, the name of the primal energy, which is spoken of as the agent of healing, the Holy Spirit –

in Hebrew, *ruach*, in Greek, *pneuma* – comes from the word for the wind. The Hebrew word denotes the unseen but incredibly powerful desert wind. The wind was understood as a very fine form of matter in motion, and in primitive times spirit was considered to be an even finer form of matter. It was not a great leap to use the analogy of the *ruach* or wind to denote the invisible yet awesome power of God. In both the Old and the New Testaments, whenever the words Holy Spirit or Spirit of God are used, the key thought is that of God "unseen but present and active in power."

It is because of the Spirit that the Old Testament prophets prophesy. It is because he receives a double portion of Elisha's spirit that the prophet Elijah is such a man of power and healing. In Genesis, it was the Spirit who moved creatively over the "face of the waters" at the beginning of time. It is in virtue of God breathing His breath (Spirit) into the nostrils of Adam that humans are said to have become living souls. The marks of the Spirit's presence are not just creativity, power, and healing, but also wisdom, compassion, and the indwelling presence of the Divine. In the New Testament, Jesus receives a special blessing of the Spirit at his baptism; according to Luke, his whole ministry has to be understood in terms of one who is filled and driven by the Holy Spirit. Jesus heals through the "finger of God," that is, the Holy Spirit; finally, he promises this same power to his followers.

The symbolism of the opening of the Book of Acts, where, at Pentecost, there are tongues of flame and the sound "as of a rushing, mighty wind" illumines by means of myth (in the sense of a truth which can only be told by a story) the experience of a huge inrush of vital energy. The healings done by the early Christians – and according to the Gospels they did even greater feats than did Christ himself – were done in and through this God-given dynamic. The Spirit or Breath of God was the pledge of their belonging to Christ and the source of all their power. As Paul says, they had been given "the Spirit of love, of power and of a sound mind." It was because he believed we all, believers and non-believers alike, are alive and exist in and by this divine energy which is through us and around us that Paul says, in his sermon at Athens, "We are all God's offspring. For, in Him we live, and move, and have our being, as certain of your own poets have said."[4]

Given this, it is only natural that Jews and Christians should speak of spiritual healing or of the body's self-healing power in terms of spirit or of the Holy Spirit. One of the reasons that Pentecostal-type churches (and neo-Pentecostal movements in the major churches, such as the Charismatic Movement) have proven so popular is because of their emphasis upon the "gifts of the Spirit," especially healing.

When we come to the vastly different culture and religious tradition of China, we have seen that the basic life-force or energy is called Chi or Qi. It flows throughout the human or animal body, but it also fills the universe. Like God, it is omnipresent. It is the essential, vital life-energy in all things. The practice of Qigong and of Tai Chi is a profoundly spiritual matter. The Taoist practitioner, for example, believes himself to be merging with the essence of the cosmos "by refining the body of pure energy" within his own physical body. I'm not saying one can simply transfer one system (Judeo-Christian) into another (Chinese) and find they are both identical; in one way the traditions are miles apart. And yet, the parallels here are quite striking.

When we come to Hindu thought and the concept of *prana*, we find the very same thing. This religion, possibly the oldest of all, holds that there is a vital life-energy that is "universal and more basic than atomic energy." In his book *Vital Energy and Health*, Edward Mann quotes S. Sivananda on *prana*: "Heat, light, electricity, are all manifestations of prana. . . . Whatever moves, works or has life, is but an expression of prana. . . . Prana is the link between the astral and the physical body."[5] In many ways, *prana* resembles not only Chi or God's Spirit active in sustaining all things, but the orgone energy of Wilhelm Reich as well.

If we extend this study and go on to consider the concept of *mana* and related forces (like good or bad "medicine") held by many aboriginal peoples, again we would find similar ideas of a cosmic energy or power. Behind the tradition of the prophet, the shaman, the yogi, or the priest, is the awareness that some people have been given an extra measure of this energy and the knowledge of how to bring themselves more in harmony with it. Modern medicine had its origins long ago in this kind of gift and wisdom. In discarding – rightly – aspects and accretions that were superstition or magic, we unfortunately threw out the founding truth of this ancient, near-universal tradition as well.

~ Faith-Healing Reviewed

I'm convinced that religious institutions should ban or at least scrupulously avoid the phrase faith-healing. Apart from the stereotypes of the television evangelists and their ilk which the words immediately summon up, these people have done immeasurable harm to some innocent sufferers and have created a communications problem for those who believe there is a reality to non-medical healing behind all the distortions. From the very first time I visited the sick in hospital as a professional cleric, I realized it is cruel and malicious to imply to or tell those who are disabled or sick that they could be cured if only they had enough faith. To their physical suffering is added the agony of believing that their failure to be cured is their own fault! In some religious circles (and, as noted earlier, it is a trap not always avoided by secular New Age writers on self-healing either), the sick are made to feel that if they'd had enough faith they wouldn't have got sick in the first place. If they only had faith now, they'd be cured.

This entire approach must be challenged and discarded. True, the Bible talks about the role of faith in healing, and we have seen – for example, in the chapter on the discoveries of Norman Cousins and his team – that the qualities of faith, hope, and a sense of purpose can have dramatic physiological consequences. But when the Bible talks about belief and faith it has nothing whatever to do with belief or trust in certain creeds, or various other religious doctrines, propositions, and rites. Certainly, Norman Cousins never uses the word faith in that sense. What is at issue is not this or that religious commitment or belief system (after all, the creedal affirmations don't appear in the New Testament in anything like their subsequent formulation in the official creeds of the early church). Jesus himself used the word "faith" mostly in the sense of confidence, trust, or expectation. It's the opposite of fear. His most characteristic words were "fear not" or, as the King James Version sometimes translates it, "be of good cheer." Indeed, in *For Christ's Sake* I have argued that Jesus saw the chief problem of humanity not as sin but as fear.[6]

Faith, then, is more a matter of the basic direction of one's out-look – towards a future that is open, no matter how bleak the present may both seem and be; the view that ultimately life itself can be trusted. It's not a question of having this or that amount of a quantifiable "stuff" called faith, it's simply accepting the possibil-ity that the universe holds options beyond the conventional wis-dom or expertise of any set of gurus. Of course, it helps and hastens the healing process if one believes in one's doctor and, similarly, also if one believes in the efficacy of the intervention of the non-medical healer. But, in both cases, because something objective is going on, something that follows specific laws, the healing is not conditional on the strength of that belief. Provided there is no strenuous opposition on the part of the healee, healing can occur. Even the Gospels record an occasion when Jesus could do no "mighty works" among the people of one region because of the opposition of "their unbelief."[7]

My own conviction is that trust and confidence in a loving God who has made us, who sustains us, and who heals us can constitute a potent factor in the self-healing process. But God "who sends the rain upon the just and the unjust alike" does not play favourites. Atheists or agnostics who believe in the power of their minds and bodies to recover health or who, to use Einstein's words, believe that the universe can be trusted, are employing a God-given force whether they acknowledge it or not. To the extent that anyone makes use of the underlying spiritual and physical laws by which the cosmos works and heals itself, the same healing resources are available to all. Thus, what I am really saying, in conclusion, is that spiritual or non-medical healing is available to all of us, whether we believe in a particular religion or in none. Antibiotics don't ask what denomination or faith we belong to before going to work. Neither does true spiritual healing. It's simply a part of the way the universe runs.

∼ Spiritual Healing and You

Being a journalist for the past twenty-one years has given me the rare privilege of meeting some of the most remarkable men and women of our time, from Pope John Paul II to Rev. Billy Graham, Mother Teresa, and Queen Elizabeth II. The point is not to name-drop – all journalists get opportunities that have nothing to do with their personal merit or lack thereof! But of all the people, all the thinkers I have met, one man made a deeper impression on me than any other; he is Dr. Viktor Frankl, the successor to Freud, Adler, and Jung in the Viennese school of psychotherapy. Frankl, who is still alive and vigorous at the time of this writing, is the author of a number of books, but none has had anything like the impact of his little volume titled *Man's Search for Meaning*, which tells of his experiences in the concentration camps of Hitler's Germany.[8]

Frankl was struck during this horrific experience by the fact that it was not always the big, strong, healthy-looking types who were able to survive these camps. Many of these simply gave up and died or threw themselves upon the electrified barbed-wire to kill themselves. The ability to stay well and to surmount even the foulest and crudest of conditions, he discovered, lay not in externals or apparent strengths but in having a meaning for one's life. It was the man or woman who in the midst of that hell could find a reason for hope, a reason to suffer through whatever came his or her way, who ultimately made it. He concluded that most people suffering from inner turmoil and neuroses need, more than anything else, to find a meaning for their lives. He formulated this as the necessity for someone to love, or to have work that has to be done. Employing the Greek word *logos*, which means a rational plan, a meaning, principle, or purpose, he coined the term logotherapy. Healing, he argued, is fundamentally connected with helping sick people to find new reasons for living. His therapeutic approach has been a tremendous success.

The reason for introducing Frankl's experience here is that, like Norman Cousins, he has demonstrated that spiritual or non-physical factors are the key to health and meaningful survival. The best medications, the best surgeons, and the finest hospitals can not on their own bring true healing to anyone. If the individual's own inner healing power is not activated, life is cut off at its source. With the inner healing power as an ally, with all possible spiritual help and in full co-operation with all the arts and technology of modern medicine, the struggle against any disease can be taken up with the most powerful tools available. There will not always be a cure, but the greatest possible healing will take place even if it is, ultimately, a healing into death itself.

Significantly, when Norman Cousins visited patients who had "incurable" illnesses and who were too overwhelmed by their condition to fight back in any way, he used to spend some time at the outset speaking to them about the miraculous ability of the body to heal itself. He would talk about the marvels of the human immune system, which is designed to meet the challenges of any illness. He would describe to them the "sentry" cells that roam the body searching out intruders or abnormal conditions and calling upon the body's own defenders – cells that can prise open malignant cells and inject poisons to kill them off, cells that can wipe out infections, and cells that can even put viruses under "arrest" and call up reinforcements. He would then show them how "practically everything" can affect the immune system – our thoughts, emotions, imaginations, diet, and exercise. "The immune system is a mirror to life, responding to its joy and anguish, its exuberance or boredom, its laughter and tears, its excitement and depression, its problems and prospects." He would point out to them that the late editor of the *New England Journal of Medicine* once wrote that fully 85 per cent of human illnesses are within reach of the body's own healing system. Body, mind, and soul are so tightly knit and integrated that every action or event affects the total organism.

Cousins would then ask the patient to do some mind-body exercises developed by Dr. Elmer Green of the Menninger Clinic to prove how the brain can directly and immediately affect the body. The simplest of these exercises involves increasing blood flow to one's hands by relaxing completely and simply visualizing them becoming engorged. The patient holds the bulb of a thermometer and is shown the actual temperature of the skin before and after the visualization so that the objectivity of the event is put beyond question. Differences of ten degrees Fahrenheit or higher are easily reached in this manner. In the same way, patients can be taught how to reduce their blood pressure significantly. Cousins was able to alter his own blood pressure, sometimes by over twenty points, by consciously directing the blood flow to his hands or his head.

What mattered to the patients he was counselling, and what matters to each of us, is that if something as obvious as skin temperature or blood pressure can be affected by our own thinking it is not a large step to realizing that we can affect every other organ and activity of our bodies. The point can not be made or reinforced too often that we are able to shape our health. The truth of the biblical saying that as we think in our own innermost being so indeed we are, is absolutely true.

One final piece of evidence, though it is scarcely needed, is a phenomenon which, once I was reminded of it, I remember witnessing frequently when long ago I had the care of a large parish. My brother, who is a doctor with a far-flung family practice in the Bruce Peninsula in Ontario, was telling me just the other day about a couple of his patients who had died recently. Both were well advanced in years and were quite prepared to die. In each case, he said, any physician would have predicted an earlier moment of death. But both of them had a particular reason for wanting to see some specific event or date before they died. In one case, the elderly patient was waiting for family members to come from a distant part of the country to take over the care of her property and affairs. She lived until they came and was satisfied they knew all that had to be done, and then she died peacefully some twenty-four hours later. The other patient, a man with advanced cancer, also defied all odds and lived until a big family celebration was over. Then he died almost as though on cue. In other words, human beings do have an ability to prolong life or postpone death until a specific purpose has been completed. Then, and only then, is death allowed to intervene.

The challenge is for us to enlarge our awareness of our own healing capacities and to strengthen by all means possible the energies and forces within us that God or nature has provided. This means taking responsibility for our own health – part of which means getting proper medical care when and as needed – through a healthy lifestyle, including a balanced diet, lots of exercise, and moderation in everything.

It means, as well, developing our spiritual resources. My own conviction is that some kind of religious commitment is an essential ingredient in this, although I am well aware one can be spiritual without being religious at all. The central thing, I believe, is to be able to see one's life in a way that connects it not just to everyone else but to the universe. It's difficult to realize the therapeutic effects of a sense of purpose without having a mythos or story of the cosmos that gives it all meaning. To me, the essence of spirituality is the vision or insight that there are ultimate realities behind the ephemeral and material things which make up so large a part of life. I believe this is grounded in God; others may have a different understanding. But to have hope, faith, and love in this life one needs a worldview which gives one, like Archimedes, a place to stand.

For myself, I find that it is of enormous help to meditate or spend some time daily in solitude when you can focus your energies and both affirm and visualize the reality of "God-power" or "Christ-power" all around you and within. Others may prefer simply to make affirmations about the life energies given to us by nature and to visualize their immune systems functioning properly. All of this will, however, be in vain unless it is seen in the wider context of living a meaningful life on behalf of others. In other words, healing is more than an end; it's a means to a fuller life shared with the rest of humankind. The ultimate test of whether spiritual healing has occurred, I believe, is whether the person who receives it in turn becomes a healing presence, first with those nearest at hand and then with the wider community. Healing that stops with the individual seems eventually to sour or to weaken and falter.

That's why I believe for each of us the final challenge in this investigation is to discover our own potential for healing others. For some this will mean learning to develop the healing energy latent in their own hands and bodies. I recommend Dolores Krieger's book on Therapeutic Touch as one guide, but it's not essential. All that is necessary is a real desire to help others and a willingness to practise the art at first with one's relatives and close friends. What is needed, as Estebany used to say, is "a pure heart" coupled with an ability to relax, focus one's mind on the reality of inexhaustible energy in and around us, and then quietly and without strain direct it through one's arms and hands into the healee. Some will have more ability in this than others. But keep a simple logbook or diary; you'll be surprised at the results.

The same will be true if you pray or meditate for the healing of others at a distance. Energy is released as you visualize them being healed. The final results, of course, must be left to God. This is not a form of magic, and so there are no absolute certainties or guarantees. But try it for yourself and you'll find it makes a difference – sometimes a quite extraordinary one. In the end, this book is not about a pious theory or an intellectual abstraction, it's about a living process and is as practical as your next breath. The ultimate challenge is to put it to the test in the laboratory of your own life and then decide. Nothing could be more scientific than that.

Finally, before closing this discussion, I want to add a personal reflection. It flows not just from the evidence reviewed here but from my years spent in pastoral ministry. When you spend time with people during their moments of crisis, when they or those very close to them are seriously ill in body or spirit, there is one cry you hear over and over again: Why did this happen? What did I (or they) do wrong? Behind this poignant *cri de coeur* are a couple of assumptions: that illness is a form of punishment, and that it is sent by God. The reader may have felt this way in the past. Indeed, if you or a loved one are facing a critical illness, you may be experiencing this particular "dark night of the soul" right now.

It is important to recognize that insofar as these questions are an expression of anger against the disease or accident, they ought never to be repressed. A priest, pastor, or doctor who expresses shock at such outbursts or who discourages a sick person from complaining against "heaven" doesn't really understand what used to be called "the cure of souls." Anyone who has read the Psalms, for example, knows that rage against God or the cosmos can be a therapeutic part of prayer. In the New Testament, Christ several times expressed anger against the ravages of disease. But, at the same time, he challenged the theology or the belief-system underlying the view that illness comes from God. Our own reason confirms this.

Theologians don't understand the reasons for disease any more than doctors do. There is such a thing as the "mystery of evil." The issues surrounding sickness are so complex that while we can do everything in our power to promote and maintain perfect health we can not always be assured of success. We are mortal beings and will all eventually die. Indeed, properly understood and prepared for, death can be understood as a form of healing. God, whose nature is love no matter how much this love may seem to be obscured at times of crisis, does not send illness. Sickness is not a divine punishment nor is it sent as a lesson or as a means of purifying character. Such a view would make a sadistic monster out of God instead of the loving source of light and energy revealed by Christ.

The misunderstanding comes, I believe, from the undeniable, observable phenomenon of the way in which suffering and illness often have the power to reshape and redefine people's values, their sense of purpose and ultimate meaning. History bears witness to this in that some of the most creative or giving individuals who ever lived had to cope with an extraordinary physical or mental challenge at one or more points in their lives. This is not to restate in a more sophisticated form the hackneyed and altogether erroneous maxim that suffering "is good for you." Pain and sickness are to be avoided, but they are a part of life. What truly matters is how they are dealt with. They can often be turned into a source of insight and strength if one determines, in addition to using all the modes of healing available, to wrestle some meaning out of them whatever the cost. It is foolish piety – and irrational nonsense – to say that what is so obviously hurtful is actually good. But it's something quite different to realize that in the end, through courage, faith, and hope, even the worst we ever feared can be made to yield some benefit and blessing. I have seen this happen in too many people's lives to ever doubt it. I assure you that, however deep the valley of the shadow through which you or a loved one may be passing, the Ultimate Ground of the universe is with you and with them. "Underneath are the everlasting arms," as the Bible says. And, in the end, as T. S. Eliot put it, echoing this same faith, "All shall be well, and all manner of things shall be well."[9]

Appendix I

An *address given by Godfrey Mowatt at a service of healing at St. Mark's Church, London, in May* 1955.[1]

I am taking as my text the fifth verse of the first chapter of John's Gospel: "And the Light shineth in darkness, and the darkness comprehended it not."

How true this is! In this material age the world is living in darkness, misery and fear, terror and bewilderment. The Light is here all the time if men and women could only realise it. I have the great joy and the great privilege of bringing this understanding to men's minds that the power of God is all round us; and I know how the Light is penetrating the darkness. I get hundreds of letters from people who have not realised God in any way, nor the living Christ, nor the power of the Holy Spirit. They have not lived – they have just existed in fear, fearing what is going to happen, not understanding that they are part of God's creation, and that God's love and understanding is with them.

Before I left this morning, I had such a heavy post that I could only open some of the letters, but thank God those letters were from people who had lived in darkness, and to whom the Light has penetrated. They have found new happiness, new understanding that we do not live by bread alone, and by material schemes for happiness – we live by the power of God and the living Christ, and the inspiration of the Holy Spirit.

Men and women alike throughout this country, and throughout other countries, are finding the happiness of realising the meaning of the Divine Love and Divine Mercy and Divine Guidance which has completely altered their lives.

Over fifty clergy have written to the Archbishop's Commission on Divine Healing to say their parishes have found new understanding, and the people are coming to church again and are also realising the Power and the Love of God in the Church. Many of the clergy who write to me say that their congregations, which were only a few in the morning and little better in the evening, have now increased, and that their parishes have found their souls. The churches are now full in the morning and absolutely packed in the evening – because they are aware of the Light shining through the darkness.

Think of the terrible materialism and darkness that has caused all this misery! The two ghastly wars we have been through, and the fear of another ghastly war more terrible than ever facing us, because we live in darkness. Yet, the Light is there all around us, and we have got to seek it; and we seek it through Divine Healing – not merely the healing of the physical body, but the healing of the understanding. There *is* the Power of God all round us. There *is* the Power of God to deliver, and if we can only believe and strive to understand, we find a harmony that we have never known before. The distress of body and terror of mind receives relief and healing – the healing that is above all, the healing of the understanding, bringing peace, comfort, and happiness to the soul and the mind. Oh, if we could realise how to live through our minds! Our minds control our bodies. . . . Don't we all know that if we get bad news, we feel sick and faint, because the mind is conveying fear to us. People can fall down in absolute distress and bewilderment when they hear bad news; and in some cases the heart will stand still, and death will come about. Oh, if we could only grasp it! When we lie awake in the night, letting our minds run about, dreading this, that and the other, it need not be, if we have the understanding that there *is* the Power of God to save and deliver. We must grasp it with our minds when we say the Light can penetrate through the darkness.

When you come up for the Laying-on-of-Hands, come up with the understanding that you must seek the Kingdom of God, you must seek the guidance and inspiration of the Holy Spirit. And then you will be free from your fears, then you will be sure that power has been given to resist whatever overwhelms you – whether it be physical suffering, or dread of material harm and difficulty. Christ definitely told us he will never desert us. He said: "I will pray to my Father, and He will send the Comforter, the Holy Spirit." The Power of God *is* on Earth, and we can receive that Power to calm our minds, to lift our minds above fear, misery, sorrow and despair.

Just kneel and seek the Power of the Holy Spirit to deliver you from all that depresses you, and to deliver you from your physical sickness, and you will be given something far more wonderful than that – you will find a peace and a happiness that the world cannot give.

Appendix II

A double-blind experiment establishing by fully objective, scientific means that the "healer effect" cannot be simply dismissed as due to the placebo effect, hypnosis, or other powers of suggestion from the healer upon the healee.

A California doctor, Daniel Worth, president and research director of Healing Sciences International, Orinda, California, set out to explore whether there would be a healer effect if the persons to be healed were kept completely unaware of the healer's presence and, indeed, unaware that any healing was actually intended or taking place. He devised the following schema and protocols to achieve total objectivity.

Worth enlisted forty-four male student volunteers (average age, twenty-six) who were told they would be part of an experiment to test a new, highly sensitive camera which could photograph the energy flowing around the human body. Under the tightest of secrecy and controls – not even the project manager knew what was really being tested – half of the group came to a rented house at regular intervals in the morning, and the other half came in the afternoon. Everyone was told the same story; everyone was treated in exactly the same way. Each volunteer had an eight-millimetre-wide, skin-deep wound cut on his forearm on the first day. The wound was dressed with gas-permeable gauze. When they went into the house, each volunteer was seated close to the wall of an otherwise empty room and instructed to insert his arm through a small, heavily draped hole – nothing was visible on the other side. Each volunteer sat there for precisely five minutes while the "camera" in the adjoining room was supposedly filming the wound. They were told that the camera was so sensitive it had to be kept by itself. The purported theory was that there should be extra energy flowing around the wound and the hi-tech camera would, hopefully, be able to pick this up and record it. The point, however, was that there was no camera in the next room. The morning group were simply hanging their arms in empty space. In the afternoon, a traditional-style healer, named Laurie Eden, totally concealed from them, sat in the alleged camera room, close to the wall, and carried out a non-touch healing session on the wound of each. Only Worth knew she was there.

At the end of sixteen days, medical experts who did not know who had been treated by the healer and who had not, examined the arms of all forty-four students. The wounds of thirteen of those treated by the healer had healed entirely; each wound had closed over and had a layer of new tissue sealing it. The rest of the afternoon group were "well on the way to total healing." By contrast, not a single member of the control group had experienced complete closing of the wound, or anything close to it. The photos showing the differences are striking. In other words, Worth's experiment showed that, as we have already seen in the case of plants, animals, and babies, belief or suggestion played no part in these healings.

The documentation for Worth's findings is contained in a special thirty-minute documentary film by the BBC called "A Way of

Healing," which was aired on March 24, 1993, on TVOntario's medical program "Vital Signs." It has also been fully written up by Dr. Worth himself, complete with all the relevant statistics and charts, plus bibliography, in *Subtle Energies*, vol. 1, no. 1, 1990, pp. 1-20.

Appendix III

One of the most effective ways of centring or focusing one's spiritual life and thus harnessing the energies for healing both body and soul is to use the Psalms as a therapeutic tool. Many of them are excellent mantras or brief prayers ideally suited to be meditations. There are times when they can serve us better than any "wonder drug." Here are a few of my own favourites (because of the beauty of the language, the text is that of the King James Version).

"I will both lay me down in peace, and sleep: for thou, Lord, only makest me dwell in safety." Ps. 4:8

"Thou wilt show me the path of life: in thy presence is fulness of joy; at thy right hand there are pleasures for evermore." Ps. 16:11

"The Lord is my shepherd; I shall not want. . . . Yea, though I walk through the valley of the shadow of death, I will fear no evil: for thou art with me." Ps. 23:1,4

"Lead me in thy truth, and teach me: for thou art the God of my salvation [wholeness, total health]." Ps. 25:5

"The Lord is my light and my salvation; whom shall I fear? The Lord is the strength of my life; of whom [or what] shall I be afraid?" Ps. 27:1

"I waited patiently for the Lord; and he inclined unto me, and heard my cry. He brought me up also out of an horrible pit [bodily illness or depression], out of the miry clay, and set my feet upon a rock, and established my goings. And he hath put a new song in my mouth." Ps. 40:1-3

"God is our refuge and strength, a very present help in trouble. Therefore will not we fear." Ps. 46:1-2

"God be merciful unto us, and bless us; and cause his face to shine upon us; . . . that thy way may be known upon earth, thy saving health among all nations." Ps. 67:1-2

"Bless the Lord, O my soul: and all that is within me, bless his holy name. Bless the Lord . . . who forgiveth all thine iniquities; who healeth all thy diseases." Ps. 103:1-3

Notes

Preface

1. Exodus 15,26. Luther translated this as, "I am the Lord thy physician."

Chapter 1: Roots of an Enquiry

1. From the documentary video "Bioenergy: A Healing Art," 1992, by Peter Walsh, New World Media Alliance, Wirkus Bioenergy Foundation, Bethesda, Maryland.
2. *The Healing Light* (London: Arthur James, 1949), pp. 30-1.
3. See H.W. Janson, *A History of Art*, 2nd ed. (Englewood Cliffs, N.J.: Prentice Hall, 1977), p. 49.
4. *The World Book Encyclopedia I*, vol. 10 (New York: World Book Inc., 1983), p. 67.
5. The association's address is: JASH, 23 Magnolia Court, Headley Rd. East, Woodley, Reading, Berkshire, England, RG5 4SD.
6. Its address is: The National Federation of Spiritual Healers, Old Manor Farm Studio, Church St., Sunbury-on-Thames, Middlesex, England, TW16 6RG.
7. See Morris Maddocks, *The Vision of Dorothy Kerin* (London: Hodder and Stoughton, 1991).

Chapter 2: Facing Some High Hurdles

1. *Globe and Mail*, Jan. 28, 1993.
2. James Randi, *The Faith Healers* (Buffalo: Prometheus Books, 1989).
3. Deepak Chopra, *Quantum Healing* (New York: Bantam, 1989), p. 62.
4. Randi, *op. cit.*, pp. 283-4.

5. (Quoted in) Chopra, *op. cit.*, p. 65.
6. For a recent study that rules out the placebo effect in adults treated by a healer, see Appendix II.
7. See Chapter 6.

Chapter 3: The Religious Roots of Healing

1. The Qu'ran, Sura 44:45.
2. Matthew 9:20-22.
3. Mircea Eliade, ed, *The Encyclopedia of Religion*, vol. 14 (New York: Macmillan, 1986), p. 578.
4. Modern doctors refer to scrofula as a tuberculosis of the skin.
5. Robert Prévost, *Montréal: A History*, trans. E. Mueller and R. Chodos (Toronto: McClelland & Stewart, 1993), p. 18.
6. *Encyclopedia of Religion*, *op. cit.*, vol. 6, pp. 226ff.
7. *Encyclopedia of Religion*, *op. cit.*, vol. 13, p. 203.
8. 2 Corinthians 12:7.
9. *Encyclopedia of Religion*, *op. cit.*, vol. 13, p. 216.

Chapter 4: The Origins of Judeo-Christian Healing

1. 2 Kings 4:32-6.
2. Visitors to Israel today can visit the restored ruins of the synagogue in question. It stands at the north end of the Sea of Galilee, not far from the traditional site of the Mount of the Beatitudes, overlooking the water.
3. Mark 8:22ff.
4. Tom Harpur, *For Christ's Sake* (Toronto: McClelland & Stewart, 1993), pp. 76ff.
5. Mark 3:22-30.
6. Luke 11:20.
7. Luke 4:17ff.
8. Mark 2:9.
9. Acts 14:8ff.
10. Acts 28:8.
11. See Dolores Krieger, *Therapeutic Touch: How to Use Your Hands to*

Help or Heal (Englewood Cliffs, N.J.: Prentice Hall, 1981), pp. 93-4. See also Chapter 10.

12. 1 Corinthians 12:1-11.
13. 1 Corinthians 12:14ff.
14. 1 Timothy 5:23.
15. John Spong, *Rescuing the Bible from Fundamentalism: A Bishop Re-thinks the Meaning of Scripture* (San Francisco: HarperSanFrancisco, 1991).
16. Revelation 21:4.

Chapter 5: The Blind Healer

1. Kathleen Lonsdale, *Forth in Thy Name: The Life and Work of Godfrey Mowatt* (Winchester: The Wykeham Press, 1959), p. 44.
2. *Ibid.*, p. 2.
3. *Ibid.*, pp. 6-7.
4. The process is known as sympathetic ophthalmia; that is, when one eye is severely injured, for reasons as yet not wholly understood, the other eye often loses vision "out of sympathy." Removal of the injured eye will prevent this happening.
5. Lonsdale, *op. cit.*, pp. 11-12.
6. *Ibid.*, p. 31.
7. *Ibid.*
8. For an example of the kind of address given by Mowatt at such healing services, see Appendix I.
9. The Churches' Council on Health and Healing is headquartered in The Healing Centre, St. Marylebone Parish Church, Marylebone Road, London, NW1 5LT.
10. Lonsdale, *op. cit.*, pp. 43-4.
11. *Ibid.*, pp. 52-4.
12. *Ibid.*, pp. 71ff.

Chapter 6: The First Scientific Evidence

1. Allen Spraggett, *The Unexplained* (New York: The New American Library, 1967).

2. Edward Mann, *Vital Energy and Health* (Toronto: Hounslow Press, 1989), p. 29.
3. Bernard Grad, "Reminiscences of Wilhelm Reich and Orgonomy after Four Decades." *Journal of Orgonomy* 26:5-17. See also the bibliography in M. Sharaf's *Fury on Earth* (New York: St. Martin's Press/Marek, 1983).
4. Dolores Krieger, in the bibliography of her book *Therapeutic Touch* (Englewood Cliffs, N.J.: Prentice Hall, 1979).
5. For further information about Oskar Estebany, see Krieger, *op. cit.*, pp. 4-6, and also D. M. Rorvik, "The Healing Hand of Mr. E." *Esquire*, Feb. 1974, pp. 70, 154, 156, 159-60.
6. "Some Biological Effects of the Laying on of Hands." *Journal of the American Association for Psychical Research* 59 (1965), pp. 95-171.
7. Grad, *op. cit.* See Grad's note 8.
8. *Ibid.*, p. iii.
9. *Ibid.*, pp. 114-9.
10. For further descriptions of Grad's work see E. Mann, *op. cit.*, pp. 54, 233, 237-40, and also Sheila Ostrander and Lynn Schroeder, *Psychic Discoveries behind the Iron Curtain* (New York: Bantam, 1971), pp. 224, 383-4.

Chapter 7: A Psychiatrist's Case for Healing

1. Reiki, the Japanese version of the Chinese Qigong (see Chapter 13), is a form of laying-on of hands. It was developed in Japan at the end of the eighteenth century. The LeShan method was developed by Dr. Lawrence LeShan in the mid-1970s. The healer using this technique goes into an altered state of consciousness through meditation and attempts to see himself as one with the healee. There is no attempt to direct or manipulate the healee, who uses the healing energy as needed.
2. See Chapter 9.
3. Daniel Benor, *Healing Research: Holistic Energy Medicine and Spiritual Healing*, vol. 1 (London: Helix Editions, 1993).
4. See Sheila Ostrander and Lynn Schroeder, *Psychic Discoveries behind the Iron Curtain* (New York: Bantam, 1971), p. 5 and passim.

5. Daniel Benor, "A Psychiatrist Examines Fears of Healing." *British Journal of the Society for Psychical Research* 56:287-96.
6. Susan Howatch, *Glamorous Powers* (New York: Alfred A. Knopf), 1988.
7. See Chapter 6.
8. "Survey of Spiritual Healing Research." *Complementary Medical Research*, September 1990, vol. 4, no. 3, pp. 9-33.
9. Justa Smith, "Paranormal Effects on Enzyme Activity." *Human Dimensions*, 1972, vol. 1, pp. 15-19.

Chapter 8: Therapeutic Touch

1. D. M. Rorvik, "The Healing Hand of Mr. E." *Esquire*, Feb. 1974, pp. 70, 154, 156, 159-60.
2. For a full discussion of the results see Benor, *Healing Research, op. cit.*, pp. 212-13.
3. Agnes Sanford, *The Healing Light*, revd ed. (New York: Ballantine Books, 1983).
4. *Ibid.*, p. 82.
5. *Ibid.*, pp. 20, 26, 109-110.
6. *Toronto Star*, Feb. 20, 1993.
7. Reported in "A Way of Healing," a thirty-minute TV documentary by the BBC, aired on TVOntario's "Vital Signs," March 23, 1993, and hosted by Robert Buckman, M.D.

Chapter 9: The Spiritual Factor

1. Norman Cousins, *Head First: The Biology of Hope and the Healing Power of the Human Spirit* (New York: Penguin, 1989), pp. 105, 245.
2. 1 Corinthians 13:13.
3. One in three Canadians feels constantly under stress and trapped in a routine that allows no time for pleasure or relaxation, according to a recent Statistics Canada study (*Toronto Star*, Aug. 12, 1993).
4. Norman Cousins, *Anatomy of an Illness As Perceived by the Patient: Reflections on Healing and Regeneration* (New York: W.W. Norton, 1979).

5. Cousins, *Head First, op. cit.*
6. *Ibid.*, p. 140.
7. *Ibid.*, p. 259.
8. *Ibid.*, pp. 260, 264-6.
9. *Ibid.*, p. 266.

Chapter 10: Energy-Field Healing

1. From the documentary video "Bioenergy: A Healing Art," 1992, by Peter Walsh, New World Media Alliance, Wirkus Bioenergy Foundation, Bethesda, Maryland.
2. *Ibid.*
3. James Randi, *The Faith Healers* (Buffalo: Prometheus Books, 1989), p. 228.
4. The address is: 9907 Fleming Ave., Bethesda, Maryland, 20814, U.S.A. Phone/Fax (301) 652-3480.
5. At the London Conference, in October 1992, Wirkus said humans from earliest times have used everything from a pool of still water to various kinds of polished, metal discs to see reflections of the human aura. The method he recommended was to stare intently, with the eyes nearly closed, into a mirror – preferably in a darkened room with a soft light coming from behind one.
6. Sheila Ostrander and Lynn Schroeder, *Psychic Discoveries behind the Iron Curtain* (New York: Bantam, 1971), pp. 200-2.
7. Edward Mann, *Vital Energy and Health* (Toronto: Hounslow Press, 1989), p. 307 and see note.
8. *Toronto Star*, Feb. 28, 1993.
9. From the documentary video "Bioenergy: A Healing Art," *op. cit.*
10. Bill Moyers, *Healing and the Mind* (New York: Doubleday, 1993).
11. *Ibid.*, p. 182.

Chapter 11: The London Conference on Healing and Energy Medicine, 1992

1. See Sheila Ostrander and Lynn Shroeder, *Psychic Discoveries behind the Iron Curtain* (New York: Bantam, 1971), pp. 202ff.

Chapter 12: Prayer

1. Larry Dossey, *Recovering the Soul: A Scientific and Spiritual Search* (New York: Bantam, 1989), pp. 44ff.

2. For full documentation of Byrd's research, see "Cardiologist Studies Effects of Prayer on Patients." *Brain/Mind Bulletin* 2:7 (March 1986), pp. 1ff. See also Randolph C. Byrd, "Positive Therapeutic Effects of Intercessory Prayer in a Coronary Care Unit Population." *Southern Medical Journal* 81:7 (July 1988), pp. 826-829; see also Howard Wolinsky, "Prayers Do Aid Sick, Study Finds." *Chicago Sun-Times*, January 26, 1986, p. 30.

3. Seán Ó'Laoire, "An Experimental Study of the Effects of Intercessory Prayer-at-a-distance on Self-esteem, Anxiety and Depression," Ph.D. thesis (Palo Alto, The Institute of Transpersonal Psychology, May 1993).

4. See "Churches Might Meditate on What Maharishi Offers," by Tom Harpur. *Toronto Star*, June 27, 1993, p. B7.

5. Herbert Benson, *The Relaxation Response* (New York: Avon Books, 1976).

6. See Neil McKenty, *In the Stillness Dancing: The Journey of John Main* (London: Darton, Longman and Todd, 1987).

7. Agnes Sanford, *The Healing Light*, revd ed. (New York: Ballantine Books, 1983), p. 21.

8. I am grateful to Dr. Bernard Grad for the following list of earlier research articles on the power of prayer:

   R. N. Miller, "Study of Remote Mental Healing (through prayer)." *Medical Hypotheses* 8:481-90, 1982.

   R. N. Miller, "The Effect of Thought upon the Growth Rate of Remotely Located Plants." *Journal of Pastoral Counselling* 6:61-63, 1971-72.

   P. J. Collipp, "The Efficacy of Prayer." *Medical Times* 97:201-204, 1969.

   C. R. B. Joyce and R. M. C. Welldon, "The Objective Efficacy of Prayer." *Journal of Chronic Disorders* 18:367-77, 1965.

   A. Carrel, *A Voyage to Lourdes* (New York: Harper, 1950), pp. 36-46.

258 ～ THE UNCOMMON TOUCH

A. Carrel, *Man the Unknown* (New York: Harper and Brothers, 1939), pp. 147-9.

F. Loehr, *The Power of Prayer on Plants – and People*, 2nd ed. (Olympia, Washington: Research Association Press, 1959), pp. 2, 3.

Chapter 13: Traditional Healing in China

1. Roger Jahnke, "Qigong: Awakening and Mastering the Profound Medicine that Lies Within." *Newsletter of the International Society for the Study of Subtle Energies and Energy Medicine* (ISSSEEM) vol. 1, no. 2, fall 1990, pp. 3-7.
2. *Ibid.*, p. 3.
3. Bill Moyers, *Healing and the Mind* (New York: Doubleday, 1993), p. 251.
4. *Ibid.*
5. For a full discussion of the scientific research that has been done on acupuncture and the range as well as the limits of its usefulness, I would recommend Edward Mann's book *Vital Energy and Health* (Toronto: Hounslow Press, 1989), pp. 160-9.
6. Jahnke, *op. cit.*, p. 3.
7. ISSSEEM Newsletter, vol. 1, no. 2, fall 1990, p. 1.
8. Elmer and Alyce Green, *Beyond Feedback* (Fort Wayne, Ind.: Knoll Publishing, 1989).
9. Kenneth Cohen, "Qigong: Cultivating the Vital Breath." ISSSEEM Newsletter, *op. cit.*, pp. 9-12, and see note 3, p. 12.
10. Jahnke, *op. cit.*, p. 4.
11. *Ibid.*, p. 5.
12. See Deepak Chopra, *Quantum Healing* (New York: Bantam, 1989), p. 93.
13. Jahnke, *op. cit.*, p. 5.
14. *Ibid.*, pp. 11-12 and references.
15. Cohen, *op. cit.*, p. 10.
16. Moyers, *op. cit.*, p. 297.
17. ISSSEEM Newsletter, *op. cit.*, p. 18.

Chapter 14: The Challenges

1. (Quoted in) Bill Moyers, *The Healing Mind* (New York: Doubleday, 1993), p. 186.
2. *Globe and Mail*, Nov. 20, 1992.
3. Dean Black, "Who Goes to Quacks?" *Edges*, vol. 4, no. 3, pp. 31ff.
4. Acts 17:24ff.
5. Edward Mann, *Vital Energy and Health* (Toronto: Hounslow Press, 1989), p. 133.
6. *For Christ's Sake* (Toronto: McClelland & Stewart, 1993), pp. 23-5.
7. Matthew 13:58, Mark 6:5-6.
8. Viktor Frankl, *Man's Search for Meaning* (London: Hodder and Stoughton, 1959).
9. "Little Gidding," *The Four Quartets*, ll. 255-6.

Appendix I

1. From the News Bulletin, No. 28, of the Churches' Council of Healing, September-October 1955.

Resources

Some Key Healing Groups

The British organization the Churches' Council for Health and Healing, St. Marylebone Parish Church, Marylebone Road, London NW1 5LT, England, has as its president, the Archbishop of Canterbury. Many pamphlets, tapes, and other resources such as study kits can be obtained from this body. It publishes a bimonthly newsletter, *Health and Healing*.

The Jewish Association of Spiritual Healers, affiliated with the British Alliance of Healing Associations, is at 23 Magnolia Court, Headley Road East, Woodley, Reading, Berkshire RG5 4SD, England. The director is Ivan Kayes.

The JASH in the United States and Canada can be contacted c/o Florence J. Horn (Director), 106 Cabrini Blvd., New York, NY 10033, U.S.A. (phone (212) 928-4275). This organization is non-denominational even though affiliated with the British JASH. Ms. Horn runs a centre, "Inner Journey," for training healers.

There are scores of Therapeutic Touch groups in cities and major towns across Canada and the United States. For information on how to become a member of the Therapeutic Touch Network in Canada, call Helen Will at (416) 274-2678, or contact the Therapeutic Touch Network, Toronto, at (416) 454-2688.

Important Journals

The Noetic Sciences Review is a quarterly journal offering serious discussion of emerging concepts in consciousness research, the mind/body connection, healing, and the changing worldview in science and society. Its address is c/o The Institute of Noetic Sciences, P.O. Box 909, Sausalito, CA 94966-0909, U.S.A.

Subtle Energies is the official publication of the International Society for the Study of Subtle Energies and Energy Medicine (ISSSEEM), Stephan A. Swartz, Editor. Its address is 356 Goldco Circle, Golden, CO 80401. Editorial FAX (213) 933-6476.

Bibliography

Becker, Robert O. *The Body Electric: Electromagnetism and Life*. New York: Morrow, 1985.

Birnbaum, Raoul. *The Healing Buddha*. Boulder, Colo.: Shambhala, 1979.

Brennan, Barbara Ann. *Hands of Light: A Guide to Healing Through the Human Energy Field*. New York: Bantam, 1988.

Brown, Brian. *The Sacramental Ministry to the Sick*. New York: Exposition Press, 1968.

Burr, Harold S. *The Fields of Life*. New York: Ballantine, 1973.

Carlson, Richard, and Benjamin Shield, eds. *Healers on Healing*. Los Angeles: Jeremy P. Tarcher, 1989.

Chopra, Deepak. *Quantum Healing: Exploring the Frontier of Mind/Body Medicine*. New York: Bantam, 1989.

Cooke, Christopher Hamel. *Health Is for God*. London: Arthur James, 1986.

Cousins, Norman. *Head First: The Biology of Hope and the Healing Power of the Human Spirit*. New York: Penguin, 1989.

Dossey, Larry. *Recovering the Soul: A Scientific and Spiritual Search*. New York: Bantam, 1989.

Eisenberg, David. *Encounters with Qi: Exploring Chinese Medicine*. New York: W. W. Norton, 1985.

Encyclopedia of Religion, Mircea Eliade, ed. New York: Macmillan, 1986.

Fleischman, Paul R. *The Healing Spirit: Case Studies in Religion and Psychotherapy*. London: SPCK, 1990.

Foster, G. M., and Barbara G. Anderson. *Medical Anthropology*. New York: Wiley Press, 1978.

Gerber, Richard. *Vibrational Medicine: New Choices for Healing Ourselves*. San Francisco: Bear & Co., 1988.

Grad, Bernard, R. J. Cadoret and G. I. Paul. "An Unorthodox Method of Treatment on Wound Healing in Mice." *International Journal of Parapsychology* 2 (1961): 5-19.

Grad, Bernard. "Telekinetic Effects on Plant Growth." *International Journal of Parapsychology* 5 (1963): 117-133.

———. "Some Biological Effects of the Laying On of Hands: Review of Experiments with Animals and Plants." *Journal of the American Society for Psychical Research* 59 (1965): 95-171.

Harpur, Tom. *Life After Death*. Toronto: McClelland & Stewart, 1991.

———. *For Christ's Sake*. Toronto: McClelland & Stewart, 1993. (Originally Oxford University Press, 1986.)

———. *God Help Us*. Toronto: McClelland & Stewart, 1992.

Hay, Louise. *You Can Heal Your Life*. Santa Monica: Hay House, 1984.

Katz, Richard. *The Straight Path: A Story of Healing and Transformation in Fiji*. Reading, Mass.: Addison-Wesley, 1993.

———. *Boiling Energy: Community Healing Among the Kalahari Kung*. Cambridge, Mass: Harvard University Press, 1982.

Kelsey, Morton T. *Psychology, Medicine, and Christian Healing*. San Francisco: Harper Collins, 1988.

Krieger, Dolores. *Foundations of Holistic Health: Nursing Practices*. Philadelphia: J. P. Lippincott, 1981.

———. *Therapeutic Touch: How to Use Your Hands to Help or Heal*. Englewood Cliffs, N.J.: Prentice Hall, 1979.

———. *Living the Therapeutic Touch: Healing as a Lifestyle*. New York: Dodd Mead & Co., 1987.

———. *Accepting Your Power to Heal: The Personal Practice of Therapeutic Touch*. San Francisco: Bear and Co., 1993.

Macrae, Janet. *Therapeutic Touch: A Practical Guide*. New York: Random House, 1987.

Maddocks, Morris. *A Healing House of Prayer*. London: Hodder and Stoughton, 1987.

Maddocks, Morris. *The Vision of Dorothy Kerin*. London: Hodder and Stoughton, 1991.

Mann, W. Edward. *Vital Energy and Health: Dr. Wilhelm Reich's Revolutionary Discoveries and Supporting Evidence*. Toronto: Hounslow Press, 1989.

Mann, W. Edward, and Edward Hoffman. *The Man Who Dreamed of Tomorrow: An Intellectual Biography of Wilhelm Reich*. Los Angeles: Jeremy P. Tarcher, 1980.

Marty, Martin, and Kenneth L. Vaux, eds. *Medicine in Health, Medicine and the Faith Traditions: An Enquiry into Religion and Medicine*. Philadelphia: Fortress Press, 1982.

McGuire, Meredith. *Ritual Healing in Suburban America*. New Brunswick, N. J: Rutgers University Press, 1990.

Meek, G. *Healers and the Healing Process*. Wheaton, Ill.: Theosophical Press, 1977.

Moyers, Bill. *Healing and the Mind*. New York: Doubleday, 1993.

Orenstein, Robert, and David Sobel. *The Healing Brain*. New York: Simon & Schuster, 1988.

Ostrander, Sheila, and Lynn Schroeder. *Psychic Discoveries behind the Iron Curtain*. New York: Bantam, 1971.

Pietroni, Patrick. *The Greening of Medicine*. London: Victor Gollancz, 1990.

Randi, James. *The Faith Healers*. Buffalo: Prometheus Books, 1989.

Reid, Janice. *Body, Land, and Spirit: Health and Healing in Aboriginal Society*. New York and St. Lucia: University of Queensland Press, 1982.

Sanford, Agnes. *The Healing Light*. London: Arthur James, 1949. (Revised edition published 1983 by Ballantine Books.)

Siegel, Bernie S. *Love, Medicine and Miracles*. New York: Harper and Row, 1986.

———. *Peace, Love and Healing*. New York: Harper and Row, 1992.

Silva, Jose, and Robert B. Stone. *You the Healer*. Tiburon, Calif.: H. J. Kramer, 1989.

Tate, David A. *Health, Hope and Healing*. New York: Evans and Co., 1989.

Torrey, E. Fuller. *The Mind Game*. New York: Emerson HallPublishers, 1972 (revised 1986).

Vogel, Virgil J. *American Indian Medicine*. Norman, Okla.: University of Oklahoma Press, 1970.

Weatherhead, Leslie. *Psychology, Religion and Healing*. London: Hodder and Stoughton, 1951.

Index